AFTER LACAN

SUNY series in Psychoanalysis and Culture
Henry Sussman, series editor

AFTER LACAN

Clinical Practice and
the Subject of the Unconscious

WILLY APOLLON, DANIELLE BERGERON
AND LUCIE CANTIN

Edited and Introduced by
Robert Hughes and Kareen Ror Malone

STATE UNIVERSITY OF NEW YORK PRESS

Published by
State University of New York

© 2002 State University of New York

All rights reserved

Printed in the United States of America

For information, address State University of New York Press,
90 State Street, Suite 700, Albany NY 12207

Production by Kelli Williams
Marketing by Anne M. Valentine

Library of Congress Cataloging-in-Publication Data

Apollon, Willy.
 After Lacan : clinical practice and the subject of the unconscious / by
Willy Apollon, Danielle Bergeron, and Lucie Cantin ; edited and
introduced by Robert Hughes and Kareen Ror Malone.
  p. cm.—(SUNY series in psychoanalysis and culture)
 Includes index.
 ISBN 0-7914-5479-7 (alk. paper)—ISBN 0-7914-5480-0 (pbk. : alk. paper)
 1. Psychoanalysis—Practice. 2. Subconsciousness. 3. Lacan, Jacques,
1901–   I. Bergeron, Danielle. II. Cantin, Lucie. III. Hughes, Robert.
IV. Malone, Kareen Ror, 1955–   V. Title.
VI. Series.

RC506 .A65   2002
616.89'17—dc21   2002017613

10   9   8   7   6   5   4   3   2   1

Contents

List of Figures

Acknowledgments

We gratefully acknowledge the sources of the following material:
Lacan, Jacques. *Écrits: A Selection*. Translated by Alan Sheridan. Schemas reprinted from pp. 303, 306, and 313. W. W. Norton and Company, 1966 by Éditions du Seuil. English translation by Tavistock Publications, 1977. Reprinted by permission of W. W. Norton and Company, Inc., and Taylor and Francis Books, Ltd. We appreciate copyright permission from Zone Books for Deleuze, Gilles. *Masochism: Coldness and Cruelty*. Translated by Jean McNeil, 278–79. New York: Zone Books, 1989.

The editors acknowledge with gratitude the encouragement of James Peltz at State University of New York Press. Also, Robert Hughes would like to give a word of deep appreciation to Henry Sussman for his early enthusiasm toward the project, to the Graduate School and the Program in Comparative Literature at Emory University for their many generosities, to Jennifer Ballengee for her timely and innumerable assistances, and to Morgen LeFaye, who was always more helpful than she could ever believe. Kareen Malone would like to thank her graduate assistant, Clayton Bohnet, and her patient family. Finally, the editors happily express their gratitude to Willy, Danielle, and Lucie, for the opportunity to work with them and for the grace and intelligence that has always distinguished their relationship with us.

Introduction

The Dialectic of Theory and Clinic

ROBERT HUGHES AND KAREEN ROR MALONE

The Parisian psychoanalyst Jacques Lacan (1901–1981) is widely considered to have been the most important and provocative thinker in psychoanalysis since Sigmund Freud. Philosophers, critics, and intellectuals across the humanities have been energized by Lacan's formulations on human subjectivity—its development, its structure, its interaction in the world. His theories have inspired many dozens of books and hundreds of scholarly articles in English alone. In the main, these writings address themselves to Lacan's conceptual edifice and to what his conceptualizations have to offer to an understanding of culture, art, and philosophy. Thus, in North America, the impression among clinicians is that Lacan is "all theory." Yet Lacan himself insisted that the greatest importance of his work lay in its contribution to the psychoanalytic clinic—which was, he said, the origin and the aim of all his teaching. Lacan's self-assessment is confirmed by the openness to Lacanian thought within clinical circles of other nations, belying the notion that Lacan is only accessible as an academic exercise (see Hill 1997). In fact arguably, the academic appropriation of Lacan can function as an obstacle to understanding key Lacanian concepts. The editors propose that it is a pernicious misconception that Lacan is exclusively for literary critics and cultural theorists—that Lacan, in other words, is "about" theory. Here is a recent example of this bias, one directed to the treatment of psychotics.

> In spite of these criticisms of Lacan's notion of psychosis, his theoretical construction has something to offer as a way of conceptualizing intrapsychic and interpersonal phenomena. It is perhaps all we

can ask of a *theoretician* that he prod our thinking in new directions.
(Martel 1990, 251, emphasis added)

Such a statement, appearing in the *American Journal of Psychoanalysis*,
represents a highly misleading view of Lacan and his importance. In
fact, Lacan's work was always addressed to some degree to clinical phenomena and to the development of clinical practice. It is a corollary misconception that Lacanian work could only be successful with highly
functioning, intellectual analysands. The work done with psychotics by
the authors of the present collection as well as the general range of their
patients are clear indications of the falsity of this reigning North American perception. Certainly differences in the theoretical understanding of
clinical work in Lacanian circles as well as the differences in technique
(variable sessions being iconic in this regard) have made some North
American practitioners wary. The warm reception by academics reinforces other suspicions. The present collection, then, aims to develop, for
clinicians and for interested readers in the humanities, a sense for the
clinical context where Lacan's formulations find their greatest force and
their ultimate justification. Indeed this book forcefully conveys that an
ignorance of Lacanian clinical innovations is maintained at considerable
cost to clinical advances and to the expansion of the scope and theory of
psychoanalysis.[1]

The authors of the essays collected here, Willy Apollon, Danielle
Bergeron, and Lucie Cantin, together lead the École freudienne du
Québec and the GIFRIC group (Groupe interdisciplinaire freudien de
recherches et d'interventions cliniques et culturelles; hereinafter cited as
Gifric). Gifric was founded in 1977 as a nonprofit organization with a
mission aiming at clinical and sociocultural research and interventions.
In pursuit of this mission, Gifric has, like numerous other associations
and individuals, coordinated the training of North American analysts in
Lacanian approaches.[2] On the Lacanian scene in North America, Apollon, Bergeron, and Cantin have distinguished themselves as among the
most clinically informed of theoreticians and the most theoretically astute and ambitious of clinicians. But their truly unique place derives
from the groundbreaking work at the "388," a clinic they run in Québec
for the psychoanalytic treatment of young psychotic adults (schizophrenia and manic-depressive psychosis). The highly successful clinical practice of Gifric at the 388 has been inseparable from the Lacanian
intellectual orientation and research represented in this collection.
Whatever the theoretical divergences among the many analysts influ-
enced by Lacan's work, the present collection can be said to stand together with a larger publishing effort underway, by the State University

of New York Series in Psychoanalysis and Culture, by the Other Press under Judith Feher Gurewich, and reflected in recent books by Bruce Fink and Dany Nobus. All these address the misperception of Lacan as an ivory-towered theoretician.

The title of the collection, *After Lacan: Clinical Practice and the Subject of the Unconscious*, suggests something more of the special contribution of these essays. With the publication of Bruce Fink's excellent books, *The Lacanian Subject* and *A Clinical Introduction to Lacanian Psychoanalysis*, the English-speaking reader already has access to general, introductory elaborations of Lacanian theory that are written with clarity and rigor as well as from a clinical viewpoint. Fink's admirable efforts have been supplemented by authors from the United Kingdom, such as Dany Nobus and Philip Hill, who are similarly focused on the clinical side of Lacan. Unlike the celebrated books of Slavoj Žižek, Joan Copjec, Juliet Mac-Cannell, Ellie Ragland, Charles Shepherdson, and other philosophers and literary critics among the New Lacanians, Fink and Nobus address their books not to the philosophical stakes and cultural manifestations of Lacanian theoretical structures, but rather to the specifically *clinical* origin and theorization of Lacan's theory as it evolved through the 1950s, 1960s, and 1970s. But the books of all these writers, including those of Fink and Nobus, have nevertheless called for, explicitly or implicitly, an even more concrete sense of the Lacanian clinic, particularly how various Lacanian concepts—however clearly or subtly explicated—bear upon contemporary clinical practice and upon the suffering addressed by psychoanalytic practice.

After Lacan: Clinical Practice and the Subject of the Unconscious aims towards addressing this need. The present book is not intended as a systematic exposition of Lacanian theory. It is, however, a remarkably unified and carefully planned collection of essays that succeeds in powerfully communicating some of the real discoveries of Lacan's clinical teaching. Certainly, too, the reader is likely to leave enriched from the collection's presentation of various theoretical concepts. For instance, the writers present a concept like jouissance or the signifier or the symptom, now in relation to the Other, now in relation to dream, and now again in relation to fantasy. Each theoretical glimpse emerges from the experience of the clinic and presents new and provocative vistas on concepts that have grown familiar in an unnatural theoretical isolation. Without doubt, the really special contribution of these essays lies in the remarkable way the authors pair a sophisticated theoretical exposition with a concrete sense of the Lacanian clinic.

Certainly it's true that the relation of clinic and theory is always, to some degree, an uneasy one. The most basic difficulty in theorizing from the clinic lies in the fundamental insufficiency of any *generalizable* theory to the experience of the clinic and its irreducibly *singular* savoir. That is, theory and clinic aim at two very different varieties of knowledge, a difference that Lacan explicitly speaks to in his formalization of the difference between university and analytic discourses. Theory aims at rational clarity, at a fixed and systematic elaboration with recognizable explanatory and predictive power, as well as some degree of general applicability (however strictly or loosely defined). Any given theory will surely fall short in one or all of these aspirations, but these are surely the ambitions of any theory worth the name—the qualities by which theory comes to recognize itself *as* theory. Through theory, we hope to *understand* something, in the ordinary sense, that we didn't understand before. As countless commentators have come to appreciate, Freud and Lacan were each superb theoreticians in this sense, and Western culture is much the richer for their efforts and their genius, as it is for the contributions of Copernicus, Mendel, Darwin, and others.

However, as is implicit in the essays of the present collection, Freud and Lacan also aimed at some other variety of knowledge, both in their clinical practice and in their pedagogy. This other variety of knowledge constitutes a "savoir" utterly particular to the subject and irreducible to the level of information. Lacan made it quite clear that interpretation is never quite a matter of understanding and that what interpretation aims to open or stage—a possible "hit" on the real—bears more on the subject's relationship to what one *cannot* know. Thus, interpretation resembles little the goal of understanding as making sense through the stringing together of signifiers. Whereas *understanding* is a reality we can master and believe in, *savior* supplies an access to subjective responsibility in the face of the Other's castration. Chapter 8, in which Willy Apollon writes of Marguerite, a woman who arrives in analysis with a complaint of frigidity, is especially suggestive of what is at stake in this savoir of the clinic.

> The Lacanian clinic favors an ethics where savoir is substituted for the quest for a jouissance that the treatment experience reveals as lapsed and thus impossible. The knowledge at stake at the end of the process concerns the cause of the lapsing. The savoir that concludes the experience is unlike the knowledge that the analysand in transference supposed the analyst knew at the outset of the experience. The analyst refers the analysand to an ethics where desire feeds on the failing of jouissance, and where the analysand takes that cause and the risks of desire as the only determinative realities for one's story, and as a source from which the analysand will draw principles of action, as the necessary support to assume one's sex and one's relation to jouissance.

Significantly here, it is the treatment *experience* that communicates the savoir of the clinic, not the semantic content of any word that the analyst could offer or that the analysand could report. It was indeed the special quality of Lacan's pedagogy to communicate to the auditors of his seminars something of this savoir of the clinic. Many of the eccentricities visible in his published seminars—their departure from the systematic *theoretical* structure that Kant and (in a still more totalizing way) Hegel aimed at—record Lacan's efforts to maneuver his auditors into some analogously productive *savoir* in relation to the particularities of the auditor's subjective relation to jouissance, a savoir necessary to assuming the risks of one's desire and therefore at the heart of a Lacanian ethics. Hence, what some have called the "poetic" quality of Lacan's own discourse, a quality that suggests to the reader some meaning being staged elsewhere—on an other scene one might say, and a quality of expression that has engendered much fascination among intellectuals in the humanities.

And yet, in working from a savoir particular to Marguerite's experience, what is the theoretically minded clinician to do? Not write? Not theorize? Not exactly. One would be ill-advised, as do some North American psychodynamic therapists, to take the concrete exchanges of the clinic as able to provide the frame of the analysis. Rather the task seems to entail an articulation and formalization of that peculiar "experiment" that one calls "psychoanalysis," an experiment aimed at provoking those signifiers, symptoms, transference, and fantasies that allow an analyst the leverage to serve the production of a knowledge that opens the path of desire.

In response to these demands, the authors strive in the essays here to communicate some of the power of the Freudian discovery by staging a twofold event in their writings. On the one hand, they must aim for a rigor and a clarity that respects the theoretical stakes of the clinic and renders these stakes understandable for the reader who has invested time and effort in the present book under the supposition and expectation that there is something to be learned here, something practical, something on the level of information. The reader will not be disappointed in this regard. The present collection, working as it does from an almost unique clinical concreteness, abounds with illuminating insights into basic psychoanalytic structures such as perversion, hysteria, and psychosis. Consequently, even the more advanced reader of Lacan is likely to arrive at new understandings of the relations of jouissance, the letter of the body, symptom, fantasy, and other concepts. At the same time, however, the present collection also strives to convey something of the analytic experience, with powerful and fascinating movements of seduction, enigma, and insight.

A second, related difficulty in theorizing the Lacanian clinic remains ultimately intractable, and must be a necessary limitation of any writing on the clinic. Namely, if one thinks of the clinical experience as the confrontation of subjective experience by the real, one must also recognize that the real is irreducible and impossible; it is an impasse in the structure of subjectivity such that even formalizations can not in themselves reduce it. The real, which lies at the heart of the clinical encounter, cannot therefore, be rationalized, as a text of theory demands, and fixed, as a published text necessarily produces. This is one reason why the clinic can never stage the application of Lacanian texts per se—not those texts by Gifric, and not those by Lacan himself. This is not to confine the importance of Freud to early twentieth-century Vienna, of Lacan to mid-twentieth-century Paris, or, for that matter, of Gifric to early-twenty-first-century North America. But it is to recognize that any theory of the clinic cannot exhaust what it aims to explicate. Theory, though it may be constrained to fix itself in writing, can only ever be a theory-in-progress. This was certainly true for Freud and Lacan, whose writings through the decades witness many substantive changes; it is also true of the texts here by Gifric, which mostly date from the early 1990s. So while *After Lacan: Clinical Practice and the Subject of the Unconscious* is, without doubt, about a clinical efficacy from a praxis initiated by Lacan, issuing from the field opened by Lacan in his return to Freud—and is *after* Lacan in the sense of deriving from his teaching, it is also marked by the fact of coming precisely *after* Lacan in a temporal or historical sense as well. Under the conviction that the savoir of the clinic remains the core event of Lacan's return to Freud, and recognizing both that clinical practice must be dictated by the terms brought by patients and that shifts in patient culture demand corresponding shifts in theoretical emphases, Gifric, despite their deep debt to Lacan, diverge from Lacan and certain other contemporary readings of Lacan's work.

Some Questions in the Lacanian Field and the Work of Gifric

Lacan's "return to Freud" is a tribute to his recognition that Freud's founding of psychoanalysis reflects the articulation of a specific field of effects. This specific field might be called the "subject of the unconscious" and Lacan remained devoted to a theoretical exposition of this subject and to the development of a clinical praxis addressed to it. Whether contextualized in terms of a tension between the imaginary and symbolic axes of "intersubjectivity" (as in early Lacan), or else as structured by language, the discourse of the Other, or a response of the real, Lacan attempts to further what he sees as Freud's discovery of this peculiar "phenomenon" called the "unconscious."

Hence, those with a Lacanian orientation often use ideas from both Freud and Lacan. Yet it must be said that the Lacanian sense of Freud is often much different than the one developed through the North American psychoanalytic context. This difference has been noted by Judith Gurewich (*Clinical Series* 1997) and is quickly evident in any reading of contemporary Lacanian work. From diagnosis to the metapsychological papers, Lacanians seek out Freud's logic as a distinct logic of the unconscious irreducible to biology, to any phenomenology, to any reality or narrative, or to environmental effects. Thus, many Lacanians see many contemporary psychoanalytic movements ostensibly "beyond Freud" as having underestimated an essential articulation within Freud and thus aimed toward a different psychological domain. Lacan stressed this throughout his writings. This is not to say that Lacanians do not move beyond Freud, but rather that there is always a dual reference in Lacanian work: to Lacan, it is true, but always also to Freud. The present volume is no exception. This dual reading sometimes generates a certain tension as to how much one stays grounded in Freud's particular articulation, how one reads "through" it, and where one moves in other directions. One can see this in Lacan's own work. For example, in *Seminar XVII*, Lacan works the issue of castration in terms of the structure of discourse and reexamines the ways in which Freud understands the Oedipal complex. Similar tensions are visible throughout the Lacanian field.

For example, Paul Verhaeghe draws a distinction between Freud's understanding of the father and the Lacanian view of the paternal metaphor in terms of how each conception will play out in contemporary culture. Even though it is clear that Lacan takes Freud's ideas and transforms them into structures, it remains an open question as to the degree to which the logic of those structures transform their original Freudian point of reference. Apollon, Bergeron, and Cantin's papers in this collection are less likely to emphasize the distinction between the Freudian configuration of the Oedipal and the Lacanian one, even as they clearly embrace a structural and linguistic understanding of its effects in relation to castration, authority, and prohibition. But there are, of course, numerous ways to think through the Oedipal. Lacan often spoke of the importance of understanding *Oedipus at Colonus*, the relationship of Oedipus to the (riddle of the) Sphinx, his function in the paternal lineage, as well as his status as a sort of remainder/object (see Laurent 1996; Zupančič 2000; and Lacan's *Seminar XVII* 1991). Broadening the usual North American reading of the Oedipus (wherein the father interrupts the mother-child dyad), suggests a number of ways to reconfigure the relationship between jouissance, the signifier, and the object. For example, considering the Oedipal in terms of the vagabond wanderings of Oedipus at Colonus, shifts the focus from transgression to Oedipus himself. Lacanians might call this the "remainder," the object that falls out of the Other.

In the structural reading of the Oedipal complex, one relates the Freudian terms to the relation of the subject to the law of language, his or her place within the symbolic, and its limits on the jouissance of the (m)Other. The absence of a signifier (which would be instated by the paternal metaphor) preconditions a failure in the phallic signifier that serves to establish sexual identity, orient desire to another, and, in the unconscious, mark the effects of loss and the jouissance thereby determining the subject. The phallus, as signifier, ties this desire to the signifying chain, offering a conjunction between the effects of jouissance and the possibilities of desire. In "On a question preliminary to any possible treatment of psychosis," Lacan closely ties the imaginary phallus to the symbolic phallus. In *Seminar XX*, Lacan refers to the phallus as a contingency, even as it serves as a ballast against the intrusion of the Other's jouissance and is essential to the formulas of sexuation. Although some, such as Tim Dean, have been led to question the significance of the phallus conceptually and turn more to the object *a*, there is still a critical phallic function in terms of the question of sexuation, identity, and its effects in founding desire (its operation as a conjunction marking loss). One wonders whether a position that articulates only the object *a* is likely to default to a phallic position wherein the function of woman as Other returns in another form or is even more radically eclipsed. Clearly, these issues are relevant to the treatment of psychosis and neurosis, and such issues, perhaps less figural in these particular chapters by Gifric, are under serious consideration by Apollon, Bergeron, and Cantin in their clinical praxis and in relationship to evolving social structures. Still, for these authors, the most intensive engagement with Lacanian and Freudian ideas emerges from their work with psychotics.

Some argue, as has Jacques-Alain Miller ("Paradigms" 2000), that Lacan's ideas on the function of the signifier shift with implications for the relationship between neurosis and psychosis, and the status of the name of the father (see also Grigg 1999). Gifric, as well, has revisited subjective structures and their treatment from the perspective of psychosis. Remarkably, within the clinic of the psychotic, the authors have attempted to elicit both a "signifier" and transference. Thus, they now conceptualize aspects of their work with psychosis outside of the frame of strategies originally developed in relation to the name of the father. However, it is also true that such contemporary readings remain under construction.

A recent text by Dany Nobus discusses the Lacanian effort to clarify how one treats psychosis. Nobus suggests that the path is not fully marked by Lacan. Lacan's most fully elaborated ideas on psychosis appear early (notably in *Seminar III*), and these initial formulations suggest a stabilization through working along the imaginary axis, using it to supplement the symbolic failure (see Fink 1997, who notes this description is a simplification). As this strategy risks invoking destructive imaginary rivalries and erotic preoccupations, one also establishes key signifiers that may function to stave off the jouissance of the Other. Here we have a sort of "faux symbolic," maintained by the desire of the analyst and his or her ethical adherence to the rule of the symbolic in a manner even more strict than in the case of neurosis.

In contemporary Lacanian thinking, clinicians have continued to explore the leverage of the signifier—the basis of the talking cure—in transforming the suffering of the psychotic. It is suggested by Roland Broca that one might use the triggering of the psychosis and the development of the delusion within the "transference" to allow the psychotic patient a different relationship to the jouissance of the Other. Here again the analyst must "hold fast to his desire" (1991, 53) to create a different relationship to the invasive signifiers of the Other. Understanding transference as based in the signifier and predicated within a knowledge, Gifric both uses and challenges the parameters of Lacanian ideas of transference (which is a matter of the *analyst's* position) in order to more radically engage the subjective structure of the psychotic. Does the psychoanalytic use of dreams allow the analyst an opportunity to introduce a new subjective position that depends on the function of the signifier? The authors here pose this very interesting, pressing question.

Lacan's theory of psychoanalysis, most especially as a clinically grounded exposition, is a precise tool for understanding the process of psychoanalysis and its object of research. But such an understanding does not come easily; it is still a work in progress. For many North Americans, this continuous interrogation within Lacanian thought adds to a confusion already fueled by differences in vocabulary and approach. It is easy to treat a theory that is foreign as both opaque and monolithic, but although Lacanian thought is difficult and is different, it is neither opaque nor monolithic, and it is far from being a settled, finished discourse ready for full appropriation. Rather Lacanian thought introduces a discipline, a certain set of inquiries, a way of understanding the stakes of the psychoanalytic process that are unique and viable for theory and, as these chapters indicate, for the clinic. Those who are aligned with Lacan bring a certain set of presuppositions to their work and these presuppositions run through many strains of Lacanian thinking.

The body is conceptualized uniquely in Lacanian thought, where it is most certainly socially constructed (see Colette Soler 1995). There is indeed a "bio-logic" of the body, but there is also another logic, introduced by the signifier, that installs a radical break between the biological body and the *parle-être*, thus rendering the subject as a lack in being—and at one level *split*, unknown to him or herself. Psychoanalysis must conceptualize this subject through the relationship between jouissance and the Other as the locus of the signifier.

Jouissance even as it is translated as "enjoyment," entails an understanding of what Lacan called the "death drive." It is surely fair to say that Lacanians are more preoccupied with this aspect of psychic structure than are many other schools in the United States, which would instead have repetition appear primarily as a pathological effect. The structure of jouissance—its effects through fantasy, symptom, transference, and the signifier—frame the economic question in psychoanalysis, the positioning through which the body is given over to being. For Lacanians, the formulations of jouissance are considered a bit more precise than the vocabulary of affect, which is seen as too unreliable, too phenomenologically based, to serve as an orientation for the position of the analyst.

As well as re-defining the economic side of psychoanalysis, a Lacanian approach re-formulates the "narrative" side of psychoanalysis. Here, interpretation neither refers to an object, the unconscious, nor does it play off reality. Rather, the unconscious and interpretation function along the same plane; they are, so to speak, co-constituted within the analytic process. One can see this dimension of the analytic process insofar as the analysis focuses on the symbolic register.

In the view of many Lacanians, other current schools of psychoanalysis are "taken in" by the imaginary axis of functioning. This axis, which may be conceived as the axis of identification, the analyst as self-object, or even as the terms of intersubjectivity, is certainly one part of the analytic (or any other) relationship. Its overemphasis, however, brokers the possibility of veering the analytic process toward normalization or might otherwise stall the psychoanalytic process. Thus, Lacanian informed work reconceives the meaning of analytic neutrality, not as a matter of analyst observer but as strategies for moving away from "little other" dynamics towards an encounter with the subject of the unconscious. This aspect of Lacanian practice could find as its precedent Freud's "Recommendations to Physicians Practicing Psychoanalysis."

Such differences from the more usual North American practices within psychoanalysis account for the specialized lexicon that marks all Lacanian accounts. Surely there is important work to be done in taking up the points of engagement where Lacanian approaches address the same clinical difficulties as are pinpointed by other schools, and thus more carefully addressing Lacanian differences in initial assumptions at points where dialogue is most possible and productive. However, it is not the task of these chapters to look to those points of convergence and divergence in relation to contemporary North American psychoanalysis or even within the Lacanian tradition. Rather, their interest is to bring the reader into the psychoanalytic clinical praxis and the questions that it evokes.

In "The Direction of the Treatment and the Principles of Its Power," Lacan calls for a critical fidelity to an "authentic praxis." Many of Lacan's notorious theoretical swerves refer to clinical issues that require a better conceptualization of the symptom, a more attuned response to the stakes of the transference; they utilize diagnosis in the most meaningful way, and articulate the place of fantasy, repetition, and the limits of interpretation. Gifric has taken its Lacanian roots and planted them in the soil of an ongoing practice with psychotics. It is from this site that one sees Gifric's theoretical formulations take their shape.

Academic Interest in the Lacanian Clinic

Scholars in the humanities have, of course, found in Lacan's writings an incredibly fertile source of inspiration as they work with problems in art and literature, ethics and philosophy, epistemology and cognition. However, it has become clear, in the decades since Lacanian theory first entered academic discourse, that a widespread misapprehension of the clinical aspects of Lacan's theoretical elaborations has led to a certain lack of grounding in increasingly abstract theoretical debates. One finds, for example, that certain debates over the phallus disappear when the phallus is situated, not as an abstraction amid debates in literary or political theory, but rather as a concrete function in the clinic.

Indeed any number of debates still swirl around the phallus and the question of authority that it implicitly or explicitly poses. The present volume certainly will not quell such debates and could not possibly settle all of the issues that arise in relation to the phallus and the place of the Oedipal. Such questions must be seen as part of a clinical and theoretical perspective that is continually in development, both inside the Lacanian field and among others in psychoanalysis. However, the clinical narratives of this text (and the function of the phallus in the concrete lives and structures of desire therein) argue forcefully against any position that might too facilely dismiss or deny the function of the phallus in the lives of men and women, as if it were purely a political function or based only in competitive masculine narcissism.

If we culturally—and by implication theoretically—retain sexual difference through a relation to the Other sex, we must understand its structural intermixing with the locus of the Other and with the genesis of desire in the Other. Insofar as that genesis in its particularity is written "in the unconscious," we are well advised not to be satisfied with academic discourse alone, but to turn as well to the clinical practices that are founded on the unconscious. Perhaps only clinical practice can adequately dramatize the starkly different logic that governs the unconscious, where the signifier is marked by its lack of "sense" and is rather held by its reference to jouissance. Here, the appearance of the unconscious in free association and its deduction from fantasy do not follow the same logic as any standards of intelligibility. As well, clinical practice situates this drama amid a very different structure of address, since the analysand is not speaking about himself or herself but about an Other.

Political promise has likewise troubled the relationship between Lacanian psychoanalysis and certain strains of feminism. At least since Foucault's reconsideration of subjectivity and subjection, feminists have recognized the necessity of articulating a relation between subjectivity and the political, but too often they have been hampered by a lack of clinical insight and as a consequence have succumbed to the political expedience that would collapse fundamental elements of subjectivity into ego ideals—where, for example, the mother becomes all good things. Clinical experience, as this collection shows, would suggest that the feminist ideological move away from Freud's perceived phallocentrism needs to be executed with greater precision and with greater respect for something crucial in the relation between the paternal function and the formation of the subject.

Especially germane to the interest of the present collection in the psychoanalytic treatment of psychosis, one finds that certain readers in the wake of Gilles Deleuze and Félix Guattari have suggested that there is a sort of liberatory potential represented by the psychotic, whom the Lacanian clinic shows to be outside of paternal law. Deleuze and Guattari, of course, wish to counter normative psychotherapy and to rethink the relation between subjectivity and the political. However, emancipatory claims for schizoanalysis must appear romantic when one sees the anguish that characterizes the psychotics in the present collection. It appears much more the case that in the absence of Oedipal triangulation under the father, the uninhibited flow of the Other's jouissance enslaves the psychotic and (at the very least) threatens to do the same to the pervert. This is not to say that the neurotic isn't equally enslaved. In fact Gifric, like many anti-psychiatrists, would recognize in the psychotic a particular savoir—one that is as true as it is unbearable to acknowledge.

The issue is freeing the psychotic to face that savoir of the absent Other, rather than to occlude it with the "mission" (as Gifric calls it) which aims at a flawless universe.

While *After Lacan* encourages the reader to carefully evaluate the significance of the paternal, it also speaks specifically to how the signifier organizes the logic of the body and of the images that organize corporeality. Through concrete symptoms, fantasies, and dreams, the authors show how the signifier operates in these seemingly nonsymbolic domains. One can see how this addresses certain problems in current discourses of media analysis and trauma-theory. To focus on the imaginary body to the exclusion of the symbolic, threatens to overlook precisely what is most interesting about trauma-theory and about our relation to the screen image—namely, that trauma above all stages a crisis in the symbolic and that the screen image speaks to us in very specific ways that are governed by the signifier and the symbolic. By grounding consideration of the body in the analytic clinic and in the very thorough discussion of the bodily symptom in this collection, the specifics of the way the body is overwritten by the signifier and the importance of the signifier as the means of the analytic process are restored to their proper importance.

Finally, although the work of Slavoj Žižek, and others have introduced the notion of the real into cultural studies, no amount of categorical description or illustration can fully convey the laborious work with signifiers, the timing of the symptom, or the construction of the fantasy that frames the encounter with the real within the clinic. Its momentary fragmentary appearance, etched in anguish, insists within the temporality of the subject and resists any purely philosophical depiction. Thus, in a way, clinical praxis itself forces certain forms of theorization—a dialectic that we see evident in the work of Apollon, Bergeron, and Cantin.

Clinical Interest in Lacanian Theory

The ideal of any school of psychoanalysis, at least, has been to interarticulate one's clinical choices with a certain theoretical integrity (see also London Part I 1988, 5–9). This ideal is characteristic of Lacanian work as well. So, although it is oriented to psychoanalytic praxis, this collection of papers from Gifric is not simply a clinical demonstration of psychoanalytic practice. Nor should the reader expect a clinical introduction to Lacan (for those one may usefully consult Bruce Fink, Joël Dor, or Dany Nobus), a guide to the evolution of Lacan's thought (see Miller "Introduction" 1996; and Julien 1994), or a comparison of concepts and techniques in Lacanian versus other psychoanalytic approaches (see Gurewich 1998; Muller 1996). Rather, both the theoretical and clinical bounties of the collection are best understood as a rigorous application and development of Freud's and Lacan's work in a strict dialogue with clinical practice. The fact that many of the chapters originated in presentations to general audiences, gives us hope that non-Lacanian clinicians will more readily understand how these concepts function within an analytic context.

While it is not advisable for one to be simply "theory-driven" in one's therapeutic practice (an accusation often leveled not just at Lacanian psychoanalysis, but also at psychoanalysis in general), one cannot merely collect techniques based on current or unarticulated ideas of human nature. Such a strategy is all too characteristic of contemporary psychotherapeutic and even some psychodynamic approaches. With theoretical apathy, therapeutic practice becomes vulnerable to a certain ideological overwriting. One evokes notions of projection or of "self-object," in a manner that depends on meanings of these terms that draw from consciousness as much as they draw from the encounter with "subject of the unconscious." Failing to attend to the specificity of the subject as "discovered" by psychoanalysis means that its notions become sustained by "common sense" rather the rigor of its own practice. This ideological problematic—covered over by technical preoccupations—haunts North American therapeutic practices and has received increasing critical scrutiny from psychologists, historians, social theorists, and even therapists (see Cushman 1990; Hare-Mustin 1997; Jacoby 1986). Concern with unintentional ideological effects—normative bias—has always been critical to Lacanian thinking and motivates Lacan's repeated efforts to formalize the specificity of the unconscious in its relation to the Other. Lacanians know that they are not dealing with simply asocial properties possessed by a given individual consciousness (a view Lacan called "psychologizing" in his *Écrits*). Rather, issues that arise in clinical practice are better understood as reflective of the human stakes in the social link (chap. 1). At the same time, neither does the Lacanian sensitivity to the centrality of the social link as constitutive of human subjectivity devolve into a politicization of psychoanalytic processes, nor does it translate the clinical encounter with the unconscious into a (democratic) interpersonal event. The imposition of the "intersubjective" and the social does *not*, for Lacanians, default to a model wherein healthy parts of analysts and analysands "communicate' and construct coherent narratives. Referring to the Lacanian affiliation with Freud's so-called classical psychoanalysis, Jacques-Alain Miller writes, "Nor is classical psychoanalysis the blend of ego psychology and object relations theory attempted by contemporary American psychoanalysts, that takes into account the semantic relationship to others while retaining the structural framework of ego psychology" (1996, 307).

The process by which one becomes a human subject does not, in the Lacanian view, reflect the maturation of adaptive capacities that ultimately refer to instinctual forces, conflictual or not. Rather, the subject for Lacan and for Lacanians, is genuinely a subject of the unconscious. In part, this means that Lacan regards the unconscious as the effects of the spoken word on the subject—a dimension where the subject determines himself or herself. Thus, it is necessary that the analyst "trust[s] nothing but the experience of the subject, which is the sole matter of psychoanalytic work" (Lacan cited in Nasio 1998, 133). The *subject*, we see, is not just a fancy word for the *person*; the terms are utterly distinct, and the ethics of the clinic require that the subject not be engaged as if it were the person. This "impersonal" quality to the subject of the Lacanian clinic is sometimes viewed as "harsh" by North American clinicians. But, for Lacanians, theorizing psychoanalysis through the Imaginary (e.g. imprinted interpersonal relations and schemas) is not inconsequential for the ultimate transformative effects of psychoanalysis either. As well, maintaining an ethics oriented to the subject of the unconscious does not preclude work with more "fragile" individuals who in being respected as subjects are more likely to respond as such. The work at "388" is a tribute to this fact.

Hence, it is the *subject* that we must theorize, not the phenomenology of symptoms (chap. 9), and it is precisely the *subject of the unconscious* that we must work with clinically. From this perspective, the Lacanian subject is perhaps even more completely "deconstructed" than the multiple selves currently being conceived as part of narrative and postmodernist trends in relational psychoanalytic approaches.

The success of Gifric with psychotic young adults is exemplary of how a Lacanian orientation can frame one's practice within a clinical setting. Although the "388" is not an intensive inpatient facility such as North Americans might think of with respect to Chestnut Lodge, it is a residential and nonresidential treatment center that is anchored in psychoanalytic theory and individual psychoanalysis with psychotics. The analysts of Gifric, much like the many therapists that followed Fromm-Reichman, Sullivan, Boyer, or Searles in the United States or Bion and Klein in Great Britain have creatively extended not only the horizons of psychoanalysis in their treatment of psychoses, but also what are now called severely borderline states. Here there is no supposition that psychosis is a biological entity (chap. 12).

As noted by Otto F. Kernberg, the psychoanalytic treatment of psychotic conditions is currently enjoying something of a renaissance in North America. In part this reflects the dissemination of recent work by psychoanalytic pioneers in the treatment of psychosis. These approaches, whether or not they see a continuum between neurotic and psychotic difficulties (London Part I 1988, 5–22), have dispelled the presumption that psychoanalysis is only effective in relationship to the transference neurosis (Rosenfeld 1998). At the same time, the ameliorative limits of psychopharmacological approaches are becoming more apparent, and the limited efficacy of simply supportive therapies is likewise becoming clear. Moreover, the increasing presence of what many call "borderline patients" further signals the importance of continued psychoanalytic consideration of psychosis. Lacanians do not consider borderlines a distinct category (see Fink 1997) but many psychoanalysts in North America see such patients as constituting a separate diagnostic entity. This category is characterized by more "primitive" object relations and by presenting a different set of transferential challenges. Clearly, a better understudying of innovative approaches to psychosis, such as described here in *After Lacan*, ought to shed light on the enigmatic category of the borderline.

Irrespective of the type of analysand, the clinical papers of Apollon, Bergeron, and Cantin demonstrate the clear interrelation between the overall understanding of subjective structures, the type of work undertaken in the clinic, and the way human suffering is alleviated and transformed. Even with psychotic patients, a Lacanian approach does not attempt to establish a therapeutic alliance. Thus, one would not invoke the ideal of a healthy person or real self. Nor would these authors divide the analysand into psychotic and non-psychotic *personalities*. For Gifric, psychosis, like neurosis and perversion, defines a form of *subjective structure*, an unconscious relationship to the structure of signification and the logic of the signifier as forged in the concrete vicissitudes of our relations with others (chaps. 1, and 3). Ideas such as "healthy self" may or may not intersect with certain Lacanian notions—it may approximate, for example, a certain subjective position in relationship to the signifying structure. But the Lacanian perspective approaches the questions of psychoanalysis from the place of a *divided* subject, not a subject that is fragmented into different agencies, with its "best" agency modeled on a notion of the self. In other words, the clinical process is conceived outside of the terms supplied by the ego (chap. 7). It is conceived strictly in the terms of the unconscious.

Given this shift, the role of the analyst is not oriented to providing "emotional" support based on a certain sort of maternal presence that would restore an analysand to a place wherein his or her ego can benefit from interpretation. Rather, issues that are defined by the concepts of demand, desire, the dream, and the signifier carve out a new clinical terrain. Although there is a de-emphasis on emotion, this is not a matter of the imputed classical view of an observing psychoanalyst *qua* scientist who "looks" at the unconscious of another and then interprets it. The authors do not think the unconscious is "inside" somebody. Nor is the unconscious something that is examined by another as might follow from the medical model. The "unconscious" is a clinical event: it requires the psychoanalytic dyad but is irreducible to it; it requires a third—the locus of the Other. Put differently, the unconscious and interpretation are of the same fabric.

The Lacanian approach seen in the work of Apollon, Bergeron, and Cantin is a carefully conceived mode of therapeutic functioning that is founded in the position of the speaking subject. Psychoanalysis operates in relation to the conditions that structure the coming into being of the subject and trace the impasses that are marked in a particular subject's repetitions and symptoms. Clearly, Lacanian clinicians are aware that they are the vehicles through which interpretation is effected. They must serve to structure the transference and the patient's encounter with the savoir of the unconscious (chap. 6). However, Gifric conceives of these clinical activities and of the patient's progress outside ideas of countertransference, emotional support, or the analyst's self-disclosure (see McWilliams 1994; Searles 1988; Boyer 1989). Countertransference, like intersubjectivity assumes two monads interacting even as such views attempt to dialecticize such a relation. The early Lacan entertained this idea of intersubjectivity, but later determined that this model could not calibrate the presence of the Other. This is especially important given that, in North America, such "relational" concerns are commonly considered the pivot of success with more disturbed patients. Certainly, the difference in praxis here and the theory that sustains it deserves the same significant dialogues that are accorded the differences between more typically British object-relations perspectives and more process-relational North American stances (see Williams 1998).

The essays in this collection show how treatment at the "388" aims to restore a sphere of subjective psychic activities to patients that will enable them to reintegrate into social life and recapture sufficient control of their personal and social lives that they can take a certain satisfaction from coexistence. The treatment aims to stabilize the delusion and to control the disorganizing effects of the psychosis. It does so in part by bringing the psychotic to take responsibility for the comprehension of that which causes his or her activities. The patient, then, is not regarded as an object of care, but rather treated as a subject of speech. The analytic listening to the experiences of the psychotic in relation to the imaginary Other and the social and symbolic Other creates a space for the expression of the truth of that psychotic, a truth other than that of the delusion and its voices, a truth that aims to reappropriate the life and history of the young psychotic. Partly in response to psychiatric advances in the treatment of psychosis, American psychoanalysts are in great alarm as biomedical approaches and short-term, insurance-driven therapies increasingly encroach upon analytic modes of treatment. This battle about human nature requires more than professional maneuvering. It needs all of the clinical knowledge it can garner and a serious theorization of the ethical and theoretical stakes of psychoanalysis.

Broader Debates

It is surely an inappropriate cliché that North American psychotherapy is only ego-centered. Nevertheless, some of the ideas presented here may be surprising or radical to North American sensibilities. Hence, the importance of the clinical material in which this book abounds. Such material, rather than the almost impossible task of theoretical translation, allows North American clinicians to gain an appreciation of these innovative Lacanian concepts. As well, gaining a sense of the Lacanian contribution may significantly further contemporary understandings of ongoing psychoanalytic debates and treatment approaches for certain populations.

For many psychoanalysts, especially in North America, psychoanalytic perspectives ultimately divide over the place of "environmental" object-relations approaches versus more classically oriented positions. The latter conceive of the psychoanalytic process in terms of endogenous drives and resultant intrapsychic conflicts, whereas the former turns the psychoanalytic process toward issues of relationship. Within the psychoanalytic community, there are certainly many blends of these two perspectives, combining what one calls "drive/structure" with object-relations and "relational modalities" (see Greenberg and Mitchell 1983). As one reads the following chapters, it becomes clear that Lacanian approaches offer a third alternative that re-conceptualizes the drive, the Oedipal and the pre-Oedipal, and thus moves both technique and theory beyond current theoretical integrations or exclusive alternatives. For if the Other is the absolute pivot in psychoanalysis and one must privilege the signifier and the object (petit objet *a*), it does not follow that psychoanalysis automatically moves to the dimension of the interpersonal. The drive and the unconscious indicate that the subject is produced on another scene (chaps. 2 and 3). The particularity of the discipline of psychoanalysis also answers to this other scene which is most certainly neither the realm of neurology or biology, nor is it located within the phenomenology of the emotions or in corrective emotional experiences (re)-lived in the relational present. Psychoanalysis does constitute a social bond, but there is an asymmetry between the Other and the subject that is not captured by the notion of intersubjectivity.

More specifically, the intricate Lacanian understanding of the function of the Other in relation to the advent of the object and of the human bondage to the signifier address in a very precise way the relationship between representation and what are called "primitive object relations." Such relations are really played out in terms of signifiers that emerge as indices of the logic of the subject. Although a number of approaches to psychosis directly theorize the representational confusions of psychotic individuals, the "deficiencies" in cognition are referred to "super-ordinate" cognitive processes related to adaptation (London Part II 1988). These process are either genetically compromised or severely disrupted by early trauma experiences, giving the patient a psychotic "personality" that must vie with a more normal one (Williams 1998). The second personality is the vehicle for identification with the analyst and is the leverage that allows for psychoanalytic progress through interpretation. In contrast, more relational practices accept the significance of a "psychotic transference" and work within that process. In this case, the emphasis is to treat the psychotic transference as defined mostly by chaotic affective responses and scarred object relations that are tolerated and repaired by a certain analytic presence. Although analytic observations on transference in psychosis indicate that they are dealing with a type of relationship with the Other in which the Other is both impervious and absolute, in North America, this relationship may be seen less as a structure and more as played out in terms of affects, persons, and perhaps styles of representation. Thus, the therapeutic presence is defined as much by its emotional tonality as it is by interpretation. In very recent developments in this relational view, one interprets "up" (McWilliams 1994) and is supportive of the healthy self (Black 1998). This reading of a psychoanalysis of psychosis would seem to suggest affinities to ego psychology even if it uses the word "self" instead. Such approaches remain quite different from a Lacanian approach or even from Searles' exchanges within "psychotic transference."

The orientation of *After Lacan*, then, should be read as marking a certain departure from prevailing North American tendencies. From psychosis to neurotic disorders, we are dealing with issues of a subject that is defined by its inception into a community that speaks (chap. 1). The effects of the signifier ground all subjective being in relationship to speaking and its logic—one does not need a super-ordinate adaptive function for language. But, as well, this condition of coming to signification is always complicated by its registration in the terms of the body and the impossibility of our fully knowing the Other (chap. 2). Thus, in a sense, the issues raised by this collection are indeed not only matters of object relationships, but also relations to the object that function much more as a matter of an effect of a structure and a location in fantasy. The object is more precisely understood as a place within a logic that creates a corporeal consistency. Thus, analytic concepts such as projective identification, which are so important to work with psychotics, do not neatly coincide with the Lacanian frame of the logic of the signifier. Rather than compiling a list of defensive postures and mechanisms, such defenses are coherently related to the genesis of human desire within the structures and registers (the real, symbolic, and imaginary) that found human coexistence. This allows one to clinically encounter the human subject rather than a normative subject that is crippled by a certain set of defenses. This encounter, if it is theorized and carefully addressed, fully exploits the possibilities of understanding offered by psychoanalysis. As such it offers a more coherent picture of the stakes of clinical practice, new clinical approaches, and an ethical position from which psychoanalysis can maintain and expand its way of seeing the human subject in an era where considerations of subjectivity are all too rare.

It will be evident from preceding sections of this introduction that there is a diversity of opinion among Lacanians on many topics; there is no supposition here that all Lacanians would agree on the parameters that define the diagnostic categories as they are presented in this text. Such differences in the Lacanian field do not devolve into eclectic laissez-faire pragmatics but constitute the tension that define Lacan's rich theory and the demands of clinical work. The essays of Apollon, Bergeron, and Cantin clearly represent how this tension informs clinical work and indicate the ways that a Lacanian orientation allows one to reconceive transference, castration, the symptom, the object, interpretation, and "psychopathology" itself. Perhaps, this clinical edge will introduce some modesty into academic debates about Lacanian psychoanalysis and encourage the long overdue recognition of the claims of the Lacanian clinic.

General Summary of Chapters in *After Lacan*

The twelve chapters of the present collection give a highly integrated presentation of Lacanian ideas in relation to clinical practice. Probably a word or two might be said about their disparate origins, however. Nearly all of the chapters included here were originally occasioned by conference presentations of one kind or another—sometimes a general conference on psychoanalysis, sometimes a conference more narrowly Lacanian in focus. Somewhat to the editors' surprise, the disparate originating contexts seemed to give to the assembled whole not a scattered feeling, but, to the contrary, a sort of rhythmic movement of deepening intensities balanced by the relief of more leisurely, more concrete pieces. The texts were originally written in French, the native language of the authors, generally in the early- and mid-1990s, and then given rough translation into English to be read at the conference. The editors of the present volume worked in close consultation with the authors to give the language a more congenial gloss, occasionally retranslating passages altogether, and, of course, editing and ordering the texts according to the necessities of published, rather than oral presentation. In the editing process, every effort was made to preserve the intended meaning of the original French texts, despite the fact that the authors' thinking has continued to evolve through the intervening years since the essays were written.

The early chapters (chaps. 1, 2, and 3) are devoted to the general concepts (for example, the jouissance of the Other, the sexual division, and the paternal function) and key terms (dream, signifier, and interpretation) that constitute the touchstones of the early phase of analytic treatment, elaborating their interrelations and their clinical relevance. The next chapters (chaps. 4, and 5) focus on the groundbreaking clinic of psychosis that Gifric has pioneered in Québec—how Lacanians theorize psychosis and how Gifric has come to treat it analytically. The next chapters (chaps. 6, 7, and 8) turn toward the second phase of analytic treatment, introducing a new set of terms—the letter of the body, the symptom, the fantasy—to understand the genesis within the transference and the ethical act of analysis in the subject's assumption of the Other's lack. The concluding chapters (chaps. 9, 10, 11, and 12) are especially rich in clinical material, and broaden the understanding of the analytic clinic by discussing the key psychic structures that describe the organization of subjectivity and thereby dictate the terms of analysis: obsessional and hysterical neurosis, perversion, and (again) psychosis.

"Language," writes Lucie Cantin in chapter 1, "has transformed us into beings subject to a logic that is other than biological or natural logic." The early chapters of the collection probe the clinical implications of this human fact. One discovers that at stake in this subjection to language is more than the way we are captured by desires, fantasies, and expectations in the discourse of others about us—though indeed one sees this dimension very concretely in Cantin's presentation of the case of Myriam, a young dancer who lives so painfully under the fantasy of a mother whose devaluation of the father and whose own refusal of loss interferes with Myriam's access to desire. As Cantin argues further, the very organization of our very bodies, our erotics, our symptoms, even our life and our death—all this has come under the law of the signifier, with the exile of our bodies from a natural logic. This exile has at the same time necessitated an essential loss in human existence; in language, human life recognizes an impossibility of a natural jouissance or a total satisfaction. As language and the laws of culture mediate our appetites and our pleasures, human desire has shown itself to be irreducible, that is, without any specific object to offer perfect and complete satisfaction of its own. And if, in our subjection to language, "father" becomes the name of this necessity of loss under the law of the signifier and the law of culture, "father"—the paternal function—also acts to limit the jouissance demanded by the Other in the imaginary of the child. Loss and lack are the law for child, but they are the law also for the Other, whose claims on the life of the subject are thereby limited.

Willy Apollon's canny and passionate chapter on jouissance (chap. 2) deepens the consideration of the irrevocable loss of natural satisfaction and the consequent impossibility of any total jouissance. When satisfaction must be routed through language and culture, when satisfaction submits itself as a demand to the Other, it becomes vulnerable to the whim of the Other, dependent upon the Other, who may or may not respond as the subject demands (by providing or withholding a desired object, say). Satisfaction comes to depend, therefore, upon the Other even more than upon the adequacy of the object itself. Moreover, a jouissance is imputed to the Other in this power of refusal—the Other may be thought to derive a certain pleasure from this power over the subject's demand. Thus, jouissance always implies the relation to the Other. An obsessional neurotic, for example, may hypothesize a lost, mythical moment in which he or she was perfectly satisfied by the Other's jouissance, but in actuality, jouissance will always prove an obstacle to satisfaction. It is the signifier that places the subject in an elsewhere outside of consciousness and in excess of need, an elsewhere regulated by jouissance and radically unknown to the subject. How the subject will relate to the Other and to jouissance in terms of the procreation of the speaking human being describes the asymmetrical terms of the sexual division, which Apollon explores in the balance of the chapter.

Danielle Bergeron's chapter on the signifier (chap. 3) scales us back from the theoretical intensity of the preceding chapter and begins in a more leisurely fashion to describe the nature of the signifier in psychoanalysis. Lacanian borrowings from linguistics are, of course, familiar territory by now, but Bergeron illustrates how the signifier in psychoanalytic discourse also represents a break from the semiotic signifier insofar as the psychoanalytic signifier is what, above all, *ruptures* meaning, to suggest the workings of some "other scene" hidden from view. Moreover, with her clinical example from the dream and subsequent associations of a young medical intern, Bergeron shows vividly how the psychoanalytic signifier, selected from the navel of the patient's dream, gives voice to the unconscious and allows for the talking cure to do its work. Hence, Bergeron's description of the signifier as both the metaphor of the subject and as the metonymy of desire.

The next two chapters by Bergeron and Cantin (chaps. 4, and 5) build upon the earlier chapters' elaborations of the signifier, the paternal function, and the jouissance of the Other, to illustrate the theory and clinic of psychosis. In the cases of John, Mr. Owens, and Mr. T., the reader gets a powerful sense of the pathos and the anguished drama of the psychotic in his vulnerability to the abuse of the Other. This exposure to being used as the object of the Other, we learn, results from a failure of the paternal function to establish the law of the signifier, the law of universal lack that would place a limit on the jouissance of the Other.

Through a graceful marriage of theory and case material, Bergeron and Cantin trace the precise positioning of the analytic acts that effect the movement from the subject's relationship to the signifier within psychotic *delusional* systems, to the logic of the signifier found in the *dream*—a movement allowing the psychotic a different relationship to his or her suffering. The delusion attempts to treat the real by subordinating scattered, aggressing signifiers with the imaginary as it elaborates a flawless knowledge that both accounts for the victim position of the psychotic subject as the object of the jouissance of the Other and signals the status of the psychotic as a privileged, elected one. The dream, by contrast, processes the real by subjugating the imaginary to the symbolic, where desire must obey the laws of language and meaning. It is by inducing the psychotic to produce a dream for the analyst, these chapters argue, that psychoanalysis can treat psychosis. Because the dream introduces the curious logic of the signifier and the signifying chain (and hence also a certain flaw or lack in savoir), when a psychotic is brought to dream, the certainty of the psychotic delusion begins to come under doubt. The consistency of the persecuting jouissance of the Other gradually diminishes as the analyst takes the specific signifiers of the psychotic's dream narrative and encourages metonymic association with the patient's past to construct a narrative of the psychotic's life that is outside of the delusion and alternate to it.

Apollon's chapter on transference and the letter of the body (chap. 6), initiates an important shift to the concerns of the second phase of analytic treatment, a phase dealing with the real of jouissance through symptom and fantasy. In this and the following two chapters, Apollon develops further the presentation of the parceled body dealt with in psychoanalysis to demonstrate how the logic of the signifier moves clinical practice beyond what the signifier can reveal in itself. Since the symptom indicates the failure of the law of the signifier to limit the Other's jouissance, the analyst's maneuver in the transference aims to instigate lack as a barrier to that deadly jouissance that repeats itself in the life of the patient. In general terms, then, the analyst's desire under the transference elicits various materials—the signifier in the dream, the letter in the symptom, the object in the fantasy—to convert forbidden drive jouissance into desire. Apollon writes of the matter as an ethical choice, albeit not a choice on the ordinary level of conscious intention. More precisely, the choice of the subject—and the maneuver of the analyst—may be said to involve an ethical assumption by the subject of the Other's lack as foundational to desire. As Apollon will suggest in chapter 8, the choice revolves around the question of the relationship to jouissance sustained by the subject: either to persist in the prohibited, fatal (impossible, lapsed, etc.) jouissance that returns in the repetition of the symptom, or else to assume subjectively the constitutive failing of jouissance, to answer the lack in the Other, a lack necessitated by the law of the signifier, and lying at the heart of desire.

The next chapters on symptom and fantasy (chaps. 7, and 8) further integrate these theoretical elaborations with clinical case material. In chapter 7, drawing from the earlier argument concerning the routing of satisfaction through the vicissitudes of the Other's response (in chap. 2), and following the case of a young anorexic, Apollon propose two dimensions of the symptom in relation to jouissance. There is, as he describes it, a certain jouissance that inscribes the symptom itself in relation to the signifier and the failure of the Other; and there is another jouissance that fails to be inscribed in the symptom and in consequence returns to seek inscription in the *repetition* of the symptom. This latter jouissance is the one that concerns the second phase of analysis, as treatment begins to orient itself in relation to the symptom and the traversal of the fantasy. Analysis attempts to treat the symptom through the traversal of fantasy, where fantasy is understood as formulating the subject's relation to the lost object that gives rise to desire. The analyst's maneuver aims, as Apollon puts it, to disengage the fantasy, to grasp the remainder of jouissance that both repeats and resists inscription in the symptom.

The next chapter on the fantasy (chap. 8) continues Apollon's theoretical work with case material to follow the clinical process through to the traversal of fantasy that marks the end of analysis. The chapter follows the case of Marguerite, a young woman whose frigidity derives, she says, from her fear of fainting during sexual intercourse. Her analysis turns upon two dreams. While the dream attempts to accommodate insistent jouissance by way of the signifier, the jouissance that the dream fails to reduce shows itself in the symptom. Her analysis shows that Marguerite's relation to jouissance has been organized according to a fantasy in which Marguerite supposes that the prohibition of her own jouissance derives not from the universal law of the paternal phallus, but rather from the reservation of a special jouissance for the mother. Through the analysis, her symptom gives way as Marguerite moves to make the ethical choice to confront the truth that was previously hidden by the fatal, prohibited jouissance at work to efface the subject

The final chapters focus on the fundamental structures of subjectivity, as defined by the Lacanian clinic: obsessional and hysterical neurosis, perversion, and psychosis. Bergeron's chapter describing obsessional neurosis (chap. 9) introduces the important Lacanian distinction between subjective structure and phenomenological features. She follows the case of Mr. Beauregard, a man whose sexual behavior and fantasies might be considered perverse by some classical and object-relations perspectives, but whose structure is clearly obsessional. Bergeron describes the anguish of the obsessional (and the obsessional's special difficulty in analysis) as that of a forbidden hope unabandoned. Mr. Beauregard's analysis illustrates the obsessional's paradigmatic seduction fantasy: events in his childhood have suggested the illusory hope that the mother may be available to him (despite the paternal prohibition he recognizes), and he feels himself therefore forbidden to desire any others, as well as guilty, fearful, and self-punishing for his forbidden fantasy. When we see this in the life of Mr. Beauregard as he symptomatically sabotages his sex life with his new partner, we understand the neurotic symptom as the jouissance of the drive seeking satisfaction in the body, when desire cannot supersede the demand of the Other—the demand Mr. Beauregard feels in response to what he imagines his mother would love (her son as a priest).

Cantin's chapters on perversion and hysteria (chaps. 10, and 11), elucidate the two structures by considering them in relation to each other, as well as by considering examples, one from the clinic, another from literature. Perversion, we learn, is characterized by a twofold movement: an initial postulation of the Father and of the signifier, coupled with a logically subsequent denial that stages the uselessness of the Father-signifier-symbolic. The pervert attempts to obscure the logic of the drive's functioning by imposing instead a logic of pure mechanism. A conflation of the natural/organismic penis and the symbolic phallus, for example, denies the phallus and symbolic castration to eliminate desire: no longer must the pervert hazard the question of a partner's desire. The perverse contract formalizes the matter by regulating exchange and eliminating the gap, as if to say: "It's not a question of what you or I might desire; it's a matter of arranging our bodies and organs as pre-arranged, as scripted." It's like a reversion to some sort of animal code: the signifier compels, but only with the evacuation of the other—as Cantin shows in the example of the Sacher-Masoch contract (chap. 11). Nevertheless, in contrast with psychosis, the phallus *does* exist in perversion, and the pervert's collusion in the denial of the law—and his or her status as the captive object of the mother's desire—is determined by some sort of unconscious choice and assent.

Hysteria, we find, also features an unsatisfied mother, but where perversion accents the failure of the paternal most generally, hysteria accents the voracity of the mother, her unsatisfied demand. Because the maternal complaint concerns the insufficiency of the paternal phallus to put an end to the jouissance at work in the mother, the hysteric seeks to satisfy the mother by bolstering the inadequate father. Castration is repressed under the supposition that it is only the hysteric's particular father who lacks, rather than fathers (and humans) universally. Consequently, the hysteric is on a quest for the phallic ideal, the Master, who might satisfy the mother and repair the inadequacy of the father—a role the pervert may feel privileged to play. Also, for the hysteric, the insufficiency of the signifier of the Father's desire for the mother means that the subject has been unable to sufficiently trust the signifier. Thus, the ability to occupy the position of a possible object of desire has been compromised. Such is the tragedy of the hysteric, endlessly addressing the Other, seeking reference points that would allow the subject to construct the ego as an object of desire. In the pervert, the hysteric may find not only the Master who embodies the accountable other, but also the one who gives the hysteric the dedicated status as object. The hysteric, however, cannot be the object-cause of the pervert's desire, but only ever an object of jouissance. The seduction fantasy, in which the hysteric's desire is forsaken in becoming the object of the desire of the Other, as well as the quest for the credible word of love that would quiet the jouissance of the Other, constitute the pathos of this subjective structure.

The final chapter (chap. 12), in which Bergeron introduces a fascinating clinical analysis of the Japanese writer Yukio Mishima, usefully generalizes discussion of the psychotic from earlier chapters to examine the life of a highly functioning, very articulate psychotic, and to propose some conclusions about the treatment of the excluded jouissance that is unrepresentable by the signifier and that constitutes the real defect of language. Bergeron finds in Mishima an exemplary psychotic who experienced his body as powerless against the jouissance of an Other. Raised by a grandmother who, it seemed, cared only for his physical preservation and refused the boy entry into the world of social interaction and masculine identification, Mishima lived a childhood organized by key images—hypermasculine images of fairy tale violence and tragic sacrifice in the cause of God (Saint Sebastian) and country (knightly Joan of Arc). The psychotic's fantasy, as we see here (and as we might recall from earlier discussions), involves the subject being brutally captured by the jouissance of the Other, and abandoned to this jouissance. Foreclosed from masculine identification under the symbolic phallus, Mishima was nevertheless able to attenuate the violence of the jouissance of the Other, through his art and through his body building. His distance from perversion is suggested by Mishima's concern for masculine ethics, for a sacrifice on behalf of the paternal emperor—concerns that would have been anathema to a pervert. Mishima shows us, too, the peculiar relationship to language that the psychotic suffers: words have power over his flesh, but though supremely articulate, Mishima cannot make words represent reality. More and more he comes to forge a flawless language of the flesh in body building, an effort that also gives him access to a powerful masculine identification, and gives meaning to his life and death.

Limited Glossary of Terms

There are several fine Lacanian and psychoanalytic dictionaries currently available in English and the interested reader may usefully consult those of Dylan Evans, Elizabeth Wright, and Laplanche and Pontalis. The definitions given below are not considered general, either in terms of the full scope of Gifric's thinking, Lacanian thought, or psychoanalysis, overall. Rather this brief list of terms is provided as a point of entry for some of the terms used in the present collection.

Castration

Castration suggests the subject's entry into the world of irreducible lack and loss, the impossibility of total satisfaction that necessarily accompanies the entry into the symbolic order of language and social law (chap. 6). Castration is therefore the result of the effects of the signifier, and constitutes the universal law for both women and men, though the masculine and the feminine positions have a different relationship to it (chap. 2), as will different subjective structures (chap. 10). One's relation to the Other is a Lacanian formalization of the "castration complex" as postulated within Oedipal dynamics in the Freudian paradigm as a mark in which a biological difference becomes a psychological inscription.

Ethics

Although Gifric certainly intends the word to describe the exigencies of clinical behavior, this isn't quite what North American practitioners know as a code of professional ethics. In their usage, the choice of the subject—and the maneuver of the analyst—may be said to involve the subject's ethical assumption of the Other's lack as foundational to desire. This ethical choice isn't on the ordinary level of conscious intention (weighing known alternatives, choosing between them, etc.). Rather, the choice revolves around the question of the relation to jouissance sustained by the subject: either to persist in the prohibited, fatal (impossible, lapsed, etc.) jouissance that returns in the repetition of the symptom, or else to assume subjectively the constitutive failing of jouissance, a failing necessitated by the law of the signifier, and lying at the heart of lack and desire (chap. 8). It's a matter relinquishing the comforts and promises of the devil one knows, in favor of hazarding the *unknown* of desire (one's own and that of the Other) to fully claim a position as desiring subject. Ethics presuppose an encounter beyond the pleasure principle.

Imaginary

Imaginary is one of the three basic, interconnected registers (with the symbolic and the real) with which Lacan describes psychic life. In chapter 1, Lucie Cantin writes of the imaginary body: the relationship the subject sustains with the image of his or her body. In chapter 4, Danielle Bergeron writes of the imaginary relations of the psychotic as being ones of strength and power, rivalrous relations unmediated by the restraints instated by the signifier and the symbolic. The imaginary is the register most firmly connected with what many think of as subjective experience, entrained to the visible world, bounded by a (false) sense of inside and outside, and functioning as correlative to an alter ego (and thus dyadic). The dimension of the imaginary presupposes some sense of coordinates within the symbolic (a place from which to see oneself—even if these coordinates fail to "overwrite" the imaginary in psychosis). The imaginary also comes into play when thinking of the object *a*, even as its functioning refers to the real and, of course, to fantasy, even as its formulation returns to the signifier.

Jouissance

Jouissance is probably the key term of the present collection and arguably one's of Lacan's most significant contributions to psychoanalysis.

Jouissance is tied to pleasure but only the sort of pleasure for which we would suffer endless pain. In fact, as one follows the trajectory of jouissance, it clearly reaches beyond the pleasure principle and is thus profoundly implicated in the ethical choices within psychoanalysis. In chapter 2, Apollon describes the paradox of this term that, on the one hand, suggests pleasure and total satisfaction, and on the other hand (since total satisfaction is prohibited and impossible), is experienced as an anxiety threatening to overwhelm the position of the subject and thus as an obstacle to desire. In this sense, jouissance is linked to the real and to the death drive. Jouissance in this collection tends to be considered specifically as the jouissance of the Other: the way the subject relates to that use or abuse by the Other, and the limits placed on that use by the paternal function.

Law

Law is written with an uppercase L. Law is here used in its philosophical sense to suggest the universal regulation of human life to which everyone must submit. The law of Law, so to speak, is that total jouissance is firstly impossible and simultaneously prohibited, that there is a limit to jouissance and that these laws apply equally to oneself and ultimately as one comes to see, to the Other. Law is aligned with the symbolic, with the signifier, desire, lack, and loss. In its absence, the caprice and strength of the most powerful are free to dictate the terms of satisfaction.

Name-of-the-Father

Name-of-the-Father refers to the installation of a certain function of the signifier in relationship to limit and to speech that is established by the paternal function: the fact that the mother seeks her object of desire elsewhere and that this loss/lack is referred to a particular suturing of the marks of the (m)other's desire by the logic of the signifier, allowing the subject to enter into the series of substitutions that found social existence.

Object a

The impossible object-cause of desire. In chapter 12, Bergeron describes the object *a* as an inadequate hallucination of a mythical lost object, supposed by the subject to be causing the real jouissance that traverses human being irreducibly in excess of any possible signification. Because that real jouissance cannot be represented, and yet insists in the subject, the subject supposes a series of substitute objects as impostor representatives of that impossible representation. The object *a* insists as a non-specular quality of another that causes desire; it is deduced from its function in the subject's fantasy.

Other/other

These terms describe the position held by an important other person (parent, analyst, society, etc.) in the psychic life of the subject. The other (small o) describes this position in terms of the imaginary register; the Other (large O) is more commonly the concern of the present collection and describes this position in terms of the symbolic order. But the Other means more than its face as the symbolic Other, for this register always implies more; language is irreducible to its properties as a system; there is more to the alterity of language. Because the subject must go through the Other for the satisfaction of needs, and because the response (or nonresponse) of the Other seems unpredictable, the subject will suppose that the possibility of satisfaction is subject to the demands, desires, and requirements of the Other, that he or she occupies a certain position in terms of the jouissance of the Other. The relationship of the subject to the jouissance of the Other is, therefore, the crucial question of the subject's life and is determinative of his or her psychic structure.

Perversion

Perversion describes not any actual or fantasized behavior in itself, but rather constitutes one of the three fundamental psychic structures (together with neurosis and psychosis). The cornerstone of this structure is the subject's attempt to deny the paternal function (the phallus, the law of lack, the signifier of desire), to demonstrate the uselessness of the Father in a maternal universe. Perversion is more fully discussed in chapters 10, and 11.

Phallus

The signifier of the Other's desire that triangulates the child in the Oedipal scenario and thus engenders the subject as, precisely, a speaking being. Hence, it is not the same as the penis. When Lacan writes that the phallus is the signifier of the effects of the signifier, one of the things he means is that the phallus signifies the effects of the definitive *loss* due to language and its incompleteness. It introduces the child to lack and desire and bears a specific relation to his or her being as sexed.

Real

One of the three basic, interconnected registers (with the symbolic and the imaginary) with which Lacan describes psychic life. The real is linked with impasses in the logic of the signifier and its formalization. Thus, the real can be associated with the impossible and what can not be (at present or ever) put into the dialectic of the signifier. The real can be connected with repetition, jouissance (in some of its formations), and the drive.

Savoir

Gifric uses the word savoir to describe the singular knowledge that comes out of the experience of the clinic. At one level, savoir is a knowledge that is utterly particular to the subject, irreducible to the level of information, concerning the particularities of the subject's relation to jouissance. The savoir at the end of analysis refers itself to fantasy and concerns the cause of the failing of jouissance. Savoir may therefore be considered necessary to assuming the risks of one's desire and hence at the heart of a psychoanalytic ethics. There are other levels of savoir that serve to inform clinical praxis.

Symbolic

One of the three basic, interconnected registers (with the real and the imaginary) with which Lacan describes psychic life. In a general sense, the symbolic order is made up of the cultural and historical demands that social life imposes upon the human being (chap. 2). Put in a more structural sense, the symbolic concerns the subject's relation to the phallus, to law and to the signifier. The symbolic is the dimension that allows access to the unconscious in that the unconscious is structured like a language and returns in the formations and mis-fires of speech.

Notes

1. James Glogowski has also argued this point eloquently in his essay on the drive.
2. Other North American associations for the training of Lacanian analysts include RSI in Montréal, Après Coup in New York City, and the Lacanian School of Psychoanalysis in Berkeley, California; there are, moreover, innumerable Lacanian trained analysts offering individual supervision. The reader should not suppose that the training provided by such associations is uniform (as with any school of psychoanalysis), nor that the list here is an exhaustive one. Less formally of course, there exists a wide network of reading groups, seminars and cartels.

References

Apollon, Willy. "Nothing Works Anymore!" *Differences* 9 (1997): 1–13.

Black, Margaret. "Fracturing Drive or Fracturing Connections: Commentary on Paper by Paul Williams." *Psychoanalytic Dialogues* 8 (1998): 493–500.

Boyer, L. Bryce. "Psychoanalysis With Few Parameters in the Treatment of Regressed Patients." *Psychoanalysis and Psychosis.* Edited by Ann-Louise Silver. Madison, CT: International Universities Press, 1989.

Broca, Roland. "The Psychoanalyst Faced with Psychosis in the Transference." *Analysis* 3 (1991): 50–54.

Cushman, Philip. "The Empty Self: Towards a Historically Situated Psychology." *American Psychologist* 45 (1990): 599–611.

Dean, Tim. *Beyond Sexuality.* Chicago: University of Chicago Press, 2000.

Deleuze, Gilles and Félix Guattari. *Anti-Oedipus: Capitalism and Schizophrenia.* Translated by Robert Hurley, Mark Seem, and Helen Lane. Minneapolis, MN: University of Minnesota Press, 1983.

Dor, Joël. *The Clinical Lacan.* Edited by Judith Feher Gurewich. Northvale, NJ: Jason Aronson, Inc., 1997.

Evans, Dylan. *An Introductory Dictionary of Lacanian Psychoanalysis.* New York: Routledge and Kegan Paul, 1996.

Fink, Bruce. *A Clinical Introduction to Lacanian Psychoanalysis: Theory and Technique.* Cambridge, MA: Harvard University Press, 1997.

———. *The Lacanian Subject: Between Language and Jouissance.* Princeton, NJ: Princeton University Press, 1995.

Freud, Sigmund. "Recommendations to Physicians Practicing Psychoanalysis." *The Standard Edition of the Complete Psychological Works.* Edited by James Strachey, 109–120. 1912. Reprint, Vol. XII. London: The Hogarth Press, 1958.

Glogowski, James. "Remark Concerning the Drive." *Umbra* 1 (1997): 53–60.

Greenberg, Jay R. and Stephen A. Mitchell. *Object Relations in Psychoanalytic Theory.* Cambridge, MA: Harvard University Press, 1983.

Grigg, Russell. "From the Mechanism of Psychosis to the Universal Condition of the Symptom: On Foreclosure." *Key Concepts of Lacanian Psychoanalysis.* Edited by Dany Nobus, 48–74. New York: Other Press, 1999.

Gurewich, Judith Feher. "The Lacanian Clinical Field: Series Overview." In *The Clinical Lacan.* By Joël Dor. Northvale, NJ: Jason Aronson Inc., 1997.

Gurewich, Judith Feher, Michel Tort, and Susan Fairfield, eds. *The Subject and the Self: Lacan and American Psychoanalysis.* Northvale, NJ: Jason Aronson, 1998.

Hare-Mustin, Rachel. "Discourse in the Mirrored Room." In *Toward a New Psychology of Gender.* Edited by Mary M. Gergen and Sara N. Davis, 553–574. New York: Routledge and Kegan Paul, 1997.

Hill, Philip. *Lacan for Beginners.* New York: Writers and Readers Publishing Company, 1997.

Jacoby, Russell. *The Repression of Psychoanalysis: Otto Fenichel and the Political Freudians*. Chicago: University of Chicago Press, 1986.

Julien, Philippe. *Jacques Lacan's Return to Freud: The Real, the Symbolic, and the Imaginary*. Translated by Devra Beck Simiu. New York: New York University Press, 1994.

Kernberg, Otto F. Forward. *The Psychotic*. By David Rosenfeld, vii–xiv. London: Karnac Books, 1992.

Lacan, Jacques. *Seminar XX: Encore, 1972–1973: On Feminine Sexuality; The Limits of Love and Knowledge*. Edited by Jacques-Alain Miller. Translated by Bruce Fink. New York: W. W. Norton and Co., 1998.

———. *Seminar III: The Psychoses, 1955–1956*. Edited by Jacques-Alain Miller. Translated by Russell Grigg. New York: W. W. Norton and Co., 1998.

———. *Le Séminaire. Livre XVII. L'envers de la psychanalyse, 1969-1970*. Edited by Jacques-Alain Miller. Paris: Seuil, 1991.

———. "On a Question Preliminary to Any Possible Treatment of Psychosis." In *Écrits: A Selection*. Translated by Alan Sheridan, 179–255. 1959. Reprint. New York: W. W. Norton and Company, 1977/1966.

———. "The Direction of the Treatment and the Principles of its Power." In *Écrits: A Selection*. Translated by Alan Sheridan, 226–280, 1961. Reprint, New York: W. W. Norton and Company, 1977/1966.

———. "Subversion of the Subject and the Dialectic of Desire in the Freudian Unconscious." In *Écrits: A Selection*. Translated by Alan Sheridan, 292–325, 1960. Reprint, New York: W. W. Norton and Company, 1977/1966.

———. "Agency of the Letter in the Unconscious, or, Reason Since Freud." In *Écrits: A Selection*. Translated by Alan Sheridan, 146–178. 1957. Reprint, New York: W. W. Norton and Company, 1977/1966.

Laurent, Éric. "The Oedipal Complex." *Reading Seminars I and II*. Edited by Richard Feldstein, Bruce Fink, Maire Jaanus, 67–75. Albany, NY: State University of New York Press, 1996.

London, N. "An Essay on Psychoanalytic Theory: Two Theories of Schizophrenia. Part I Review and Critical Assessment of the Development of the Two Theories." In *Essential Papers on Psychosis*. Edited by Peter Buckley, 5–22. New York: New York University Press, 1988.

———. "An Essay on Psychoanalytic Theory: Two Theories of Schizophrenia. Part II Discussion and Re-statement of the Specific Theory of Schizophrenia." In *Essential Papers on Psychosis*. Edited by Peter Buckley, 23–48. New York: New York University Press, 1988.

Martel, J. "A Linguistic Model of Psychosis: Lacan Applied." *The American Journal of Psychoanalysis* 50 (1990): 243–252.

McWilliams, Nancy. *Psychoanalytic Diagnosis: Understanding Personality Structure in the Clinical Process*. New York: The Guiford Press, 1994.

Miller, Jacques-Alain. "An Introduction to Seminars I and II." *Reading Seminars I and II: Lacan's Return to Freud*. Edited by Richard Feldstein, Bruce Fink, and Maire Jaanus, 3–35. Albany, NY: State University of New York Press, 1996.

————. "On Perversion." *Reading Seminars I and II: Lacan's Return to Freud.* Edited by Richard Feldstein, Bruce Fink, and Maire Jaanus, 306–322. Albany, NY: State University of New York Press, 1996.

————. "Paradigms of Jouissance." *lacanian ink* 17 (2000): 10–47.

Muller, John P. *Beyond the Psychoanalytic Dyad: Developmental Semiotics in Freud, Pierce, and Lacan.* New York: Routledge and Kegan Paul. 1996.

Nasio, Juan-David. *Five Lessons on the Psychoanalytic Theory of Jacques Lacan.* Translated by David Pettigrew and François Raffoul. Albany NY: State University of New York Press, 1998.

Nobus, Dany. *Jacques Lacan and the Freudian Practice of Psychoanalysis.* London: Routledge and Kegan Paul, 2000.

————, ed. *Key Concepts of Lacanian Psychoanalysis.* New York: Other Press, 1998.

Ragland-Sullivan, Ellie. *Jacques Lacan and the Philosophy of Psychoanalysis.* Chicago: University of Illinois Press, 1986.

Rosenfeld, H. "On the Treatment of Psychotic States by Psychoanalysis: An Historical Approach." In *Essential Papers on Psychosis.* Edited by Peter Buckley, 147–176. New York: New York University Press, 1988.

Schneiderman, Stuart, ed. *Returning To Freud: Clinical Psychoanalysis In The School of Lacan.* New Haven: Yale University Press, 1980.

Searles, Harold. "Transference Psychosis in the Psychotherapy of Chronic Schizophrenia." In *Essential Papers on Psychosis.* Edited by Peter Buckley, 177–232. New York: New York University Press, 1988.

Soler, Colette. "The Body in the Teaching of Jacques Lacan." *JCFAR* 6 (1995): 6–38.

Verhaeghe, Paul. "The Collapse of the Function of the Father and its Effect on Gender Roles." *Journal for the Psychoanalysis of Culture and Society* 4 (1999): 18–31.

Williams, Paul. "Psychotic Developments in a Sexually Abused Borderline Patient." *Psychoanalytic Dialogues* 8 (1998): 459–492.

Wright, Elizabeth, ed. *Feminism and Psychoanalysis: A Critical Dictionary.* Oxford: Blackwell, 1992.

Zupančič, Alenka. *Ethics of the Real: Kant, Lacan.* London: Verso, 2000.

Chapter 1

The Trauma of Language

LUCIE CANTIN

Human Beings as a Product of Language

Human beings are living creatures capable of speech and, as such, have been exiled from the animal kingdom regulated by the logic of the natural satisfaction of needs. Lacan described as "real jouissance" such unmediated satisfaction as is sought by the animal who pounces on its prey out of hunger or follows the rhythms of its mating instinct. But however far back one goes in the life of a human being, one cannot find any trace of access to that real jouissance. Language has transformed us into beings subject to a logic that is other than biological or natural logic.

Knowledge of this other logic lies within everyone's grasp. One need not be a psychoanalyst to see it. Animals have communication systems, a code of more or less sophisticated signs to which they respond. However, their signs are univocal. Lacan has pointed out the fixity of the correlation of these signs to the reality that they signify.[1] Darkness from a midafternoon eclipse of the sun will send birds back to their nests as if actual night had fallen six hours early that day. By contrast, human beings speak, and their language signifies "*something quite other* than what it says."[2] Human beings can speak nonsense or make jokes and puns that make others laugh. They write poetry, represent existence metaphorically, ennoble, or debase the reality of the world. A patient, who is a painter, once said to me: "For the last few days, I have been fighting with colors to make them say what I mean to say but don't

This chapter was presented, in different form, at a workshop entitled "Lacanian Psychoanalysis: The Process of Working Through and Dreams," at the Center for Psychoanalytic Study in Chicago, February 1993.

know." For human beings, language evokes the invisible and the inexpressible. The most evocative words that bear the weight of the greatest meaning: words of love; significant words addressed to a child; poetic words spoken by a political leader, promising hope and justice to a people who have turned to him; consoling words that can help us bear suffering or death. Another patient, worried about his passion for the art of warfare, finally managed to express what he found fascinating in those things. He described how enemy generals, who respected each other, had a drink together and shook hands before facing each other across the battlefield. Such situations, he said, bring out the paradox of the meaning of life, which suddenly appears in those moments when death looms on the horizon. The idea that death awaits every living being and becomes, for those capable of speech, the driving force of life—such was, for that patient, the paradox of the human condition. "How can one chase away the anxiety of death? How can one find pleasure in this absurd life?" he asked, thus gaining access, little by little, to the idea that it is precisely that radical *lack* of meaning that creates the desire to live despite everything.

Human beings speak and language has certain effects—perhaps most significantly, the body. Only humans have bodies. This, too, is something that anyone can see. Animals, by contrast, have an organism, a biological machine regulated by needs that must be satisfied. The body is contrasted from the organism insofar as it is a body that is spoken of (*un corps parlé*), carved up and made visible by language. It is the image we look at in the mirror, an image built up of the look, the words and the desire of the Other. The body is always the body as it has been eroticized. Moreover, the sight of the organism always yields a feeling of strangeness. An X-ray of an organ strikingly demonstrates the difference between the real of the organism and the imaginary of the body. The imaginary of the body results from the signifiers that have left their mark on it throughout its history. Thus, for example, the body is a neck that is too long, hips that are too broad, legs that are too short—in brief, the body is what an anorexic might (mis-)perceive in their mirror. Here, too, one senses the gap that exists between the real of the organism and the body. Manic psychotics and insomniacs, who for days are bursting with energy and defy the logic of the organism, offer yet another example. Hence, the body is a series of pieces that no longer function according to the organic logic of the organism, that are marked by the Other, by language. Freud has designated as "erotogenic zones" these cutout pieces that have been diverted or perverted from their biological function. In *Three Essays on the Theory of Sexuality*, in a note added in 1915, Freud said that any part of the body, all the organs, can thus become erotogenic zones.³ These zones are also fragile spots, hysterogenic zones, according to Freud, who remarked that hysterical conversions lodge themselves in these elected places where that body starts speaking, as it were.

A whole series of examples, known to everyone, illustrate the radical distinction between body and organism. In the ecstasies of the mystics, which transport and maintain them in a second state for days, in the exploits of contortionists and, of course, in the realm of love and eroticism, the body appears as an object shaped by the requirements of culture or fashioned by the effects of signifiers and speech, or of the Other's desire. The body results from the exile of a biological logic, which speech has irrevocably driven from a human being.

Thus, the human subject is a creature of language. For humans, the most natural events, such as birth and death, are wholly caught up in the symbolic web created by language. Human beings have reasons to live and to die. At birth, one is already linked to the realm of symbols and words that define one's future destiny. Long before conception, one is born as a subject, subjected to the discourse and the desire that resulted in one's conception and birth. One is born of a parental desire, which often predates one's birth by many years, and which may even date back to the desires of the parent's own childhood, now buried in the unconscious, of the little girl, for example, playing with her doll twenty or thirty years before becoming a mother. One sometimes replaces a dead child or comes after the death of someone loved. One's "place," whether spoken of explicitly or not, always precedes one's birth: one is expected there. Bound to the unsatisfied desires of parents, to their fantasies and to the expectations built up through past generations, the child is born as a subject by this very capture into signifiers coming from the Other.

The family saga told in *The Godfather* movies by Francis Coppola illustrates suggestively the nature of a human subject's destiny, caught from the beginning in a narrative woven well before birth, in which a definite place must be assumed. The first Godfather (played by Robert De Niro in *Part II*) is as a child witness to the death of his father, who is executed by the Mafia. This child of modest origins, who finds himself orphaned and poor, becomes engulfed in a desire for revenge, which will henceforth become the vital thread of his life. As a result, he becomes the uncontested head of a family empire, the Godfather who commands fear and respect, who can give the order to kill and who rectifies the affront done to his father and family. The Godfather's own son (played by Al Pacino) must, against a wish to distance himself from the family destiny, take over and carry on the requirements of his father's path, when his father (repeating history) is wounded in an assassination attempt.

The son then takes over and is caught, in turn, in the duty to avenge his father. The third generation shows Al Pacino's son, who has become an opera singer against his father's will but who, in fact, follows the path of his father's unsatisfied desire to retire from illegal business. Pacino's character is in fact a caricature. All his life, he tries to escape his fate, and each time it comes back. One sees this, for example, in the attempted murder aimed at his father or at the end, in the death of his daughter at the very moment when Pacino's character tries to reestablish peace between the families.

The symbolic order, the world of signifiers and meaning created by the fact of speech, is foremost for human beings. One has only to imagine the account that a being from another planet might give when describing the strange world of human life. Such an account might read something like this:

> Human beings give a name for their children to bear, a name that their unconscious desires select without their knowing and that puts a stamp on the existence of the name bearer. They bury their dead and write their name in stone. They strive to immortalize the signs of their passage in life in writings and artifacts that they amass and keep for future generations in halls that they call "libraries." They plant a piece of material that they call a flag on the territories that they occupy. They write Laws and Constitutions. They live on hope and love and on illusions, and readily die for honor or get killed for ideas that they consider true and that they put above everything. To make life bearable, each culture devises particular ways to answer the questions posed by existence. Thus, they have invented God, deities, religion, science, art, literature, poetry, music, love, honor, and dignity. Obviously, these creatures have satisfactions other than natural ones. They idealize certain principles, whatever they may be, and not only are they willing to die for those principles, but they also find in them the very reason for living or dying.

A less fanciful example is provided by the Italian judge, Giovanni Falcone, whose legal campaign against the Mafia resulted in his assassination. Prior his death, Falcone granted a series of interviews to a French journal. There he outlined the norms and rules that govern the *Cosa Nostra*. The judge gave a striking analysis of the beliefs and modes of operation characteristic of the Mafia's so called men of honor. The relationship with life, with death, with the sense of honor, and with one's word is a microcosm, even a caricature, of the primacy of the symbolic order in human society in general. Speaking of these men's relationship to death, Falcone said:

The attitude toward death is even more revealing. Why is there no one to mourn over the death of Salvatore Inzerillo, assassinated at the age of forty? It is not because he had no friends or because no one wants to avenge him. On the contrary, it is because everyone in the Cosa Nostra respected and admired him: he lived like a lion and he died standing up. We must not forget this: for a man of honor, it is an annoying thing to die assassinated, but it is also a very prestigious one. His descendants will be proud of him. Inzerillo's own brother, Santo, was strangled with a rope in 1981, a few days after his older brother. He had been caught by the Corleonese at the same time as a friend, who was crying out of rage during the execution. Santo told him very calmly and very dryly: "Quit your weeping, and tell these cuckolds to be quick." That is an important sentence for his children, to whom it was repeated. They will be able to boast a father who did not fear death.[4]

Even death itself can no longer be natural. The usurpation of the biological by the symbolic, exemplified in the concept of an honorable death, demonstrates how even death is transformed in human experience. The last words of Santo were addressed to future generations. Not only does he accept that ultimate loss of satisfaction that defines the very essence of death, but he also gets another satisfaction from death, namely, an opportunity to immortalize his dignity for his children. War or espionage movies, or certain British or Japanese novels, offer some eloquent examples of that primary relation to the signifier which goes right through human life.

Language Makes Real Jouissance Impossible

A certain number of satisfactions are inaccessible to a being capable of speech. As Lacan would say, language makes impossible real jouissance, or jouissance of the need. In *Civilization and its Discontents*,[5] Freud had already remarked that civilization not only forces human beings to give up instinctual satisfactions in the name of a cultural ideal, but also substitutes for instinctual satisfactions various other satisfactions which are mediated, partial, and delayed. What Freud attributes to the renunciations inherent to civilization is understood by Lacan as an effect of language. The symbolic world of myths, beliefs, laws, moral and human values—which forms the very tissue of civilization—is created through language.

A need aims at its satisfaction by searching for a specific and adequate object. Satisfaction implies a total appropriateness of the object; satisfaction is by definition complete. The originary capture of human being in language diverts the subject from that form of satisfaction. Hunger and thirst call instead for particular sorts of objects according to cultural dicta; the development of specific tastes and distastes results from the hazards of the subjective history. Culture imposes rules and behaviors; it dictates the framework, the places, the times, and the objects from which it is acceptable to gain satisfaction. Thus, people eat sitting down or squatting, with sticks or with metal tools. The preparation of food leads to the development of an art, a gastronomy, and of particular habits and customs. From birth, all the needs of a child are ensnared in these various mediations and practices, which function as so many conditions imposed upon satisfaction by the law of the culture where the subject is articulated.

But the child is not directly confronted with the lack of satisfaction imposed by language. Rather, the child encounters parental demands which are in turn related to the prescriptions of culture. The familial and Oedipal prohibition that inscribes the child in a culture becomes the mode through which the child will experience castration. The prohibition configures "the impossible" per se. Its function is to serve notice to the child that there is something impossible, to support for the child the loss imposed by language until the child can face it and assume it, without being forced by a law. Only with adolescence will the subject face that which is beyond the arbitrary Oedipal and cultural prohibitions in all their forms by encountering that which is impossible to any human being. The subject's own desire *as* a subject will then become the way to claim a relationship to the lack of satisfaction, as it results from the human condition, and not just from some seemingly arbitrary parental or cultural prohibition.

Thus, it is language that imposes a radical lack and creates the "human real" by imputing a real or natural jouissance as what is lacking. It is that lack, which is inherent to the ability to speak, that creates desire, that feeds it, and sustains it. Thus, there is desire because there is something impossible. Desire is therefore irreducible, without specific object, and without any possible satisfaction. Desire becomes the unrelenting quest for that which is lacking, for the impossible that human beings cannot, however, renounce.

The Introduction of an Other Jouissance and the Paternal Function

Freud insists on the fact that the child accepts the loss imposed by civilization only out of fear of losing the love on which the child depends for survival. At birth, one is in a state of total dependence, at the mercy of the other for the satisfaction of primary needs. According to Freud, the child accepts what civilization stands for only through the repression of that aggressivity directed against the parent who imposes the sacrifice of satisfaction. Thus, for Freud, civilization rests on the repression of the death drive, which is the primary aggressivity directed against anything that stands in the way of the quest for instinctual satisfaction in human beings. Such a provocative thesis opens the question of the relation to the Other, and demands that we examine what this relation introduces in the movement of subjectivization that language imposes on human beings.

The law of the father is what represents, for the child, the law of culture—what culture imposes, allows or forbids, in establishing the conditions of everyone's satisfaction in coexistence. More fundamentally, however, the function of the father is to represent the law of the signifier and its primacy for the human subject. Indeed, the Father that we are confronted with in psychoanalysis, is a creation of civilization in that the notion of father is essentially related to the existence of language. Paternity exists because we speak. The father has no raison d'être other than to represent the law of the symbolic. He represents this law insofar as his position as father is not a position given by the order of things. The father is thus whoever is named as "father." He is *not* the father, strictly speaking, merely because he may have impregnated the female.

The father, when postulated as such, links up the child with what Freud has called "civilization" and with the cultural ideals that have replaced the laws of instinct and need. Paternity cannot be reduced to a role or a function to fulfill, which could be delegated to the mother who might then occupy both the father's and mother's position. The mother is necessary, she is part of a direct, natural link with the child; she is part of a logical continuity. To say to a child: "Here is your father" is to choose a man to occupy a position where the only link with the child is that created by his having been designated as the father. It is like electing someone to the function of President, who is required to represent authority. Authority is granted and it is precisely insofar as it is granted that it can represent the law of the signifier, the primacy that human beings have decided to give to the symbolic order. Thus, the father is purely a signifier. He is a metaphor; for the child, he represents the signifier of cultural law, the signifier of the effects of language on human beings.

It is through the parental Other that the child encounters culture. But what is required of the child according to the cultural rules is inevitably grasped as a demand and as reflecting the will of the Other. In addition, the parent introduces something other than the cultural requirement. With or without knowing it, what the parent demands from the child is fraught with the dissatisfactions that have marked the parent's own life. Such demands carry unconscious and unsatisfied desires from past generations;

intermingled with them is a complaint against or the refusal of the assumption of lack. In brief, the parental demand addressed to the child in the name of culture always carries some surplus meaning. It represents a lack other than that which is imposed by culture, a parental lack, which manifests itself as such to the child. The child can only grasp it as a lack of jouissance on the part of the parent; such a lack calls the subject to that place where one could or should respond to it. Here, a jouissance is introduced by the signifier of the Other's lack. This could be expressed as a question: "What does the Other wants out of me?" or "What jouissance would my mother have if I became this or that?"

Beyond the Ideal postulated by culture and which we call "Ego Ideal" (*Idéal du Moi*), the child will respond to the parental lack. By imagining the object that the Other lacks and by identifying with that object, the child will construct the Ideal Ego (*moi idéal*), in order to respond to the parental demand; in other words, the Ideal Ego is formed as the imaginary of the object that the other lacks. The question that stems out of that logic obviously is: How far will this demand go? To what extent will the subject devote a lifetime to responding to the demand of the parent or to the demand of anyone who would occupy that place during the course of a lifetime? Language only eliminated the jouissance of the need by replacing it with partialized or mediated satisfactions. But here, the signifier introduces another jouissance, a jouissance of the Other which subjugates the subject to the point of diverting completely the logic of satisfaction. The prototypical example of this subjugation is provided by psychotics, who are subjected to the Other, caught in the demand or the injunction that dictates their conduct, decodes their thoughts, orders their actions, and even threatens their life. What is lacking in psychosis is the Father's function, in other words the representation of an irreducible lack that is inherent to language and culture and cannot be filled. The law of the Father limits the jouissance demanded by the Other in the imaginary of the child; it states that the Other is not to be satisfied; that the lack it signifies refers to something that is beyond any relationship with others.

Each culture has ways to represent the impossibility of total jouissance. The signifier of the Law, arbitrary and diverse in nature from one culture to another, is represented by the father and serves to link up the child with the lack inherent to human nature. As for the signifier introduced by the Other's demand, it rather refers to the imaginary of a possible jouissance, that the Other requires. When that demand of the parent is not linked up with the requirements of the culture, we say that the child is exposed to the other's caprice. The imaginary of a possible jouissance, as it is claimed by the Other, blocks any possibility for the subject to claim the lack in being as something that results from the link-age to language. From that, one can see how important it is that the parent—in this case the mother, since she is in a position where she can refuse to give a father to her child—has assumed the impossibility of jouissance and, accordingly, that she does not expect from a husband or from her child the satisfaction of her unfulfilled desires.

The Case of Myriam

Myriam is a young dancer in her thirties. During treatment, she discovers that her parents "wish her to be sick." At seventeen, she was hospitalized for a delirious and paranoid episode. She was at that time treated as a psychotic and put into the care of a psychiatrist, who was a friend of the family. For Myriam, that experience is the acme of her subjective alienation: members of her family speak in her place, organize her hospitalization, and entrust her to the care of a doctor who, they believe, will return to them the obedient daughter they have always known. This is Myriam's interpretation of her present, acute crisis, which developed as she was beginning to see the possibility of fulfilling her dream of becoming a dancer.

In the patient's discourse, the father is presented as being like a child who cannot take care of himself and who needs the presence, the love, and the continuous care of his daughter; as for the mother, she is presented as thinking of and being only interested in herself. From what Myriam says about her father, it is hard to imagine that socially he occupies a position of authority in politics, as, in fact, he does. Myriam's relationship with her mother is clearly one of conflict and is marked by a morbid rivalry. The mother is presented as a woman, who despite her advancing years has refused to age, and who is still constantly preoccupied with her looks. Myriam complains of the barely disguised arrogance and contempt her mother has for her. She describes how her mother, like a teenager, flaunts her beauty to her daughter who is rather less favored by nature, and how the mother almost exposes herself in postures which are staged as relaxed, but are suggestive and even vulgar for a woman of her age. Without knowing it, Myriam unconsciously responds to the provocation of her mother.

Myriam does not see the vexation that this provocation disguises in a woman who denies her age and thus reveals her profound dissatisfaction with life. The mother is caught in a mirror relation with her eldest daughter, who has become a top model of international renown and perpetuated her mother's youth and beauty, but the mother never fulfilled the dream of *her* life, which was . . . to be a dancer. It is Myriam who possesses that talent and who develops it. Accepted into the finest per-forming arts schools in Paris, Myriam was little by little taking the di-rection that, in her family, she was not supposed to take. She was becoming a dancer and was, in the opinion of her trainers, among the most promising. Just when everything was opening up for Myriam, she became ill, thus unconsciously abiding by her mother's interdiction that the daughter was not to surpass the mother by becoming what the mother had failed to become.

In her treatment, Myriam talks about her unhealthy rivalry with her mother. Recognized very early for her special talent in music and dance, she became, without knowing why, she says, her mother's scapegoat. Myriam was ignored by her mother, even as the first signs of her mother's rejection began to appear in her body. Amenorrheal until the age of twenty-five, Myriam saw her adolescence go by without her mother worrying about that disorder. That symptom, which was accom-panied by an increasingly pronounced case of facial acne, was not sub-jected to any medical investigation despite the professional environment in which the family lives. The constant derisive remarks of her mother about her physical appearance only aggravate Myriam's symptom. Myr-iam believes she is resisting the ideal image of "top model" with which she believes her mother wishes her to identify. But, in fact, she is uncon-sciously responding to her mother's demand, which gives her a specific place to occupy, where she will be "out of play." It is as if the degradation of her body and the impossibility of becoming a woman, expressed by her amenorrhea, forced her to remain a little girl, both guardian and ser-vant of her father—a man presented as incapable of taking care of him-self and to whom her mother has abandoned her. Her hapless father is a general topic in family gossip; the father is recognized by all as a child. He is a character who is kept inoffensive and ridiculous within the fam-ily, and who becomes a man only when he leaves the house.

Myriam clearly doesn't have access to her own desire. She only re-sponds to the prohibition imprinted in her unconscious: she must never surpass her mother. Myriam's failure and the symptomatic degradation of her body, like the oldest daughter's success, we might say, would seem to be responding to an injunction coming from the mother. This injunc-tion, located (at the very least) at the level of Myriam's fantasy, might be formulated as: *The mother must not be confronted with her rightful lack.* Nor was Myriam's possible success as a dancer able to return the mother to her proper lack. It is only gradually in treatment that Myriam discovers her alienation within that demand which she imputes to the mother. Al-most to the point of caricature, the father is diminished in the family, where the maternal ideal has replaced the authority of the paternal phal-lus. The entire family organization revolves around the mother's fantasy, which is maintained and sustained by the mirror relation of the mother and her eldest daughter—the only one of her children, by the way, who has never seemed to require psychotherapy.

This particular clinical example allows us to make certain remarks. First, it speaks very eloquently to the fact that the position of the father is strictly linked to the place that it receives in the mother's discourse. The prestigious professional and social position of that man does not give him any authority in his family. In our clinical example, a maternal ideal based on the denial or the repression of the lack has taken the place of the authority of the paternal phallus. The phallic authority, resting on the primacy accorded the signifier of law and culture would confront the subject with a lack that must be assumed. These limitations are inscribed, interrupted, and run counter to what Freud calls the "search for individual happiness." But, in the patient's words, the mother remains an unsatisfied woman, who refuses to grow old and who watches as the possibility of becoming a dancer vanishes with every passing day. That lack, which has certainly been the tragedy of the mother's life as a woman, is still unassumed, so she can't bear to see her daughter succeed where she has failed. That "demand" of the maternal Other to which Myriam responds, "not to become a recognized dancer," is inscribed in the knowledge of her unconscious (*le savoir de son inconscient*). So that when, during the treatment, she gains access to that knowledge, that savoir, she recognizes the truth of it and sees it as something that has directed her life without her knowing. By stopping her career as a dancer, she bears the loss that her mother cannot assume and thus maintains the fantasy of an ideal woman that her mother exhibits and that the eldest daughter supports.

Myriam's clinical problem leads us to examine the relationship of women to castration, to irreducible lack. This relation is an essential element in the way a woman will recognize the father as the representative of the phallic authority for the child. Certain feminist discourses, ever more widespread in North American society, promote an Ideal that would deny the importance of phallic authority. According to such views, a woman could both be the mother and play the role of the father for the child. The father would thus be reduced to a progenitor, a function that science might replace by some reproductive technique. The social struggle of women, justified when it is a matter of recognizing rights and responsibilities that are incumbent to all subjects as citizens, begets the dynamics of perversion when it is displaced from its initial aims in order to justify a refusal of phallic authority in the relation of the mother to the child. Deciding to do without the father as signifier of the cultural law necessarily nurtures, in the unconscious of the child, a particular subjective position for the mother, who could "be total," without lack, uncastrated. What is then refused to the child is that possibility to experience an irreducible lack which is common to every human subject. It would be as if the world of the mother would attest to a place where one could escape castration. The refusal of the authority of the phallic signifier would thus support, in some way, the illusion of a *self-sufficient* maternal universe where one might foment the fantasy of a jouissance that would be accessible to some.

One last remark concerning access to desire. As long as Myriam cannot help but respond to the demand of the maternal Other, she has no chance to gain access to her own desire. Her mother's relationship to lack, the way her mother has failed to assume what increasingly appears as impossible in her life, subjects Myriam to a demand that is all the more irrevocable because it is unspoken. The subject's access to her desire, and this applies both to the daughter and her mother, implies that the lack inherent to the human condition be accounted for without evasion. The mother's profound dissatisfaction with her life is doubtless part of a series of circumstances related to her own history and to that of preceding generations. She has no choice but to take on this history like a tragic heroine shouldering her fate if she wants to have any chance to make her mark in life. Access to desire implies the leaving behind of adolescence, that time of life where revolt feeds on the discovery of the arbitrary and which also supports the accusation brought against the other as the one who hinders satisfaction. The quest for satisfaction or individual happiness, to use Freud's words, is not in the logic of desire. Desire is what drives the mountain climber to surpass himself or makes the race car driver risk his life; it is what makes Mick Jagger or José Carreras sing; it is what makes one produce a work, whatever it is. The results these people achieve have nothing to do with a natural satisfaction. Desire has no object. It creates one—one which is always inadequate and insufficient and which ultimately serves only to maintain its movement. Desire is inscribed in the logic of the loss imposed on us by language, which introduces an other mode of satisfaction that is no longer natural. Desire is what drove Judge Falcone in his fight against the Mafia. His testimony gives the impression that the finesse, the shrewdness, and the intelligence with which he waged his war became more important than the Mafia-object he fought. Desire is what holds the life of human beings; it is what make us live longer or die prematurely.

Notes

1. Jacques Lacan, *Écrits: A Selection*, trans. Alan Sheridan (New York: W. W. Norton and Co., 1977), 84. Original edition (Paris: Éditions du Seuil, 1966), 297.

2. ———. *Écrits: A Selection,* trans. Alan Sheridan (New York: W. W. Norton and Co., 1977), 155. Original edition (Paris: Éditions du Seuil, 1966), 505.

3. Sigmund Freud, *The Standard Edition of the Complete Psychological Works of Sigmund Freud, Volume 7: Three Essays on the Theory of Sexuality,* ed. James Strachey (London: The Hogarth Press, 1953), 184.

4. Giovanni Falcone, with Marcelle Padovani, *Costa Nostra—Le juge et les hommes d'honneur* (Paris: Éditions de la Seine, 1991), 84.

5. Sigmund Freud, *The Standard Edition of the Complete Psychological Works of Sigmund Freud, Volume 21: Civilization and its Discontents,* ed. James Strachey (London: The Hogarth Press, 1961).

Chapter 2

The Jouissance of the Other and the Sexual Division in Psychoanalysis

WILLY APOLLON

Individual Satisfaction and the Jouissance of the Other

Anyone who approaches psychoanalysis through Lacan is immediately struck by the central place occupied by certain concepts. Among these is surely the concept of jouissance. In current use, this concept refers most globally to the notion of a sexual satisfaction that is full, complete, and without any remainder. And yet the reader is confronted immediately with the unsettling fact that in Lacanian usage, the concept of jouissance is fundamentally related to what Freud elaborated under the concept of the death drive. This paradox suggests that there is an irreconcilable incompatibility between the psychoanalytic concept of jouissance as it has developed since Lacan and anything that might be understood as having to do with the domain of the individual's *satisfaction*. The first contradicts and presents an obstacle to the second; that is, jouissance seems to introduce into the domain of satisfaction something that takes on the dimension of anxiety.

This clinical fact is crucial to the discussion in the present chapter. Indeed jouissance and satisfaction manifest themselves in two dimensions distinct to such an extent that the relationship between them is in no

This chapter was presented at a workshop entitled "Lacanian Psychoanalysis: Jouissance, A Concept at the Core of Lacanian Clinical Practice," at the Center for Psychoanalytic Study in Chicago, February 1995.

way self-evident. Satisfaction concerns the individual. The etymological derivation from the Latin *satis-facere* suggests rather nicely that what satisfaction asks is that the Other "make enough" of it. The implication of the Other in the individual's satisfaction is thus structural, so there is no way around it. In the individual, satisfaction invokes a need that is subjected to a demand addressed to an other. But for this other, satisfaction invokes a power of refusal concerning the object adequate to this satisfaction of need. This power to refuse, that every demand gives to the person to whom it is addressed, raises this other to the stature of the Other, with a capital O. This minimal structure highlights the ambiguity and misunderstanding that, for the human subject, already hover over the question of the satisfaction of need. Satisfaction, then, is dependent upon the Other's power to refuse. The child's radical experience of this truth is a kind of primal scene, in which the possible satisfaction of the individual depends upon a jouissance imputed to the Other. Thus, the difficult relation between jouissance and satisfaction is founded on the very fact of speech, that is, on the signifier of the Other in language.

Indeed, the implication of the Other in the satisfaction of needs—needs not only of the child, but also of the individual as a member of society—means that this satisfaction is expected from the *Other* even more than from the *object*. Considered from this angle, the demand addressed to the Other, and the Other's response (or non-response) are of decisive importance for the adequation of the object to the satisfaction of need. For the speaking being—that is, for the subject of psychoanalysis—the Other's importance is articulated within the structure of the signifier, or more precisely, within those elements of language in which the demand and the Other's response to it assume their ultimate form. The mere fact of the Other's implication in the satisfaction of the speaking being means that, unlike for an animal, this satisfaction can never be conceived of as immediate or total, since if such a thing were possible it would be equivalent to the subject's jouissance, a purely imaginary jouissance. For the speaking subject, the very structure that conditions the *satisfaction* of need is thus an obstacle to jouissance. And jouissance, in turn, is antithetical to satisfaction. Perhaps surprisingly, the Other's jouissance, whether imputed or not, logically goes to the foundation of the subject's castration, creating an obstacle to the satisfaction required by need.

Something presenting itself as a jouissance is thus introduced into the subject through the Other of the demand. Freud theorized the Superego to account for this exigency on the part of the Other that conditions the satisfaction of the subject's demand. Even though it is logically contained within the demand addressed to the Other, the Other's power to refuse is perceived by the subject as a capacity for jouissance. The obsessional illustrates this trait of the structure with a characteristic repugnance felt for the demand: the obsessional fears being used by the Other as an object of jouissance. In the same way, the obsessional experiences perhaps more acutely than anyone the trait Lacan identified in the Superego, its propensity for cruelty. Above and beyond love, the Other always has the *potential* to inflict cruelty when the subject seeks satisfaction. This is no doubt why Lacan emphasizes that every demand the subject addresses to the Other is a demand for love.[1] Only love could compensate for this cruelty, for the commanding of jouissance aroused in the subject by the signifier of the Other and by the necessity of passing through the Other's desire. Because the demand that the subject addresses to the Other makes the satisfaction of a need contingent upon the Other's desire, good will, and even caprices, any condition that the Other imposes by way of a response assumes for the subject the status of an absolute, of an inescapable command to jouissance.

This commanding and absolute character of the Other, which evokes for the subject both the feeling of a jouissance as well as the possibility of the Other's cruelty, is reinforced by the subject's primal experience of childhood immaturity and thus complete dependence upon the Other— that is, upon an adult who has moreover been granted full power over the child by society. Furthermore, the child's first experience of satisfaction from the Other—whether obtained, imputed, or merely imagined by the child—takes on the allure of a mythical jouissance, that returns to the child later on, in repetitive fashion, in the form of a hallucination. According to both Freud and Lacan, this first logical and hypothetical encounter with jouissance during childhood will provide the model for the lost cause of desire that for the subject is unconscious. At this mythical moment, the subject was in a sense *satisfied* by the Other's *jouissance*, because there was a hypothetical—but perfect—coincidence between the subject's satisfaction and the Other's command to jouissance. For the obsessional this coincidence sometimes seems beyond doubt, while for the hysteric its fundamental absence renders existence meaningless. This hypothetical, primordial experience becomes the model of satisfaction for the subject, while its absence, if not its lack, becomes the unconscious cause of the desire to recover it.

As the locus of the signifier and the authority of language for the child, the Other thus becomes the conduit through which jouissance introduces itself into one's life as an individual, as that which contradicts and creates an obstacle to the satisfaction of needs. This jouissance is therefore called "real" by Lacan, the theoretical equivalent of what Freud called "*das Ding.*" It comes from beyond the individual life of a being, and penetrates into it through language and through the demand for satisfaction addressed to the Other, who itself through this demand assumes the stature of a big Other with absolute power. This jouissance, which comes from beyond the sphere of individual needs, traversing being through the paths of signifiers and through discourses linking the subject's existence to the will and the whims of the Other, and becomes for the subject the object par excellence, the primary and most fundamental preoccupation, the first Problem to solve. Faced with this unavoidable intrusion of the breaking in of jouissance experienced as a trauma, the subject responds to the Other with drive. Beyond the instinctual satisfactions of the individual's needs, drive articulates the subject to the jouissance introduced by the signifier of the Other. Drive defines the subject's relation to this jouissance—a bit of the real, an object *a*—in the response to the Other that the signifier demands of the subject.

The Sexual Division: Procreation, Jouissance, and the Ethics of Masculinity

The sexual division is where the subject's relation to the Other and to jouissance, which is dictated by language, manifests itself and recurs in repetitive fashion. But this division also articulates a particular dimension of jouissance, that of procreation, which Freud attributes to the phallus and which Lacan designates as "phallic jouissance."

In Lacan's discourse, procreation as such refers to the engendering of the speaking being as a specific act having to do with the phallus, which is the signifier of the father's desire. In this characterization, Lacan returns to Freud's position in order to justify and reinforce it, positioning the father as a procreator and not merely as the one who forbids. Seen from this perspective, in fact, the father is the one who forbids *because* he is the procreator. Lacan draws out of Freud's work a theory of the sexual division in which sexual difference is articulated logically not as inscribed within the unconscious, but as overdetermined by each man's and each woman's *particular* relation to jouissance. This difference is marked by the relation to the phallus, the signifier of the desire to engender within the very process of procreation. The desire to engender is to be understood here as the father's desire, as distinct from the mother's desire to give birth.

The concept of *procreation* is distinct from the biological concept of *reproduction* in that for humans, unlike for animals, *to engender a speaking being* from the infant (*infans*, from Latin, literally the one who does not yet speak) is distinct from the reproduction of the individual animal. For the subject, subjected to the signifier of the Other, what is at stake is no

less than an act, a creation: which is why we speak of procreation, as opposed to the simple repetition of biological processes in the reproduction
of the individual animal. Procreation presupposes an ethics, and thus for
each partner has to do with the hazards and uncertainties of the Other's
desire. It is a singular act, whose unique features cannot be repeated. In
contrast, reproduction is a biological phenomenon that can be verified
scientifically, and therefore submitted to repetition, as the agricultural in-
dustry demonstrates. Creation, on the other hand, is singular; it happens
only once, without any possibility of repetition, and therefore eludes scientific control. This distinction accounts for the theoretical import of the
concept of the phallus, which has to support the creation of a speaking
being. The phallus introduces this ethic that language dictates when it imposes upon the speaking subject a relation to a jouissance that comes
from beyond need and satisfaction, a relation that links the subject's destiny to the uncertainties of the Other's desire. As a result, one can see that
the phallus refers to a specific jouissance at stake in the production of the
speaking subject. For both Freud and Lacan it is a sexual jouissance, although Freud relates it to the procreative function of paternity, while
Lacan proposes instead the concept of phallic jouissance. This concept is
central to the Lacanian understanding of the sexual division and of the
subject's relations to jouissance. Lacan is trying to do away with an imaginary and false understanding of the Freudian concept of sexuality.

Lacan distinguishes *drive*, which represents the subject's response to the
signifier that introduces the Other's jouissance, from *instinct*, which refers
to the repetition of biological mechanisms in the autonomous sphere of
the individual. But as part of the same argument, Lacan also distinguishes
paternal jouissance, as procreative, from the biological mechanisms of
individual reproduction. Consequently, the status of sexuality is raised to
another level. It moves beyond the mechanisms of individual reproduction, to the problem of the sexual division as condition for the procreation
and engendering of a subject of speech. As a result, the notion of the individual's sexual satisfaction loses the misleading sense that the imaginary
held up against the structure in order to repress it. Instead of a hypothetical satisfaction of the individual, the subject's encounter with the Other's
jouissance actually leads to an inhibition of all satisfaction, or even to an
introduction of anxiety into need, as is evident in adolescence, or in the
process of falling in love. For Lacan, then, what is at stake in Freud's position? Strictly speaking, it is the definition of paternity as procreative, the
fact that the father's desire is what engenders. What this position means for
psychoanalysis is that both masculinity and femininity must be understood as subjective positions taken up in language with regard to jouissance, instead of being misunderstood as biological pregivens.

As I have argued elsewhere,[2] a man, whose jouissance is structurally reproductive, is in the position with regard to his partner of *not knowing* anything about her jouissance, nor about her reproductive possibilities. Only the woman's word can alleviate this mystery, this non-knowing for the man. Moreover, the word that might alleviate it, comes without any guarantee for the man. His decision to believe or not believe her word is purely ethical. Such is the structure determining what can only be designated as the sexual act. This structuration of the sexual act defines the ethical position of each subject in relation to a jouissance that engenders, and that psychoanalysis therefore characterizes as phallic. At the center of this structure, at a minimum, is an ethics of masculinity, which is something like walking a tightrope without a safety net, since it bases a decision on a word without guarantee, and which may or may not be articulated to a woman's word, depending upon whether she turns out to be, or is reputed to be, credible.

When Lacan refers what Freud designates as sexuality to a jouissance that he calls "phallic," he is engaging the entire problematic symbolized by the phallus. The phallus represents a desire that engenders to the extent that this desire is sustained by a minimal word that alleviates a man's question about that which is at stake for a woman in jouissance and procreation. In this structure, masculinity is therefore defined as that relation of the subject to the Other's jouissance that is characterized by *not-knowing* and by the absence of any guarantee for the word that would alleviate this lack of knowledge. Out of this structure an ethics can be deduced that puts the masculine in the position of having to rely on the Other's minimal word concerning the act in which he engages a considerable part of his life. The other side of such an ethics is the position subsequent to this one, but already anticipated in advance, in which the man must make do with and assume the consequences of his act, in spite of the absence of guarantee that presides over it. The position of masculinity in this structure is all the more radical and inevitable in that the man's lack of knowledge concerning the Other's jouissance in procreation is overdetermined by yet another fact, which he cannot help but be aware of: namely, that the Other is *not* without knowledge concerning *his* jouissance. Within this logic, the sexual act takes on a very particular ethical dimension. It is conditioned and decided by the position that each subject assumes in relation to a *savoir* about jouissance insofar as it engenders and procreates. And because the phallus names this jouissance that procreates, one must conclude that the sexual act is conditioned by the *savoir* that each person has concerning the phallus. Moreover, since a woman's relation to procreation means that, for her, jouissance does not necessarily imply procreation, it follows that only the phallus engenders. This reinforces masculinity's relation to the phallus as a double inhibition, both of the man's relation to satisfaction in sexual jouissance and of his ethical responsibility in procreation, making it a source of anxiety in the face of the lack of any guarantee for the Other's word.

The Sexual Division: Feminine Jouissance Beyond the Phallic

The position of femininity in the structuration of the sexual act, and in relation to the jouissance that determines it, is something altogether different. To begin with, one must underscore that the singularity of woman's relation to jouissance lies in the fact that for her, jouissance is *not* linked to reproduction. Historically it is the cultural imperative, sustained essentially by the demands of the great religions, that has linked (or attempted to link) woman's jouissance to procreation. Cultural anthropology has taught, however, that those cultures which have remained beyond the scope of these religions have managed to develop spaces and forms other than procreation for anchoring and inscribing feminine jouissance in their modes of existence. For a woman, it is the *absence* of a relationship between jouissance and procreation that is the basis of a structural failing that marks her relation to man in the sexual act. Lacan renders this structural failing in his lapidary formulation: "there is no sexual relation."[3] Such is the definition of castration in femininity.

Woman's relation to jouissance does not imply reproduction, since she is only fertile for a few days each month. But man's relation to jouissance, as has just been demonstrated, is something else entirely, since the concept of the phallus is central both to masculine sexuality and to the procreation of the speaking subject. If the phallus is what gives meaning to jouissance, by articulating jouissance to the symbolic order made up of the cultural and historical demands of a given society, then woman's relation to jouissance is positioned *beyond* meaning. Feminine jouissance is thus beyond the phallus from the outset, and without any direct relation to whatever the symbolic order of the law might impose in the way of a demand in the order of procreation. Because the phallus articulates jouissance to procreation, it also offers a support for anything that might be understood as a symbolic imperative controlling the social and historical conditions of this procreation. Feminine jouissance, therefore, eludes the effects of the phallus as an "excess." Lacan emphasizes this excessive character when he speaks of a "supplementary jouissance" in the woman.[4]

But more precisely, the supplementary character of feminine jouissance is what both gives the sexual act this air of mystery, overflowing the limits of the structure, and at the same time introduces into procreation an other space, apprehended as a "beyond" of the symbolic order of the law and of cultural rules, an "elsewhere" that has always been related to the spiritual, and sometimes to the divine. But the excess and overflow of feminine jouissance in relation to phallic jouissance is also what fuels the feminine complaint of a jouissance abandoned and set adrift by the division that the sexual act effects under the sway of the phallus. The hysteric speaks to us indefinitely of this leftover jouissance, and of the satisfaction it inhibits. The hysteric becomes exemplary of the relationship between jouissance and satisfaction, and in fact testifies that the particular relation to desire and to the Other's caprice in which jouissance entangles the subject is *not* reducible to the individual's quests for satisfaction. As the anorexic demonstrates, the subject's failure to obtain any satisfaction from this jouissance attests that the Other of the signifier, far from responding to the satisfaction of need, actually introduces the being to a specific lack, motivated by the Other's fundamental failure to provide satisfaction. . . . Which is the true and structural definition for castration.

Castration: The Inadequacy of the Other and the Insufficiency of the Word

Feminine jouissance, cut loose from the phallus and from its role in procreation, forces the subject into a specific relation to the Other whose signifier introduces this jouissance. In the discourse that articulates her unmediated relation to the mother, the little girl confronts for the first time this jouissance that does not pass entirely through the phallus, or that in some way overflows it. Or it could just as easily be that the little girl hears in the discourse of women a conviction or a complaint about men, and that through this "girl talk" she becomes aware of the existence of a jouissance proper to women, of which men are both ignorant and distrustful. Initially the girl may experience this discovery as a traumatic primal scene, leaving her prey to a *savoir* that with time furrows her being and leaves hanging in the balance any dimension of personal satisfaction in her life. The beginning of a woman's analysis often presents this face. The aimless wandering to which the subject is reduced by such a relation to excessive jouissance defines the very mode of the demand for love that will articulate her relation to the Other. What she asks of the Other is the offer of a space in which this excess can find its limit: the singular forms in which to make itself recognized, and the aesthetic conditions through which the failure of satisfaction might transform this jouissance into a desire.

To conclude, it should be stressed that in either case, whether one is dealing with masculinity or with femininity, there is one thing that appears with a certain logical clarity—namely, that the Other is inadequate to the subject's demand for satisfaction. The Other's failing is twofold. As has already been discussed, the subject experiences the failing of the Other first through the encounter with the Superego, to the extent that the subject regards the Other's response to a demand as dependent upon the Other's love or good will. If the hysterical structure is exemplary of the woman's position, it is no doubt because the hysteric, more than anyone else, is sensitive to the dependence of satisfaction upon the good will and whims of the Other, because the hysteric has experienced (or at any rate complains of) the absence of this good will, and because experience has convinced the hysteric of the Other's lawless caprice.

But beyond any experience the subject might invoke as cause to distrust the Other's word, because of real or imputed failings, there is another, more crucial factor. The signifier itself is fundamentally inadequate to any representation, whatever it may be. How could anyone stake one's life on the mere word of the Other, unless one were operating under the illusion of being the object of the Other's desire? What guarantee could discourse as such offer the subject, even if it were presumed that the Other is not lacking? This is precisely the question that arrests the feminine subject. A woman calls into question the signifier that articulates the Other's word. She protests, and with good reason, that language cannot say all. She is profoundly aware of her inability to put into words the jouissance adrift in her body, a jouissance which causes her to stray outside of the paths of the phallus and away from the order of language. She is aware of the insufficiency of language and the inadequation of any discourse when faced with this jouissance that furrows her being and that the signifier is impotent to anchor. She exists in the manner of Saint Teresa of Ávila, or of certain women at the end of analysis, as the unavoidable figure of a castration that reaches beyond even the father's failing.

Hence, for a woman, even more than for a man (or at least more inevitably), the Other's failing may assume the double form of a structural inability to respond to her demand, above and beyond the failing of the Other's love. From a Lacanian perspective, this is the most radical form that castration can take, because the Other's signifier, which introduces a jouissance into the subject that creates an obstacle to the satisfaction of need, is also impotent to respond to the demand that makes this satisfaction dependent upon the Other's good will. The subject's relation to the Other thus becomes the logical framework for the subject's structural encounter with the impossible, or what Lacan calls the "real."

Notes

1. Jacques Lacan, *Écrits: A Selection*, trans. Alan Sheridan (New York: W. W. Norton and Co., 1977), 286–287. Original edition (Paris: Éditions du Seuil, 1966), 690–691.

2. Willy Apollon, "Féminité dites-vous?" *Savoir: Revue de psychoanalyse et d'analyse culturelle* 2.1 (May 1995).

3. Jacques Lacan, *Le Séminaire, livre XVII: L'envers de la psychoanalyse* (Paris: Éditions du Seuil, 1991), 134

4. ———, *The Seminar of Jacques Lacan, Book XX: Encore: On Feminine Sexuality, the Limits of Love and Knowledge*, trans. Bruce Fink (New York: W. W. Norton and Co., 1997), 73. Original edition (Paris: Éditions du Seuil, 1975), 68.

Chapter 3

The Signifier

DANIELLE BERGERON

The Signifier: A Structure Behind the Scenes

In thinking of the question of the signifier, a question not unlike a hidden door leading to the subject of the unconscious, my own thoughts were stirred by two memories, one of the wings of the Paris Opera House, the other of the sewers of the City of Lights. Several years ago, a musician friend, then a consultant for the Paris Opera, invited me to visit the wings and the backstages of that historic cultural site. For two hours we meandered through one hallway after another, taking backstairs and riding in ancient elevators and dumbwaiters, covering the equivalent of some ten stories. I discovered there a complex and infinitely precise mechanical organization of pulleys and ropes used to raise the curtains and magnificent backdrops of the season's musical program.

An immense gap seemed to separate my increasing interest in the preparations and necessary technical means used to stage the operas from my overwhelming awe in the performance of Mozart's *Magic Flute*. As a member of the audience, I was struck first by the pure majesty of the old building, the refinement of the ancient friezes, then by the glistening of the imposing crystal chandelier suspended in the main opera hall and the ceiling frescoes of Chagall, and above all by the sumptuous music of Mozart. However, there was nothing fundamentally incongruous between the dazzle of the stage and the convoluted, awkward and dusty character of the wings: the "Opéra," not only a palace of culture

---

This material was first presented, in different form, as a lecture given at the "Symposium on Lacanian Psychoanalysis," organized by the Center for Psychoanalytic Study and by the Chicago Open Chapter for the Study of Psychoanalysis, February 1993, Chicago.

but also an artistic concept of musical production, was possible only thanks to the existence of the other scene, silent and hidden, but nonetheless absolutely determinative in the staging of the opera. Simply, the signifier *opera*, is a condensation of multiple elements: some, apparent, support the official definition of an opera as "a dramatic work or poem set to music composed of airs, recitatives, choir and dance." Other elements, necessarily secret and concealed in technically sophisticated wings, preserve the mute memory of the artists, their stage fright, their emotions, and the anguish that had marked their bodies. The only vestiges of these hidden dramas are the names of the performers, marked by music, historically enshrined, but seemingly far removed from the backstage production that shadowed each famous performance. For its adepts, the opera is both the magnificence of the place and the musical work. But for me, ever since that day, the word *opera* has also taken me into the entrails, behind the scene, where a maze of all sorts of unaesthetic material structures and organizes the theatrical production.

My second memory may seem more amusing. I had just arrived in Paris to complete my specialization in psychiatry when a fellow physician asked if I would be interested in going with him on a visit of the Paris sewers. At first I thought he was jesting with me—after all, wouldn't a stroll to the Eiffel Tower or the splendid vista from Notre Dame de Paris be more appropriate? But finding he was dead serious, and intrigued by the idea of such an unusual tour, I accepted his invitation.

I arrived at our prearranged meeting place to find some thirty other people, each clutching a guidebook, standing in line to see the sewers. The stairway led down to an underground area that had been transformed into a museum. There a guide explained the major events in the city's history since the French Revolution. We then walked along the dark sidewalks of a humid and gloomy underground Paris, along canals of wastewater upon which sewer workers were floating in their pneumatic canoes. Despite the guide's reassurances, a feeling of uneasiness prevailed in the group as we imagined the possibility of being overcome by nauseous odor or by the shock of a rat darting out suddenly from the shadows.

At intersections we could read the names of the streets five or six meters overhead, streets that charmed their pedestrians: Champs-Elysées, avenue Montaigne, Place de la Concorde. Immensely odd and unusual, this internal Venice had nothing in common with the City of Lights but the parallel tracing of the streets whose sewers, carrying away the trash and remains of citizens' pleasures and satisfactions, recall by their names a history and attempt through language to signify meetings with the real that had been inscribed and lost in the silence of bodies. The street names of Paris, metonymically falling into place for those who walked along them, are signifiers perpetuating the memory of past revolutions, wars won, popular uprisings, and the lives of writers and artists, but words offered by language must ever fail to succeed in matching the events as experienced. In the manner that the evocative names mark off and delimit in the sewers, the remnants of everyday events in the lives of Paris residents, the signifier constitutes a spoken trace, a track that enables the subject entrenched in the real to be delimited. The street and place names of Paris repress an underground scene that repeats those very names, but this time they are organized in a structure that is far from brilliant, but that nevertheless serves to carry away the remains of daily jouissance of anonymous subjects. For an analyst, the signifier is revealed in a slip of the tongue that pierces the compact mass of the narcissistic parade. Such traces are the ribbing of precious metal leading to the subject's unconscious. Put technically, the signifier is the writing of a loss establishing the subject as a real, a position determined by the Other.

In inventing psychoanalysis, Freud lifted the curtain on an "other scene," another stage, different from that maintained on the social scene by the society man through his narcissism. As an exceptionally astute clinician, Lacan understood the complexity of Freud's texts and introduced us to the specificity of the psychoanalytic discovery: "Impediment, failure, split. In a spoken or written sentence something stumbles. Freud is attracted by these phenomena, and it is there that he seeks the unconscious."[1] As the backstage to appearance, as the sewer of vanity, the unconscious scene sustains the subject, and reveals the subject through incongruities on the scene of social coexistence: slips of the tongue, wit, dreams, symptoms and the like that trouble the scene of the ego. Every social character would like to keep this backstage under lock and key, under the wraps of the clandestine when, for instance, it throws a lapsus in a formal speech that illuminates a desire heterogeneous to the "moral self."[2] At odds with meaning and functioning and under a logic other than that of the conscious and the rational, the signifiers that give voice to the unconscious always stand as non-sense in the usual narratives that make of the ego their hero.

Take the example of Mr. Brown's slip of the tongue. Long bothered by his director, M. Jodoin, an obese and ruddy-complexioned man, who easily lost control of his hand in the presence of young secretaries, businessman Brown addressed M. Jodoin during a monthly company meeting as *Monsieur Jambon* (Mr. Ham). Note that the signifiers *Jodoin* and *Jambon* have close consonance in French. The slip of the tongue, revealing the "pig" Mr. Brown imagined his director was, not only had an effect similar to the one that would have been produced by unveiling the backstage of the opera in the middle of the performance of *The*

Magic Flute, but also of a fall into the sewers while looking up and mar-veling at the architectural genius of the Arc de Triomphe.

How is this other scene set up? The other scene of the subject is pro-duced by language, by words. Lacan teaches that "Language and its structure exist prior to the moment at which each subject at a certain point in his mental development makes his entry into it."[3] What makes the human unique is being subjected to a fundamental trauma recorded at birth: capture as a living being within the coils of language. A new-born is brutally subjected to cultural and symbolic constraints through parental demands while still in a state of biological prematurity. Having to go through an other person—and through the interpretation that that other person makes of one's needs—results in a loss for the newborn of what Lacan calls the "jouissance of need." This permanent and irre-versible loss of what could be imagined as the nirvana of the intrauterine symbiosis in which every need would be immediately satisfied, this rerouting of the organism's biological functions to the regimen of parental demands and educational constraints, remains marked for the subject precisely by *words*, by signifiers that have accompanied the loss.

One's proper name is an illustration of this inscription, as Lacan noted: "Thus the subject, too, if he can appear to be the slave of lan-guage is all the more so of a discourse in the universal movement in which his place is already inscribed at birth, if only by virtue of his proper name."[4] Bearing a name and having a sex imposes an ideal that conditions the newborn's insertion into a sociocultural group; it also in-scribes the child in the regime of loss of need satisfaction. Furthermore, the parental words to which the child responds in attempting to identify with what is perceived as their lack (what they expect from the child) forms a chain of signifiers for the subject that repress the unnamable experience of traumatic situations in which the loss of satisfaction is en-countered as an anguishing real. As evidence of successive losses expe-rienced in early childhood, the signifiers sustain the subject of the unconscious. The subject mobilizes in a movement of desire around ob-jects that act as substitutes to lost satisfaction—and whose failure per-petuates the movement. Thus, the signifier engages the individual in a structure of repetition over which the ego has no control. In treatment, the chaining of signifiers through the removal of repression will lead the analysand to the precise formula of the loss sustaining the subject's par-ticular desire and signing the terms of the subject's "own" death.

In opposition to desire, which is individual and original, culture im-poses laws to ensure coexistence and to counter the insistence of the subject of the unconscious who would introduce a break in social orga-nization. Culture insists that one seek out something other than that real jouissance made impossible by language.[5] Likewise, the magnificence of the streets of Paris named to represent the famous men and events which shaped its history repress, under those very names or signifiers, a continuous structure for discharging waste linked to satisfaction, as a body marked by jouissance. The failure of the discharge would jeopardize Paris, bringing on contamination and the spread of fatal disease, and would destroy the community. In a manner reminiscent of Paris street names, the signifier functions *as* the signifier by the fact of being an element in a structure of rejection of jouissance by the symbolic Law. The signifier is the vestige in language of this loss of need satisfaction that has marked the body so indelibly.

The Signifier of Analytic Discourse as a Rupture in Meaning

In several of his texts (*Jokes and their Relation to the Unconscious, The Interpretation of Dreams, The Psychopathology of Everyday Life*), Freud posits the primary processes of condensation and displacement as fundamental to the logic of the unconscious. In this, Freud unknowingly anticipated the way in which modern semiotics would come to understand the structure of the linguistic sign. Using the linguistic theories of Ferdinand de Saussure and Roman Jakobson, Lacan reframed Freud's ideas as metaphor and metonymy. In his well-known formula that "the unconscious is structured like a language" Lacan showed how metaphor and metonymy were the two modes whereby the psychoanalytic signifier linked to the real to delimit the space of desire housing the subject.

Still, there remains a fundamental distinction between the signifier as developed by the linguists and the psychoanalytic signifier as devised by Lacan. For the linguist, the chaining of the signifier generates an overall signification. When we speak, for example, the listener seizes the sense of what we intend to say only once we have finished the sentence. The signification generated by the chaining of the words is connected to reality as a metaphor of it. For instance, the poetic lines "Love is a pebble laughing in the sunlight," or "you are as beautiful as the morning dew," constitute a metaphor of the feeling an individual experiences in the body. What in emotion does not lend itself to speech takes on a signification for the mind through the metaphor of it that gives it meaning, even if the metaphor is able only to half say it.

In distinction from the linguistic signifier, the psychoanalytic signifier, as developed by Lacan, is characterized by the rupture it creates in meaning. As the sign of what sustains and represents the subject as discontinuous with sense, the signifier creates a cleavage in the social ideal, the Ego Ideal. It splits rationality and disorganizes any attempt at reference to a reality. During treatment, the chaining of the signifier leads to a delimiting of that jouissance which marks the subject in the real and reduces the subject to an object upon which the death drive feeds. In treatment then, the signifier appears as both the metaphor of the subject, representing the subject approximately in speech, and as the metonymy of desire, repeatedly failing the lacking object causing it. In either case, the signifier conveys a dimension of rupture in the narrative as a phonemic, syntactic, logical, and rational structure. According to Lacan: "We must bring everything back to the function of the cut in discourse . . . discourse in an analytic session is valuable only in so far as it stumbles or is interrupted."[6] In treatment, the analysand's word runs up against the meeting with jouissance, with the real, that cannot be said, that can only be "half said," as Lacan teaches.

While Lacan was interested in the analysand's signifiers, the chaining of which encircles lack, Freud strove to uncover the unconscious representations that, from a scene other than that of consciousness, traced out an unsuitable destiny for the individual, one that would send his ego into exile. "Since Freud the unconscious has been a chain of signifiers that somewhere (on another stage, in another scene, he wrote) is repeated, and insists . . . "[7] With the Rat Man, for example, Freud tracks the representation of words which, so foreign for a man of his social standing, structured his helpless alienation in a desire with an inexplicable origin, a desire originating from an other scene, so to speak. His unconscious was triggered by what Freud called an "aggressive transference" vis-à-vis him, and the patient began to tell of facts, omitted until then, built on a chaining of associations based on the *rat* phoneme: *Ratten* (rats), *Spielratte* (gambler), *Rate* (debt installment), *heiraten* (to be married), *Rattenmamsell* (Rat-girl), and so forth.[8]

In following the outpouring of facts brought to consciousness through the metonymic succession of the signifier "rat," Freud enabled his patient to come to a knowledge—a "savoir"—of what was unconsciously directing his life, from his metaphoric identification with the disgusting and filthy rat up to the wish to murder his father. In tracing this path, Freud countered the symptom of obsessions about the corporal punishment with rats, of torture with rats, a symptom that was ruining the Rat Man's social and love life. The signifier *rat* cleared the path for the Rat Man to constitute memories that allowed the emergence of a new savoir in his analytic treatment.

The Navel of the Dream: A Hole in Meaning
Where Jouissance Returns

According to Lacan: "If linguistics enables us to see the signifier as the determinant of the signified, analysis reveals the truth of this relation by making 'holes' in the meaning of the determinants of its discourse."[9] The signifier is the remnant in representation, in the unconscious memory, of a series of anguishing and traumatic experiences that have transformed the body but that have remained in the unsaid, in the unspeakable. The unspeakable is palpated through the psychoanalytic signifier, provided by a dream or a slip, and flushed out through associations and memories. Freud believed that the analyst should carefully attend to the representation of words that contained, in a condensation, a multiplicity of elements.

A young woman just beginning analysis, and currently interning as a medical student at a home for terminally ill cancer patients, came to treatment with the following dream:

> My superior, Doctor X, asks me to prepare the meals for the patients. I say to myself: it's not up to me to make the meals because there is a cook for that. After hesitating for a few minutes, because my superior is also the person who fills out my intern assessment report and I don't want to displease him, I leave. I come back a bit later, the supper is not ready but there is lasagna in the oven. But I didn't make it and I feel badly about it. It looks good. The next day, my superior criticizes me for not performing the tasks required of me.

Because the analysand does not know what to think of her dream, the analyst questioned the most bizarre element in the dream—that of cooking lasagna. Associations were then jostled. The word *lasagna* turned out to be a signifier in the subject's history to the extent that it constituted a junction of events, of memories, of places, and of emotions that until then had been repressed or had remained in the real, in the non-said. It was in analyzing Irma's dream that Freud for the first time delineated the key concept of the "navel of the dream:" that point of non-sense that the narrative delimits. In the sequence of associations that follows, one sees that *lasagna* is definitely the element that constitutes the navel insofar as it is a condensation of various elements that, metonymically converge towards a real that cannot be assimilated.

First association: "I should have made the lasagna to follow the advice of my superior, Doctor X, who knows better than I do how to treat patients. Working in a center for the terminally ill is new and unusual for a student in medicine. With dying patients, I never know quite what to do or say. Its unnerving and agonizing. It reminds me of the suicide of one of my uncles who was very important to me. I think I could have prevented his suicide because I spoke with him two days before. I never was able to speak about his suicide because I felt guilty."

Second association: "I didn't do what I was supposed to do. My intern's report and final mark are going to be affected. Usually I'm the one who makes the lasagna. That's my specialty—I don't know whether I am making a mistake in my plans for eventually going into geriatrics. I don't know if this is really what I want my specialty to be. In the dream, someone else made the lasagna and it looks just as good or even better than mine."

Third association: "Why do they say that lasagna is my specialty? Other people in the dream bake it without 'making such a production of it' and without putting so much effort into it. Why am I forever wondering about existential questions when it is not necessary in order to be a good doctor? Why am I choosing to work with people who are going to die? This takes me back to the terrible anguish I have when the people around me die, as if I were somehow responsible for their death."

Fourth association: "Lasagna is also a cheese dish, one for special occasions, the sign of a holiday. The first time I made it was to celebrate a college friend's moving to another city. She died in a car accident a week later. Another friend who was at that dinner committed suicide the year after. After the lasagna party, there were funerals."

Fifth association: "'Lasagna' is also the name of a dissident Mohawk Warrior often in the news during events in Oka, Québec. He was arrested and imprisoned for his radical views. As for me, in my field I'm sort of on the fringe. I had to get special authorization to do my training in a terminally ill center. It was first decided that such training was outside the framework of traditional medicine and the curriculum for a student in medicine. I always liked doing nonconformist things, which seriously puts my future career in jeopardy."

Sixth association: "The dream reminds me of another dream where I'm with my mother who prevents me from marrying the man I love. My mother's requests meant she was always interfering in my life, thwarting my ambitions and attempting to control my relationships."

At this point in the analysis of the dream, the analysand takes a deep breath, and then says that she never imagined one word could contain so many memories and conflicts. She said she had begun to realize the hold certain words could have over her life and her lack of control over what they secretly conveyed. Removing her from the harmonious space of the holiday, the signifier drags the analysand onto the scene of death, of anguish, and of jeopardy, where her desire leads her. What *lasagna* brought back as a memory to the shore of consciousness for the young woman no longer had any connection with the pasta dish everyone enjoys. For the analysand, the word *lasagna* in the future will evoke a series of events that may be resumed in one sentence: baking lasagna is to concoct a death dish, as much socially as physically. As with this analysand, the signifier cracks the varnish of narcissism, severing the order of cultural demands and ideals. The signifier of the dream attempts, through representation, to have emerge and to delimit in words something that had been unbearable—an unbearable lack of words to say the real, a lack where jouissance reappears as the impossible in the form of the death drive. Analysis of the dream from the perspective of the signifier eventually uncovers this savoir of repetition.

In the words of Lacan: "The unconscious is always manifested as that which vacillates in a split in the subject, from which emerges a discovery that Freud compares with desire—a desire that we will temporarily situate in the denuded metonymy of the discourse in question, where the subject surprises himself in some unexpected way."[10] To be designated as a signifier, a word, a phoneme, or a fragment of a narrative, must be attachable to a dream, a trauma, a piece of the body, a symptom, a memory, a fantasy, and so forth. The word *lasagna* partially met these conditions. In order to be considered a psychoanalytic signifier, *lasagna* will have to repeat itself on other occasions during the treatment, and metonymically chain with other signifiers. Only then may one conclude that it is a compelling component of a structure circumscribing the subject of the unconscious.

Eve of Destruction: The Signifier as Metaphor of the Subject and Metonymy of Desire

The science fiction movie *Eve of Destruction* by Duncan Gibbins (1991) evokes the manner in which following the track of the signifier may lead the analysand to a savoir about the unconscious. In the film, a distinguished and successful woman scientist, both intelligent and beautiful, creates a human robot in her own image for use by the CIA. She programs her double with her own history, memories, and fantasies, and succeeds in having the double experience her emotions. But in the course of a holdup, the human-looking robot is wounded by a bullet and, defying all rational explanation, no longer responds to CIA directives and begins to function independently.

Eve the android sets out to satisfy her fantasies and settle her accounts without any of the usual moral restrictions. Dressed in sensual leather, she cruises a man in a motel and invites him to her room. There she deals with the sexual preliminaries with relative ease. When the man persists—despite her warnings—and repeatedly calls her a *bitch*, she suddenly castrates him with one bite of her teeth. On the road again, she becomes annoyed with a businessman in a hurry, who is trying to get around her in traffic. He signs his death warrant when he gives her the finger and calls her a bitch. She then drives full speed into him and he dies, crushed in his car. Then, after Eve the robot succeeds in tracking down the father of Eve, the scientist (he was living under an assumed name), she coldly kills him by snapping his neck. Anyone in her path meets with an element of the real that escapes any rationalization through the signifier. Finally she goes to the home of her ex-husband, who has the custody of Eve's son. She kidnaps the child—does she intend to kill the child too?

In *Eve of Destruction,* the colonel who is in charge of the investigation, realizes the nonrational motives that trigger the android's action. He decides against any attempt to determine so-called objective—mechanical—causes of the malfunction. Rather, he takes on the role of an analyst and questions Eve the scientist about her childhood and adolescence. Impervious to the narcissistic wounds she might experience and totally disinterested in her social status as a brilliant engineer highly valued by her country, the colonel tracks the scientist's meetings with the real. There, he uncovers a signifier, the only remnant in language of the repressed traumas of her childhood. Using this signifier that sustained lack and absence, he devises the type of fantasmatic construction that will enable him to determine the exact trajectory of the android's insensate movement. On the heels of the censured in the scientist's life, he will constrain her to seek out her truth as a subject.

What proves to be the key to Eve's unconscious is the signifier *bitch.* Unknown to CIA specialists, the holdup at the bank had restaged Eve's meeting with an unbearable real. During the holdup, after senselessly beating up a defenseless woman, the bandit aimed at the android, calling her stupid and yelling "fuck you, lady." In doing so, the bandit removed the repression of the condensation of the following traumatic representations: when Eve was a small girl, her father would beat her mother in her presence while calling her a stupid bitch. The father ultimately precipitated the mother's death by pushing her in front of a moving vehicle. One may deduce that the signifier *bitch* is what for Eve, identifying with her mother, constituted her as the object of her father in a fantasy of seduction. But because the signifier recalled the atrociousness of her mother's death and abuse that Eve herself had witnessed, while standing by anguished and helpless, it was unbearable to her. The lifting of the repression sustained by the signifier *bitch* transformed the android robot into a machine of death, a pure inexhaustible drive of death, propelled by the Other. In the end, the colonel succeeds in using the signifier *bitch* to destabilize the android and thus, finally causing a short circuit in the mechanism of its automatic functioning.

The event in the motel and the explanations given by the scientist enable us to comprehend exactly how the signifier *bitch* functioned for Eve in adolescence to allow her to take over a jouissance, a fatal enjoyment, that up until then, had been attributed to her mother. The scientist tells the colonel that in her youth, the motel bar was a meeting place for prostitutes. She and her friends often walked by it without daring to enter. Still, she had always wondered what went on inside and this curiosity nourished many fantasies. As an adolescent, when she walked by the motel, Eve met with a feminine jouissance, waking in her the memory of the fascinating terror she supposed her mother experienced when her father, a frequent patron in such bars, mistreated her and called her a stupid bitch. The scene in the motel between the robot Eve and the man stages the scientist's relationship to her mother's jouissance. This jouissance, first attributed to her mother, became for Eve, through her fantasies, something that implicated her. It was an horrifying enjoyment, a jouissance that constituted Eve as a bitch for men in sleazy bars. And it is this excess, this jouissance, which will be her and her android's downfall.

For Eve, the signifier *bitch* is the metaphor, the condensation of an inexpressible meeting with a terrorizing and anguishing real, where as Lacan might say, the repressed meaning of her desire expresses itself. The destructive path along which the android travels is linked with the signifier *bitch* which determines a metonymic succession of events in which her desire is marked as a desire for an other thing that is always lacking. The subject at stake is constituted by the other scene, that of the *bitch*, where "desire is borne by death."[11]

Like the colonel's efforts in *Eve of Destruction*, analytic treatment is a strategic space in which the calculation of the signifiers of desire as determining the subject's position is the sole stake of speech. A quote from Lacan aptly illustrates the active role that the analysand must play in this voyage to encounter this savoir of his or her own unconscious and in doing so, to recover some degree of liberty:

> In the recourse of subject to subject that we preserve, psychoanalysis may accompany the patient to the ecstatic limit of the '*Thou art that*,' in which is revealed to him the cipher of his mortal destiny, but it is not in our mere power as practitioners to bring him to that point where the real journey begins.[12]

Notes

1. Jacques Lacan, *The Four Fundamental Concepts of Psycho-Analysis* (New York: W.W. Norton and Co., 1978), 25. Original edition (Paris: Éditions du Seuil, 1973), 27.

2. Sigmund Freud, *The Standard Edition of the Complete Psychological Works of Sigmund Freud, Volume 10: Two Case Histories*, ed. James Strachey (London: The Hogarth Press, 1955), 177.

3. Jacques Lacan, *Écrits: A Selection*, trans. Alan Sheridan (New York: W. W. Norton and Co., 1977), 148. Original edition (Paris: Éditions du Seuil, 1966), 495.

4. ———, *Écrits: A Selection*, trans. Alan Sheridan (New York: W. W. Norton and Co., 1977), 148. Original edition, (Paris: Éditions du Seuil, 1966), 495.

5. On this point, see also Lucie Cantin's chapter 1 in this collection, "The Trauma of Language."

6. Jacques Lacan, *Écrits: A Selection*, trans. Alan Sheridan (New York: W .W. Norton and Co., 1977), 299. Original edition (Paris: Éditions du Seuil, 1966), 801.

7. ———, *Écrits: A Selection*, trans. Alan Sheridan (New York: W. W. Norton and Co., 1977), 297. Original edition (Paris: Éditions du Seuil, 1966), 799.

8. Sigmund Freud, *The Standard Edition of the Complete Psychological Works of Sigmund Freud, Volume 10: Two Case Histories*, ed. James Strachey (London: The Hogarth Press, 1955), 200–220.

9. Jacques Lacan, *Écrits: A Selection*, trans. Alan Sheridan (New York: W. W. Norton and Co., 1977), 299. Original edition (Paris: Éditions du Seuil, 1966), 801.

10. ———, *The Four Fundamental Concepts of Psycho-Analysis* (New York: W.W. Norton and Co., 1978), 28. Original edition (Paris: Éditions du Seuil, 1973), 29.

11. ———, *Écrits: A Selection*, trans. Alan Sheridan (New York: W. W. Norton and Co., 1977), 277. Original edition (Paris: Éditions du Seuil, 1966), 642.

12. ———, *Écrits: A Selection*, trans. Alan Sheridan (New York: W. W. Norton and Co., 1977), 7. Original edition (Paris: Éditions du Seuil, 1966), 100.

Chapter 4

The Work of the Dream and Jouissance in the Treatment of the Psychotic

DANIELLE BERGERON

The Tyranny of the Jouissance of the Other and the Absence of the Symbolic Father

According to Lacan, the newborn "drops" into a world of language[1] and is consequently diverted irrevocably from the immediate and total satisfactions that answer biological need, and is submited instead, through the use of signifiers, to cultural requisites and parental demands. These signifiers, linked one to another by the signifier of the Father, repress the impossibility of jouissance—that is, complete and immediate satisfaction for the human being—and introduce the prohibited as the principle of coexistence and social link. The navel, that indelible imprint on the human body, stands as a metaphor for the infant's introduction and capture in the universe of language. In it we see the dual dimension of the infant's entry into the world. On the one hand, the navel indicates the obturation of the umbilical cord through which the fetus directly secured everything essential to its continued life. On the other hand, the navel persists as the scar of the "fallen" cord. As the latter, it functions as a knot symbolizing the passage to subjectivity, a passage that begins by the severance of an immediate, but problematic access to an other—problematic, that is, in

This chapter was presented in different form at a workshop entitled "Lacanian Psychoanalysis: The Process of Working Through and Dreams," at the Center for Psychoanalytic Study in Chicago, February 1993.

the bidirectionality of this cord, and in the many psychic traps that lie in the other's responses. The cutting of the umbilical cord by a third party, even prior to the expulsion of the placenta following delivery, elevates that customary gesture to the value of a symbol. In this symbol, we recognize the consecration into existence of a new human life.

To ground these theoretical speculations in relation to the clinical question of dreams and psychosis, let us look at an actual dream reported by John, a young psychotic brought in for treatment. This is the first dream he brings to the analyst.

> I was playing volleyball with my father and some of his friends. I wasn't playing very well, and my mother told me, in a worried tone, "I hope you're not seeing Jackie Baker." I became discouraged, stopped playing, and flew onto the fence. I was atop the fence surrounding the volleyball court, when I said, "No!" I got a grip on myself in thinking I had to continue the game with my father and his friends. I told my mother, "It's you, mom, who has to leave." She then left.
>
> Later Peter, my father's best friend, came and talked to me. He said, "There's something traumatizing your life, but I don't know what it is. . . . It's not normal for you to cry so much at your age. We cry when we're young, but not at your age."

This first dream, so beautifully paradigmatic, sets in motion the undertaking of the psychotic's treatment. The dream tells John he must give up his mother if he wants to be a man, if he wants to enter into the social competition and not give up the game. She must leave in order for him to stand face-to-face with the Law of the Father.

In the ordinary, non-psychotic, course of subjectification, long before the infant's birth, the mother introduces the Father as the symbolic instance, the outside instance, necessary to the social game.[2] Given to the child by the mother, the Father ordinarily assures the child that the rules of the family are the same as those for society, and that the familial demands made do not reflect idiosyncratic whims of the parent but, rather, are linked to the cultural order and are consistent with its requirements. The Father is, therefore, the entity that makes symbolic castration the kernel of coexistence and guarantees that the child will never be enslaved as the exclusive object of the jouissance of an other to whom the child must be devoted. The father's function is to represent the necessity of prohibition and, in so doing, to guarantee that complete and total satisfaction—jouissance—is impossible for everyone. We might further note that the symbolic Father is also a fiction that in language sustains a meaning for life by repressing the absence of any justification for *loss*, that traumatism at the root of the human experience.

Without this fiction that Lacan called the "Name-of-the-Father," one would be thrust face-to-face with the emptiness of meaning in human existence—a confrontation that would rend apart one's life. In short, the symbolic Father is constituted both in the *paternal function* that guarantees the limits of jouissance and in the *paternal metaphor* (Name-of-the-Father) that sustains the fiction of meaningfulness on which the neurotic's life rests.

It is precisely the installation of the symbolic Father that has failed for the psychotic child, who is thereby maintained in a dual relation with an imaginary other. In the clinic, we find that this relationship, as elaborated in the discourse of the patient, is set in motion by a perverse denial of castration by one of the psychotic's parents. Despite the real cut of the umbilical cord, the psychotic continues to live, in his or her imaginary, as the object which completes the Other, the object that manifests this Other as uncastrated or uncastratable. The psychotic feels, as we shall see later in another of John's dreams, like a robot, sacrificed to the Other's jouissance, a slave of special laws and capricious demands that may jeopardize his or her life. The mission we find at the heart of the psychotic delusion—often abruptly appearing as a summons served by an all-powerful Other—operates to mitigate the insensate life the psychotic has been leading in the service of an unforgiving master.

Symbolic Frame for Treatment: Delusion to Dream, Knowledge to Ignorance, Object to Subject

The framework of the psychotic's treatment must from the outset be anchored on the side of the symbolic Father, where castration, as we have said, is the law for all. The treatment must sever the psychotic from his or her imaginary relationship with that other being who dictates every action. Consequently, at the first interview, once the treatment framework has been devised, we bring the analysand to engage a personal responsibility in the process of analysis. We ask, as means of payment, that the analysand give the analyst at each session a written account of a dream which will form the basis of the work; moreover, we ask that the analysand bring memories of events never before spoken of or things that cannot be spoken of elsewhere. These may seem extraordinary requests to make of a psychotic, but in our experience, the psychotic readily complies with this sometimes very painful, very stringent ethical requirement in hopes of regaining control of life. It is as if the dream, in conveying suffering and horror, is paying the symbolic debt for the person's right to exist and to speak. Thus, in treatment, the dream will function as the psychotic's "ticket to ride" to subjectivity and individuality.

For years, some analysts have suggested that psychotics do not dream or else cannot dream in relation to the psychoanalytic process because their imaginary is so wholly engrossed in delusion. Such has not been our experience in Québec. Let us emphasize here, then, that it takes an analyst's desire-to-know, a *désir de savoir*, for the psychotic to dream, since the psychotic will produce dream only in response to this desire. But, one might ask, why demand *dreams* in particular? Dreams prove valuable because, with the signifiers they offer, they are the best clinical tool for gaining access to the analysand's history. "It's a good thing we can tell you our dreams," exclaimed John after a few months of treatment, "otherwise, it would be hard to speak. I would have nothing to say." Furthermore, in contrast to the *delusion*, to whose certainty the psychotic clings for survival against the void, the *dream* is a sort of neutral territory. Here, from the outset, both the analyst and the analysand are in a position of questioning. The strangeness of the dream, its eccentricity, its unreal allegories, and its absurdities—all this turns the dream into a foreign object capable of sustaining the psychotic's curiosity. Whereas with the telling of the delusion the psychotic is in the position of teaching something to the analyst and of displaying totalitarian knowledge, with the telling of the dream, the psychotic, like the analyst, is in the position of searching. If the analyst were to question the delusion directly by confronting it with social reality, the analyst would be pitting his or her own knowledge against that of the delusion—a confrontation which, in the end, would only maintain the psychotic in an imaginary relation of power.

With the dream, however, both analyst and analysand lack knowledge; they lack "savoir." The work with the dream yields signifiers which, even if they are picked up by the analyst from the psychotic's speech, lead to memories extracted by the psychotic him- or herself, from the psychotic's own history. It is these memories, linked to what the analysand has experienced (and therefore originating from the "inside"), that undermine the certitude of delusion. Delusion is a closed and dense imaginary construction that discharges any surprise by the real because it can be entirely told with words. In delusion, signifiers are "absolute" and words have only one closed meaning. In the dream, by contrast, signifiers open up other signifiers. The dream, moreover, yields signifiers which recall events that marked the psychotic's life because they operated a rupture in that life by remaining nonrepresented, unassimilable, and unspeakable. These memories derived from dream-work, then, uncover gaps, loose threads in the fabric of the delusion, and thereby put the delusion into question.

In the treatment of the psychotic, the dream and its enigma, which according to Freud should be tackled as a rebus or riddle,[3] contribute to make *ignorance* the driving force behind the analysand's work and the analyst's interrogative listening.[4] The enigma of the dream enables doubt to creep into the delusion and certitude to be pierced. A "passion of ignorance," to use a Lacanian term, maintains the analyst in the position of a lacking and castrated Other, a position that sustains the Absence of any Other. It constitutes the knot around which a new history will be organized for the psychotic—only this time, the psychotic's history will be based not on the logic of the delusion that makes the psychotic the object for the Other, but rather on signifiers that will allow access to his or her truth as a human subject marked by lack. The analyst grounds the analytic ethics in the fact that there is a symbolic order and that it is incomplete. There is, therefore, no absolute knowledge, as the delusion would assert. The work of the dream limits the jouissance of the imaginary Other and allows for symbolic castration and the emergence of the Law of the Father.

The Dream as Staging the Structure of the Subject's Relation to the Other

The dream in analytic treatment quickly sets the psychotic to work. John brought to his second session an intricate dream that, as we shall see, clearly illustrates the structure of his relation to the Other.

> I'm helping my father renovate one of his shops. A Christian friend tells me it's still possible for me to renew contact with them. I finally use their code. He discovers that I have extraordinary aptitudes. We're going to see his guru to give him the following demonstration: my friend hits my hand with a stone and I feel nothing. Later he is surprised to discover my father personifies adversity.
>
> Some men are after me. The watch I'm wearing on my wrist warns me of their presence. They sift through the remains of our shop and find me. They screw a device on my watchstrap to decode my language. Thanks to the device, they can understand the meaning of my speech and locate my friends. They take me away with them, but I manage to escape. They search for me everywhere and I hurry to find my friends. I tell them to leave their hideouts—they've been discovered. A young colleague reveals his identity to me. . . . He tells me he's a robot . . . that he repaired his arm . . . he's therefore just like me. But I let them know that I'm the only one who can lead them out of this.
>
> Those who were after us have caught up with us. There's going to be a showdown. Not long after, we succeed in neutralizing them.
>
> Later, I rejoin my friends in a huge room in front of a TV that is going to announce news that's too difficult to bear. I suggest we

kneel down and cross ourselves. Once the news is out, I get up to see
if I have enough strength to bear this new burden. My friends try to
do the same, but they realize that I'm the only one who can fit into
this new consciousness. I announce to them that they will have eter-
nal life. They explode with joy and are full of compassion for me because they understand I am offered up in sacrifice. Now I'm no
longer afraid. All I have to do is carry my cross.

Considered as a dream addressed to the analyst, the narrative acts
out the structure of the relation of the subject to the Other. The hero
of the dream, with whom John identifies in his associations, is a robot.
Like any machine, he has no feelings: he can be hit on the hand without
feeling a thing. In his association on the dream, John reveals that when
he was young, he thought he was Arthur the Robot. An additional indication that John does not regard himself as a human being is that the
basis for his relation to others is a "code." In "The Freudian Thing"
Lacan tells us that "there is no speech that is not language," and that
language "is not a code . . . it is not to be confused with information."[5]
Whether in a computer program or in the behaviors of an ant colony,
there is always a specific, unvarying response to a code. Language,
taken here as the fact of speaking, is by contrast something very different. To a demand expressed by one person, the answer—if there is
one—may take one of several forms and will never perfectly match what
was demanded. In human language there can be no equivalence between the word spoken and the thing asked. Moreover, every demand is
subject to interpretation and acceptance by the person expected to answer. In John's dream, however, his enemies are able to decode his language and seize possession of his thoughts merely by installing a device
on his watchstrap. The dream is suggestive of the subjective position of
the psychotic. The psychotic lives as if managed from the outside. He
does not consider himself master of his own fate and free will. The notion that John's body may be freely accessible to others who compro-
mise his privacy will come up in subsequent dreams in the form of
secret microphones used against him, devices placed in his mouth to
cause his teeth to rot, and suppositories inserted by God that keep him
from temptation. The psychotic does not experience his body as a space
personally belonging to him for his own subjectivity. On the contrary,
the body of the psychotic is experienced as an access route used by the
Other to act directly on him. It is as if, imaginarily, the umbilical cord
still existed and as if its severing failed to symbolically determine the
knot of his individuality: he is, within and without, the extension of an
Other who derives jouissance from him.

The dream reveals another aspect of the psychotic's relation to the Other. Even though he is offered up in sacrifice, John is the Chosen One among the robots, "the only one" as he says, "who can fit into this new consciousness"—and thanks to his offering, the one who will ensure that the others will be able to enjoy eternally. The dream that gives John the occasion to tell us he converted religiously at the age of twenty-one, has already begun to trace out the form of his delusion that he will fill out with a later dream.

Without the Father as guarantor of each person's freedom and upholder of social law, the psychotic experiences every relation as an imaginary one of strength and power. We see in John's dream that the men who want him don't negotiate. They kidnap him. In the psychotic's imaginary world, democracy does not prevail. Autocracy rules. In psychosis, the father "personifies adversity," as John's dream puts it, rather than being the third party that insures a limit to the Other's demands for jouissance.

Bandages on the Knees: The Dream, the Chain of Signifiers, and the Unrepresented

The delusion responds to superego demands (for perfection and for the gift of the psychotic's entire being) by freezing the psychotic's life in fulfillment of a mission. In this mission, the psychotic is to make a supreme, uncompromising sacrifice on behalf of a worldwide or universal Cause or of a Being. The interest of the *dream* with the psychotic, as we have said, consists in the fact that, through the signifiers, a savoir of the unconscious—in the form of fragments of the signifying chain encircling a hole—is substituted for the dense certitude of delusion and for the delusionary knowledge that blocks any representation of lack. Lacan taught that the signifier is "that which represents a subject for an other signifier."[6] One implication of this well-known dictum is that the signifiers noted by the analyst during the narration of a dream lead metonymically, in the analysand's associations, to new signifiers that are in turn directed towards an unrepresentable. As part of a group, each signifier in a segment of chain expends itself around the void it encircles, around an element of the real that in the analysand's life had remained unassimilable. The act of the analyst, then, lies in going from signifier to signifier, encircling the real, and progressively symbolizing the untold moments of the analysand's life. In this way, analysis is able to force an emptying of the jouissance left stranded in the traumatizing event of the analysand's history.

With the neurotic, the very structure of the dream chains the signifiers around the lacking signifier, that unacknowledged thing in the navel of the dream. With the psychotic, by contrast, the signifiers may reorganize but will not fully chain. It is rather the analyst's maneuver that directs these segments of signifying chain to an inevitable confrontation with whatever in the psychotic's history has remained without representation. The analyst in the position of object *a* is necessarily the link between the chain segments and the real in the case of psychosis. At the end of treatment, according to Willy Apollon, it is the "externalized object"[7] that will replace the analyst-as-object-*a* to serve as the link between the chain segments and the real. At the place of the impossible object of desire, the object *a*, the analyst contests the position of the psychotic as object of the jouissance of the Other, and engages the psychotic in the construction of a subject history that is detached from the Other and has its own proper object.[8]

Another of John's dreams illustrates the work of symbolization as it leads to the construction of bits of history that may serve the psychotic as a basis to sustain a meaningful existence in the world—but a meaning this time *within* the social link, something the delusion could not offer. The segments of the signifying chain will produce a new logic to the subject's life, a history he may rely on, a new knowledge to be substituted for the delusion and its closed logic. This new knowledge, however, will be a pierced one, since words will never be commensurate with his experience.

> On the steps in front of the college, a student interviewed me about my projects for the future. His microphone was hidden in his left sleeve. I told him my age and told him that my intention was to take a few courses at college. I then walked down a hallway sitting in a wheelchair. I had bandages on my knees.

The signifier "projects for the future" gave an occasion for John to speak of various courses he had registered for at the university, of his own incapacity to choose a career, and of the fact that up until his conversion, he had thought of becoming a merchant in his father's trade. He added that as early as his secondary school years he wondered why he was here on Earth. He felt left to himself and perceived no interest in him on the part of his parents. "They never helped me with my homework to give me a chance to succeed in life. My father was too busy with his business. Whenever he went out with me, he would lecture me. As for my mother, she packed my lunch. On weekends, when I should have been doing my homework, my father made me do work in his shop. I did it to please him, but I couldn't understand why."

During the next session, John said that in realizing his parents had not spent much time with him, he became, for the first time, aggressive towards them. This sense of aggression distressed him, and John questioned the usefulness of pursuing his treatment. Here, memory works as a past that returns and ruptures narration. The rupture of narrative is evidence that it did constitute a historic moment in the life of the subject.

The analyst then pursued the analytic work by inquiring after *les pansements aux genoux*, the "bandages on my knees" concluding John's dream narrative. John explained that he'd suffered two serious knee injuries in his late adolescence. Recollection of these events led John to childhood memories of parental misunderstandings based apparently on conflicts surrounding his education. "My father was for strictness; my mother for flexibility," he said. "My mother would encourage me to lie to my father so that he wouldn't punish me. When I would come back from the swimming pool, mother would say, 'Don't forget to tell your father you did eighty laps this afternoon, not just fifty.'" John's mother required him to *penser à mentir*, to think of lying, so that *nous*, we the family, may continue to exist. John's words in French suggest the workings of the signifier: the word for bandage, *pansement*, can be heard in his formulation of *pense-ment*, his thinking of lying. Also, the *nous*, the family that John is to save, resonates with both *genoux*, knees, and with *je-noue*, I knot. John's parents had failed to knot together around their parental function because the mother had entered into a special, perverse contract with him to deny paternal authority. Those associations opened onto the unease and anxiety John had experienced in those circumstances where he "could not manage to trust."

For the first time, John also spoke of discovering masturbation, something that would later constitute a *symptom* for him, as an episode of rupture in his life, a moment when he had not succeeded in relying on his father for the words that would have enabled him to bear the anguish of unknown jouissance. "At fourteen years old," he said, "something broke. I wanted to know what masturbation was. Somehow it didn't seem right. I later found some pornographic magazines in one of my father's filing cabinets. I thought that he himself had problems and that he wouldn't be able to do anything for me."

John's discovery of masturbation, however, was overshadowed that same year by the drama of his parents' separation. In particular, John recalled that his father, who was unable to speak to John's mother, took the boy to see her. She sat in her lover's car, and while John's father waited in his own car, the boy was to try to persuade her to come home. John could never explain his father's reasoning, which he found very strange at the time, but we can see that, in essence, his father was asking John to be the one to *re-nouer*, reknot, the parental couple. From John's standpoint, the bandaging was to be done to the *je-nous*, the "I-us" that resonates with the *genou* signifier, the knee of the dream image. In going over those painful memories in treatment and in articulating them verbally, John began to gain access to the fact that something had been lacking on his parents' side in their parental function and he had been thrust, wholly despite himself, at the core of a failed knotting. From the signifier "bandages on the knees" extracted from the dream by the analyst, John began to perceive his parents' failing. In discovering confusing memories of unassimilable situations—situations which had threatened to overwhelm him with inarticulate emotion—John first began to grapple with the idea that his parents were not beyond reproach.

John's dream of bandaged knees clearly shows how the work with a signifier and its modifications enables a history to be constructed both of recent and past events and of memories that had ruptured the organization of sense in the analysand's life and had been maintained in the unspeakable. With the metonymic link of the signifier "bandages on knees," fragments in John's history began to cohere together, providing him with markers for his life other than those of delusion, and constituting for him a savoir about those dark encounters with the real during his childhood and adolescent years.

Dreams of the Hand: Bringing the Symptom to Pierce the Delusion

> I was shoveling gravel in front of the shop. The father of a friend showed up and told me that he was going to purchase the shop in co-ownership with his son. I told him it was an excellent deal. When I asked him if he planned to retire soon, he told me he was going to work a few years longer. I wanted to know whether spirituality and science were compatible. He answered "absolutely . . ." I continued to work. I discovered bits of my clothing under each shovelful.

This dream was a pivotal point in John's treatment in that it connected events from his history with the triggering of his delusion. The construction, maintenance, and renovation of his father's shops here emerge as a signifier hiding major traumas of John's life. "When I was young," he said, "I agreed to work in my father's shops with the understanding that, when I became an adult, I would take over and become responsible for managing them. When I saw that I wasn't succeeding at my school work, I told myself there would always be the shops if I couldn't work at anything else. At twenty-one, my first venture into my father's field came when I bought one of my father's shops. Then, without telling me, my father suddenly decided to sell all of his other shops to a perfect stranger. He told us he'd had enough of all the responsibility. It was about this time that God began to speak to me. 'Agree to give yourself to Me,' He said in one phrase. I then decided to realize my own goals. I got rid of everything that belonged to me—records, stamp collection, bike, and the shop—to become God. He told me I should leave because He was getting old. And so I set out to abide by His will, to be His instrument, His tool, just like Jesus had been. I thought that God was a father who realized His strength was slipping away. That troubled me because for the first time I felt He was vulnerable."

By selling the shops, it seemed to John, his father had taken away his last chance to succeed in life. During his childhood and adolescence, John had served his father to the detriment of his own goals, and had trusted in his father's word. When his father made the impulsive decision to sell his shops, John found himself before a void, a terrifying absence of either foundation or reference for a given word. He had identified with the ideal that his father had set for him—that of becoming a merchant in his father's field—at the expense of his own future as an independent citizen relying on stable studies; and his father had abused this trust in using John as cheap labor. As time went by, John had identified with what he believed his father lacked: a son to take over from him when he became too old. But at age twenty-one, John found he had been exploited for nothing. Against this defect, the voice of John's delusion addresses itself as a reparative effort. Being in God's service while waiting to take over from God functions to repair the failure of his relation with his father and to give meaning to his life. Once he had been of no great value to his father, but no more. With the onset of the delusion, the whole world had come to depend upon John.

Selling the shops was not the first time John's father had left him on the edge of the void. In telling a dream where a man told him *take my hand*, John brought up two memories that show that the foreclosure of the signifier of the Father was already at work in his childhood. The first memory was quite brief: "Once when we were visiting Inverness Falls, my father pushed me forward toward the edge of a precipice, but then held me back at the last moment. It was a joke in bad taste." The second memory, though similar, was a little more elaborate than the first: "We had gone with my father to look at my uncle's house that was under construction. I was five years old. There was a plank over a ravine. My father said 'Take my hand.' He walked across on the plank, but when he got to the other side, he kicked out the plank from under me. I was left hanging in the air, holding on to his hand. It really scared me."

Even when his real father was there, John felt he was alone, suspended over the void. He was uncertain of his father's capacity to protect him against the void. Moreover, John's becoming God in his delusion was an attempt to obviate the destructuring of the imaginary that had been occasioned by the absence in his life of the signifier of the Father as bearer of the requirement for a limit to abuse. The caprice and peculiarly individual aspects of the paternal demand were mitigated, to some degree, in the signifier "God" with which John identified in his delusion. "God" was stabilized through its link to the discourse of culture, and through the way it offered John a social cause. Also, situated as it was amid a series of signifiers put together by the analyst during treatment, the signifier "God" extracted from the delusion took on the role of a symbolic ideal. "God" would be the master signifier that would serve to lead to the symptom, John's masturbation, the rock of jouissance (as we shall see below). This jouissance was inconsistent with John's delusion and directs us to the subject of the unconscious.

The call of God for John served as a foundation where the Name-of-the-Father was lacking. In answering the call, he became someone who filled out God, who gave Him back His invulnerability. Taking over from God, however, entailed two further requirements—namely, that John be entirely in His service and that he match the ideal of perfection. As we see, the psychotic's delusion clearly demonstrates that what governs the universe is an Other who demands total and immediate satisfaction—in other words, jouissance.

Another dream led John to speak of this incompatibility between *delusion*, where the Other demands total jouissance and undivided subservience of the person, and the *symptom*, as a space limiting jouissance in an object internal to the body:

> We were part of a tribe. The invaders arrived and we fought. They were too many for us and we lost the battle. A young boy on a bike gave me a sword. I visited a shop. In it was a chainsaw on which you could cut off your hand. One of the invaders picked it up and carried it off with him.

The associations made from the signifier "cut off your hand" enabled John to speak of the times he had doubted the rationale behind God's requirements of him, times which had shaken the delusion in relying on the analyst as the judge of the abuse in the sacrificial demands. The associations also enabled him to address the symptom that was coming to breach the integrity of his delusion. "At twenty-two years old, I read 'if your eye or hand makes you fall, tear it off and cast it far away.' I masturbated and was haunted by the idea of cutting off my hand. Every time I masturbated, I felt I was offending God."

John associated these memories with three other wrenching moments in his life where he not only had to take over from God, but also had to answer unconditionally to all His orders. One day, alone at the country house, John had a "flash" that instructed him to set the woods on fire. He interpreted the flash as God's will, and by the time his cousin arrived to visit, everything was ready, gas and matches. Another time, after hearing on the radio "Poor Canada," a parody on the Canadian national anthem, John interpreted the lyric to mean that "the one who was supposed to personify the Word of God"—John himself—had failed and that, therefore, God wanted him to commit suicide. But then, he asked, how could God ask anyone to commit suicide? In that same session, while pursuing his associations on the "cut off your hand" signifier, John brought out a memory that had remained inscribed as particularly traumatic for him. One evening, God asked him to swim nude in the city pool. "I thought He wanted to humiliate me or send me to the hospital." But, being too proud, John remembered telling God, "Ask me anything but that." Later that evening, John was overcome by remorse and masturbated. Upon ejaculation, he said he felt *the explosion of Christ's heart beating in his belly*, he said, "as if I had fallen from a ten-storied building." That day, getting up to leave the session, John turned to the analyst and asked: "What do you feel when I tell you all this? I hadn't realized before that words could do that much good, be so freeing."

The unbearable anxiety experienced in these moments of struggle has finally now found a way out in speech. But more specifically, the work with the signifiers "cut off your hand," "renovate the shop," and "bandages on the knees," and the connections the analyst made between the fragments of his history and the elements of his delusion—all of this was undermining the delusion by making it possible for John to call into question the omnipotence of the imaginary Other. At the same time, the analyst's work of doubting meant that the ideal set up by the delusion—to become God and to be the savior of the world—began to shatter in the presence of the symptom of masturbation, an action inconsistent with the perfection required for John's mission to become God.

In psychosis, the symptom appears as the subject's resistance to the Other's demand for jouissance. It situates inside the body a knot of jouissance and partializes this knot within the body. The symptom effectively told John: "You cannot be God because to satisfy yourself, you perform acts that are incompatible with that ideal." The symptom of masturbation encircles a kernel of the real. In the sensation of Christ's heart exploding within John's belly upon ejaculation, we recognize God's heart as an object internal to the subject but exterior to the delusion. The symptom represents the subject as a piece of the real in terms of the signifier "to become God" extracted from the delusion intended to discharge all lack, and in particular, the lack making the human subject a desiring being.

While the *neurotic's dream* yields signifiers that encircle a navel, a knot of the real insisting within the dream, the *psychotic's symptom* sets itself up as an irreducible, unassimilable rock of jouissance piercing the delusion which would proclaim the imaginary existence of an Other who, filled out by the psychotic, does not lack. The symptom is to the delusion what the navel is to the dream: something unrepresentable that cannot be assimilated, an "unsoundable zone," as Freud would say.[9] John's symptom encircles an object internal to the subject, the heart of Christ beating in John's belly and exploding when John expresses himself as a subject (and opposes the demands of the imaginary Other) by masturbating. In the treatment of the psychotic, this internal object needs to be externalized in a form which will support the psychotic's social link when, at the end of treatment, the analyst must stop functioning as that external and lacking object that guarantees for the psychotic the castration of the Other and the link between signifiers. The symptom that appears during treatment is a first step in the constitution of the Other's castration. The internal object the symptom includes will need to be externalized to drain the body of the Other's jouissance.

Notes

1. Jacques Lacan, "Réponse de Jacques Lacan à une question de Marcel Ritter le 26 janvier 1975," *Lettres de l'École freudienne*, no. 18: 10.

2. Danielle Bergeron, "The Lost Body of the Schizophrenic," lecture given at the San Francisco Society for Lacanian Psychoanalysis (Berkeley, CA: Wright Institute, 1992). See also Danielle Bergeron, "Le corps perdu du schizophrène," in *Le corps en psychanalyse* (Montréal: Éditions du Méridien, 1992), 134–151.

3. Sigmund Freud, *The Standard Edition of the Complete Psychological Works, Volume 4: The Interpretation of Dreams*, ed. James Strachey (London: The Hogarth Press, 1958), 184.

4. Danielle Bergeron, "Enjeux dans la cure du psychotique," *Traiter la psychose* (Québec: Collection Noeud, Editions du Gifric, 1990), 139–159.

5. Jacques Lacan, *Écrits: A Selection*, trans. Alan Sheridan (New York: W. W. Norton and Co., 1977), 125. Original edition (Paris: Éditions du Seuil, 1966), 413.

6. Jacques Lacan, *The Four Fundamental Concepts of Psycho-Analysis* (New York: W. W. Norton and Co., 1978), 207. Original edition (Paris: Éditions du Seuil, 1973), 188.

7. Willy Apollon, "Psychanalyse et traitement des psychotiques," *Santé Mentale au Québec* IX.1 (June 1988): 171.

8. As an illustration of externalization, consider the case of Mr. Wiseman, who for some time, said he was controlled by NASA by means of an electronic receiver that had been installed in his brain. NASA would give him orders and transmit, without spoken word, information concerning urgent matters. In this manner, Mr Wiseman one day received a dispatch announcing the immanent explosion of a nuclear bomb over Québec City with countless dead and wounded expected. With treatment, however, there was an "externalization" of the object for Mr. Wiseman. This was objectivized in the job that he had found for himself: he was given a position of responsibility at the central console of a regional hospital. In his new capacity, Mr. Wiseman received urgent dispatches, from various departments, and then contacted the necessary doctors, making his own judgments regarding clinical priorities. To become more proficient, he had memorized the complete medical code. No longer controlled by NASA, Mr. Wiseman himself now controlled the system, albeit enclosed within a structure of rules, but rules issuing out of the social bond for the care of healthy coexistence.

9. Jacques Lacan, "Réponse de Jacques Lacan à une question de Marcel Ritter le 26 janvier 1975," *Lettres de l'École freudienne*, no. 18: 7–12.

Chapter 5

From Delusion to Dream

LUCIE CANTIN

It is tempting, at first sight, to emphasize the similarity of form that exists between dream and delusion. In dreams, as in delusions, one often finds a content that seems bizarre or impossible to common sense. Moreover, the narrative of the dream, like that of the delusion, is full of logical gaps that barely disguise where the cuts—the signs of something missing—show through, as if the dream or delusion were a crudely censored movie. As a child reveals the place of the object that he or she wants to hide by standing in front of it, in a dream, logical gaps and nonsensical elements signal where the dream-formation has failed. Similarly, in a delusion, the "hiccups" direct us to its governing principle. But while both dream and delusion try to treat the real with signifiers, with representation, they nevertheless bear fundamental differences in the way that treatment of the real is achieved. Indeed their difference in this regard is so great, that to bring a psychotic subject to *dream* implies a breach of that knowledge, that "savoir," that the psychotic is developing in the *delusion*. In other words, dream-formation sets up a logic that is different from—or even counter to—the logic that rules the consolidation of delusion. We shall examine here the clinical consequences of the passage from delusion to dream in the psychotic.

Dreams Treat the Real with Something Symbolic

In *The Interpretation of Dreams*, Freud lays out two essential aspects of his dream theory in describing the principles that govern the elaboration

This chapter was presented, in different form, at a workshop entitled "Lacanian Psychoanalysis: The Process of Working Through and Dreams," at the Center for Psychoanalytic Study in Chicago, February 1993.

of the dream, and in showing that the fundamental aim of the dream is the fulfillment of an *unconscious wish*. At that time (1900), Freud saw the psychic apparatus as composed of three systems: the Conscious, the Preconscious and the Unconscious—a conception that has been referred to as the First Topography. Because Freud took the unconscious system as the starting point for dream-formation, that is, that "the motive force for producing dreams is supplied by the unconscious,"[1] it would seem important to recall how, precisely, Freud considered the Unconscious and how, then, we might describe the function of dreams.

When Freud describes the unconscious system, the dream's "entrepreneur," as he puts it, that is responsible for the elaboration of the dream,[2] he is careful not to call *unconscious* that "which has not yet become conscious,"—as would be the case, for example, of a repressed desire that the interpretation of the dream would bring to consciousness. Such a repressed desire, accessible to consciousness after interpretation, is *preconscious*, that is, a desire which has found a possible representation, disguised by the elaboration of the dream and revealed by its interpretation. What Freud calls the Unconscious is rather the driving force, the "motive force," or the mnemic trace, excited and mobilized, which strives to structure itself and causes the formation of the dream. This energy must link itself to representations and then transfer its energy into them. These representations, under certain transforming conditions, can reach the dream and become its manifest content.

In a dream, the drive is structured through the dream images, a figurative process whose laws of elaboration Freud sought to describe in terms of condensation and displacement, and so forth. From an economic standpoint, the chosen representation must be trivial, "insignificant," says Freud, so that they can serve as a "cover," since censorship allows the subject to go on sleeping.[3] Comparing dreams to a rebus, Freud opened the way to their interpretation: To each image must be given back the word, the formula, the proverb that the dream image sets up. Thus, the interpretation of the dream reveals the laws that govern its elaboration, whether we call these laws condensation and displacement, as Freud did, or metaphor and metonymy as Lacan did to emphasize the linguistic structure of the dream's elaboration.

The representations invested by the energy of the "motive force" and therefore serve to structure the real of the drive, are part of what Freud calls the "Preconscious system." Here is how he explains the relation between the Preconscious and the Unconscious:

> The new discovery that we have been taught by the analysis [of
> the dream] . . . lies in the fact that the unconscious (that is, the psy-

chical) is found as a function of two separate systems and that this is the case in normal as well as in pathological life. Thus, there are two kinds of unconscious, which have not yet been distinguished by psychologists. Both of them are unconscious in the sense used by psychology; but in our sense one of them, which we term the *Ucs.*, is also *inadmissible to consciousness*, while we term the other the *Pcs.*, because its excitations—after observing certain rules, it is true, and perhaps only after passing a fresh censorship, though nonetheless without regard to the *Ucs.*,—are able to reach consciousness.[4]

From the conception of the Unconscious as that which is "inadmissible to consciousness," one can more easily grasp the concept of the "dream's navel," which Freud describes as a dark spot that reaches down into the unknown, amidst a tangle of dream-thoughts which cannot be unraveled.[5] In his analysis of the dream of Irma's injection, Freud remarks that "there is at least one spot in every dream at which it is unplumbable—a navel, as it were, that is its point of contact with the unknown."[6] It is often precisely this point that disrupts the narrative, the point in the dream which seems absurd, nonsensical according to the logic set up by the representations of the dream.

According to Freudian logic, the dream's navel is therefore what, in the motive force, can in no way be structured by a representation. It is the point where the unrepresentable real emerges through, despite the signifiers elaborated by the dream. Hence, when Freud studies the rules that govern the elaboration of the dream, he takes great care to demonstrate the role of the preconscious system (*Pcs.*) in the structuration of the motive force at work in the formation of a dream.

> Thus, there are two possible outcomes for any particular unconscious excitatory process. Either it may be left to itself, in which case it eventually forces its way through at some point and on this single occasion finds discharge for its excitation in movement; or it may come under the influence of the preconscious, and its excitation, instead of being *discharged*, may be *bound* by the preconscious. *This second alternative is the one which occurs in the process of dreaming.*[7]

Actings out, failed acts, and even symptoms and crises can be understood, then, as the setting in action of the real of the drive that representations have failed to treat. Thus, what Freud calls "unconscious desire," whose motive force results in the formation of a dream, is what Lacan calls "the real." We might schematize it this way, beginning in the upper righthand corner:

Figure 5.1
Schema I

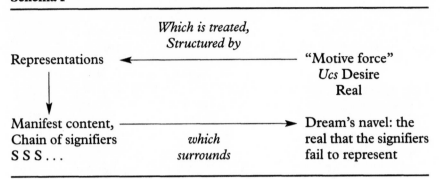

The Function of Delusion in Psychosis: The Case of Mr. Owens

Dreams, then, treat the real with signifiers. This, of course, is also what the delusion tries to do, only the delusion is doomed to fail where the dream succeeds, inasmuch as the delusion does not follow the laws of language that structure the real at work in the formations of the unconscious. Freud notes that:

> Even the deliria of confusional states may have a meaning, . . . they are only unintelligible to us owing to the gaps in them. . . . Deliria are the work of a censorship which no longer takes the trouble to conceal its operation; instead of collaborating in producing a new version that shall be unobjectionable, it ruthlessly deletes whatever it disapproves of, so that what remains becomes quite disconnected. This censorship acts exactly like the censorship of newspapers at the Russian frontier, which allows foreign journals to fall into the hands of the readers whom it is its business to protect only after a quantity of passages have been blacked out.[8]

Delusion does have a function in psychosis: it is an attempt to treat some part of the real. The triggering-off of the psychosis—often accompanied by revelations, by the upsurge of insulting and intrusive voices, or by beliefs of persecution—corresponds to the moment when the subject confronts some distressing and unassimilable part of the real. Delusion builds itself up as the elaboration of a revealed knowledge, a *savoir*. It attempts to link together scattered aggressing signifiers by elaborating a theory that would account for the victim position taken by the psychotic as the object of the jouissance of an Other.

The following are the first paragraphs of a letter we received from a psychotic subject, Mr. Owens, addressed to the Foreign Affairs Minister of the Federal Republic of Germany:

Dear Sir:

I am writing to you as a private man to inform you of an experience that has happened to me, since I believe it is of interest to the citizens and nationals of your country. It is a matter of words that were mentioned, which I leave to your appreciation (*laisse à votre appréciation*).

There is a French social cohesion game known as The King- or *The Fag-Game*. Some call it The Child. In Québec, the name is The English-Game. Among other things, it is part of the usages and reproductive practices of the French.

Since at least 1980, I have been the subject of the English-Game in the Québec City area. First, it took the form of thought-listening at Laval University and very likely at other places in the city.

In the Fall of 1984, I was taken during the night, as I was sleeping in my apartment. It was as if someone had taken a slice off the left side of my head and then inserted a vacuum cleaner. The experience was very painful and much disturbed my life. My knowledge of the existence of the sonar and of thought dates from that period.

I was taken a second time, in the Fall of 1985. It also happened during the night, as I was sleeping in my apartment. That time, the attack was made on the right side of my head. I am not an homosexual and I have never bothered any woman or child.

During the days preceding and following the 1984 attack, a number of members of the public and others made some comments to me. Many times at the University and on the city busses, some people whispered: "It's the German." At least three times, gangs of youths walked in front of my apartment chanting: "Hey Teuton! Hey Hun!"

This was incomprehensible to me, since I have no relationship with the Germans. The Owens came only from Wales, four or five generations ago, and so forth . . .

In these first few paragraphs, Mr. Owens lays out his position: he is the victim, the object of some Other's jouissance. He relates a personal experience, which he refers to as "mentioned words." Lacan would describe these as "imposed words," to recognize in the mental automatism described by Gaëtan Gatian de Clérambault, the central experience of the psychotic subject as aggressed by isolated and insulting signifiers. In his delusion, Mr. Owens elaborates a theory to explain or to justify those intruding signifiers: someone has taken a slice off his head to insert a vacuum hose. This, for him, explains the "mentioned words." As he writes: "My knowledge of the existence of the sonar and of thought dates from that period." Additionally, Mr. Owens is the victim of what he calls the "English-Game" or the "Fag-Game," which he describes as "part of the usages and reproductive practices of the French." Mr. Owens is victim, then, of the jouissance of some Other, to which he is subjected. He was "taken" in his apartment, during the night, in his sleep. However, he is not a homosexual, as he assures his reader, and it is following that aggression in his apartment that he is mocked by people on the bus. In these few brief paragraphs of Mr. Owens' letter, one sees how the delusion of the psychotic represents an attempt by the psychotic to build a theory that will explain, among other things, the position of the psychotic as the object of the jouissance of the Other. Beginning again in the upper righthand corner:

Figure 5.2
Schema II

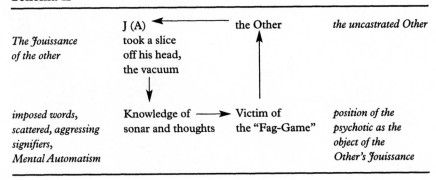

The Jouissance of the other	J (A) ← the Other	the uncastrated Other
	took a slice off his head, the vacuum ↓	↑
imposed words, scattered, aggressing signifiers, Mental Automatism	Knowledge of → Victim of sonar and thoughts the "Fag-Game"	*position of the psychotic as the object of the Other's Jouissance*

But delusion is not simply an explanatory effort; it is also a tentative *solution*, an attempt to escape from the position of being the object of the jouissance of the Other. It is in this way that delusion can be seen as what Willy Apollon has called, the "spontaneous work of psychosis" to treat the real with signifiers, with representation.

Mr. Owens continues his letter. In order to prove that he is in no way related to the Germans, he retraces the origins of his family since the arrival in Canada of the first Owens from Wales. Since he is not even one bit German, he explains, this whole business doesn't concern him; he must have been mistaken for someone else. He is, therefore, the victim of some unjust persecution. Moreover, in the third section of his letter (below), Mr. Owens explains that, while traveling in Europe, he was the victim of the very same game, which he this time calls the "German-Game." This third part of the letter represents a sort of plea, a series of complaints in which he describes the multiple attacks made on him and which are, as we see, the various forms taken by his capture as an object of the jouissance of the Other. Thus, according to Mr. Owens:

> In August of 1985, I traveled for ten days in Belgium and Luxembourg. On the plane, the sonar didn't stop. While I was waiting at the baggage counter, a young woman asked the man who accompanied her: "Why did they do that to the guy in the plane?
>
> I found in these two countries the same sonar, the same thought and the same game as in Québec. More surprisingly, I was again the subject of their game. . . .
>
> In the Flemish cities of Ghent, Bruges and Antwerp, many youths who were strangers to me spoke to me openly in the streets. They told me: "He's whoren gamen. The kinggen es doomeden. The faggen es doomeden. The faggen es kaputen.* (sic)

These aggressions erupt everywhere Mr. Owens goes. Some of the European youths come to understand, however, that he, a law student, is there to make a new law that will forever stop the German-Game and thereby make international unity possible. Moreover, it is towards international unity that Mr. Owens is sending his letter to the German Minister. Mr. Owens wishes to warn the Minister that the German-Game "still exists in the memory of Europeans, since someone played the game at least once recently, in Canada." Thus, he concludes, "the act of aggression which he suffered is part of Euroterrorism," against which he warns the German Minister, so that an end might be put to it.

Mr. Owens' letter illustrates for us a number of important points concerning delusion and its function for the psychotic. First, it is clear that the psychotic's delusion is a work, a process. Second, we see that this process is governed by a central experience, an encounter with the real, which takes the form precisely of imposed words, mental automatisms, persecutory certainty, voices of which the psychotic is the object. As the encounter with the real results in the formation of a dream that processes it, an unassimilable experience triggers off the elaboration process of delusion. Third, delusion works on the signifier. That is, in its very formulation of a theory to explain *why* and in which modes the psychotic is the object of the Other's jouissance, delusion is *also* simultaneously an attempt to find a solution. Through the delusion, the psychotic tries to escape the hold of that Other who derives jouissance from him. Beginning again in the upper righthand corner:

---

* Mr. Owens is fabricating Flemish-sounding words.

Figure 5.3
Schema III

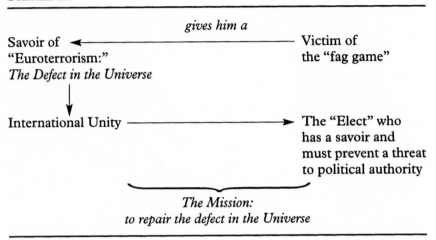

The Mission:
to repair the defect in the Universe

Mr. Owens, attacked by voices that call him "fag" and "whore," finally understands that these acts of aggression are part of Euroterrorism. His position as a victim is thus reversed and becomes the sign and confirmation of his mission to establish international unity. He has a knowledge, a savoir, that he must transmit to the political authorities. The delusion enacts a reversal of position for the psychotic; once a worthless object of abuse for the Other, the psychotic now becomes the Elect one, chosen specially by the Other since the psychotic is the object of its jouissance. Moreover, it is this new position that grounds the delusional certainty so central to the psychotic's savoir. Thus, delusion is a solution that attempts to escape the position of object to which the psychotic is reduced in his relation to the jouissance of an almighty, uncastrated Other.

While it is true that the formation of dream and the elaboration of delusion are both governed by the need to treat the real with representation, dream and delusion do not work in the same manner. The formation of a dream is governed by the laws of language, by the logic of the signifier. The specific signifiers proposed by the dream—however pocked by holes a dream may be—are always and necessarily subjected to the logic of the signifying chain. It is as if the dreamer were still subjected to the law of the Other seen as a place where the conditions of meaning are stated. Delusion, by contrast, treats the capture of the subject in the jouissance of the Other (the real) by elaborating a theory (a system of representations) of a flawless savoir. However, as Freud observed, this arrangement does not appear to be subjected to rules that would give coherence to its content. It is as if the elaboration of delusion were not subjected to or governed by the laws of language, but rather by the underlying fantasy that the delusion serves to support—the fantasy, that is, of the *omnipotence* of the Other to which the delusion responds and which the delusion works to maintain, though all the while trying to escape from it. Delusion leaves untouched the status of the uncastrated Other and contributes to consolidate and encyst the psychotic's flawless savoir in delusional certainties that end up putting a stop on the workings of the imaginary. So, in contrast to the *dream*, where the processing of the real is done through subjugating the imaginary to the symbolic (where desire must obey the laws of language and censorship imposed by Sense in order to be expressed), one could almost say that *delusion* treats the real by attempting to subordinate the symbolic to the imaginary.

Introducing Dream Work in Place of the Workings of Delusion: The Case of Mr. T.

The analyst's position is a crucial factor in allowing the psychotic to gain access to the castration of the Other and the impossibility of jouissance. In a reversal of the usual analytic positions, it is the psychotic subject, not the analyst, who takes the position of the one "supposed to know." It is the psychotic who has a *savoir* about the jouissance of the Other, a knowledge supposed to be flawless. In order, then, to reintroduce the castration of the Other and the necessary hole in the savoir, the analyst must have abandoned any position that would refer to an ultimate Sense. Indeed, the analyst cannot contest the truth of the psychotic's delusional certainty for the sake of common sense or commonplace reality any more than the analyst may question the psychic reality underlying a neurotic's fantasy. With psychotics, the problem lies not with the *knowledge* itself, but rather with the fact that the savoir aims at being *complete and flawless*. The knowledge theorized by delusion in fact attempts to use a construction of the imaginary to fill in and to repair the defect, the dis-order which the psychotic confronts in the order of Sense, and which the psychotic regards as a defect in the universe.

The analyst must try to reintroduce the hole in the psychotic's savoir in an effort to reinitiate treatment of the real—only this time treatment of the real must fall under the constraint of the law of the symbolic. To require *dreams* in place of *delusion*, mobilizes the unconscious to treat the real with an other logic than the one which governs the elaboration of delusion. The dream, in being subject to the laws of language, reintroduces the logic of the signifier. Importantly, in this regard, dreams are subjected neither to the whims of an Other (who could be represented by the analyst in the subject's imaginary), nor to the requirements dictated by the savoir formulated and founded in the delusion. The lack that reappears in the point of the real reintroduced by the dream, can no longer be attributed to someone and is no longer intrusive and persecutory. In place of the imaginary Other seen as persecuting, dreams substitute the law of language, the symbolic Other. Dreams represent the flaw in language, the impossibility of expressing everything with words. It is as if dream work itself, by confronting the subject anew with the traumatic events in his past, which have remained without meaning, breaches the savoir deployed by delusion, and shakes it up. The case of Mr. T. will serve to illustrate this point.

Mr. T has sought analysis because he has found that his problems are of an emotional nature. He reports that he feels "knots" in his plexus, where his emotions are "blocked." He dates his difficulties back to an evening of his early adolescence when, after having done some drugs with his older brothers, he found himself alone at home. There he read in a tabloid the story of another teenager who killed his parents while on drugs. Mr. T., then just thirteen years old, thought to himself that he, too, could do such a thing, and his thoughts strayed to the large knife in the kitchen. Mr. T. panicked at this sequence of thought, fled the house, and for some hours sat alone in a nearby field, terrified that he might act out. The idea that he might kill his parents remained with Mr. T., however, and he reports that "it poisoned my adolescence." To counter the impulse, he has devised a set of strategies and, above all, has made a decision that eventually calms him. Namely, he has decided that if he found himself possessed by parricidal impulses, he would "turn the knife against himself."

During the period of his adolescence, Mr. T. was beset regularly by strange, distressing experiences he was unable to articulate. These states he now considers "pre-psychotic." He adds that, when they happened, his mental processes became preoccupied by insistent ideas of "boundaries between the worlds." When he emerged from such states, he would return to "everyone's reality." At age fourteen, his sister's boyfriend gave him books by Carlos Castaneda and Mr. T. began to take an interest in Native American spirituality, in which he detected a "new way of thinking." He learned from Castaneda that "there is another reality than the one we perceive, something different from the state we are in every day." It is clear that during that whole period of his adolescence, Mr. T.'s interest in Native American spirituality and his interest in its vision of the world allowed him to link the singularity of his experience to a framework where it assumed a meaning that could not be considered delusional, since it was shared by a

number of people. Native American spirituality offered a system of representation that allowed him to treat the real of a distressing experience
unassimilated by the "reality" marked out by common sense. Native
American spirituality offered the signifiers and a referential framework to
symbolize the real of Mr. T.'s adolescent experience.

Native American spirituality fulfills for Mr. T. the same function that
the Name-of-the-Father fulfills for neurotics. One might say that Native
American spirituality, then, has substituted for the foreclosure of the
Name-of-the-Father during the period of Mr. T.'s adolescence. This substitutive function will inevitably fade as its role is to produce an ir-
refutable basis of truth to fix a definitive meaning on the distressing and
absurd experiences that have marked his life. The fact that Mr. T. cannot
question the truth he seeks in esotericism suggests the certitude that he
must find there. While adolescence is indeed the age when we discover
the absence of definitive truth about the vision of the world that has
been proposed to us, and while it is also the time when we gain access to
the arbitrary dimension of the reasons behind the prohibitions and the
ideals, psychotics prove unable to question the basis of whatever serves
as a substitute for the foreclosure of the Name-of-the-Father. To confront a logic that differs from the one set up by the psychotic's system
can, therefore, only lead to crisis.

Mr. T.'s first psychotic episode came about when he was finishing his
masters thesis in cellular biology. His biology studies had, by this time,
taken over the substitutive function from Native American esotericism.
His very precise goal in his cellular biology studies was to gain employ-
ment in clinical biology and cancer research. But suddenly, when he was
finishing his master's degree research on an enzyme involved in cancer,
he lost all interest in everything related to research and the sciences. He
once again took up spirituality and the humanities, thinking that he had
chosen the wrong path. Obviously, Mr. T. had not found in science what
he was looking for. So, as at age thirteen, when he had an episode which
was resolved through the books of Castaneda, Mr. T. now has a crisis in
his science studies, which he resolves by giving up the whole realm of the
sciences to devote his time and energy to spiritual life, humanities, and
esotericism.

There are no words for Mr. T. to meaningfully express what he experienced at age thirteen, when his body and his mind were invaded by something he knows nothing about. Likewise, he can find no meaningful
relationship between his highly focused research on an enzyme and what
he is looking for as he desires to eradicate cancer. All along this progression, the same logic takes shape, where we can see the appearance of the
subject's choice, of his ethics, and of the way he takes a stand. Mr. T. is

searching for a basis, an ultimate reason, an unquestionable truth, a science that would account for all the real, a complete language. Delusion attempts to produce that completeness. It aims at accounting for everything, at producing certainties that would act as stopping points for meaning. Dreams, by contrast, produce a sequence, a chain of signifiers that hits upon a hole, upon Freud's unknowable "navel." Obtaining dreams from a psychotic subject therefore implies that the delusional certainty has been shaken. Dream-work implies the re-introduction of a point of real, of something that reveals the failure of delusion.

We will now analyze that passage from delusion to dream with the help of a series of Mr. T.'s dreams reported during his analysis. Often, the first dreams told by a psychotic patient are indistinguishable from the logic of delusion, which they more or less reproduce. These early dreams have the same objective as delusion, and the associations to which they lead to cannot be distinguished from the work of delusion. This was case in the first dreams told by Mr. T.:

> I am in my mother's house. A room full of flowers. Marie arrives,
> looks at me and screams. I feel a stitch in the plexus and I fall down.
> I have not fainted, but I crawl toward the door to call for help.

Mr. T.'s associations suggest that the woman in the dream has been in contact with him for some time. She is nice to him, he says, but under that niceness, she deals him only "blows below the belt . . . She tries to drive me to suicide, she introduces bugs in my head." He associates further that he is sitting somewhere and that she walks in front of him. "I look at her and then I am lost. Someone must come and take me back." After being asked what then happens to him, he adds: "A part of me stays there and the other goes as if it had dissipated; I get paralyzed. What gets me paralyzed is that I don't feel like seeing her and that her vision is imposed on me. The two feelings mixed together paralyze me." Indeed, Mr. T. regularly has such episodes where he remains immobile, silent and indeed even catatonic.

A second dream:

> There is a Western atmosphere. There are people who are sitting.
> There was a question of energy. I was lacking energy for something.

In his associations, Mr. T. reports that he lacks energy these days. "To lack energy is to be naïve," he says. His naiveté causes him to receive many blows of an unknown nature. Then, he must heal all these pains precisely *as* they occur—and that is what takes so much of his energy. After such blows, he must go to his room to meditate and to heal. People are always trying to trap him. People suck up his energy; he feels this physically. Thus, in his first psychosis, he says, his head was affected.

A third dream:

> I see a cleaning lady dressed in white. She is rather pretty. I don't know how she did it, but she got me with her face. It is as if she had gained my confidence. She goes by the bed, I see her and then I completely lose sight of her and it is as if she were going through my forehead.

In his associations, Mr T. says that seduction is a trick to freeze him, so that he can no longer move. It is the same with words, with the way people use words with him, he says. The woman in the dream goes through his forehead, through the place of the third eye, the spiritual eye. I then intervene and ask him whether he has any childhood memories related to his forehead. He recalls an accident when his brother suffered a forehead injury.

The intervention takes the form of a question. In asking him whether the forehead is related to a childhood memory, something different is introduced into a system that until then has been closed up. "The woman who goes through his forehead," a representation provided by the dream, is traced back by him in his associations to an element of delusion. There, its meaning is fixed, closed: the forehead is the place of the third eye, the spiritual eye. It is as if the dream-work brought nothing more, as if it didn't come from an Other Scene, from a place Other than his imaginary universe. The analyst's questioning, however, brings back the subject's history—and even more importantly, it establishes for the psychotic subject that dream-work is governed by laws *other* than those of consciousness or imaginary creation.

At the next session, Mr. T. relates a dream and then, for the first time, produces associations linked to elements of his history. The dream therefore brings signifiers and elements that are no longer linked exclusively to the delusion, but rather are linked to events of the previous day, to memories, and to important events in his life. Thus, little by little, the psychotic subject enters the logic of dream, a logic which had escaped him and which is no longer that of delusion, a logic which therefore disrupts his imaginary position of certainty and savoir.

One day Mr. T. arrives with the complaint that he cannot remember his dream because he did not manage to get his morning meditation session. Since he had previously associated these meditation periods with healing sessions, I ask him to explain to me what these sessions were, to describe their objectives and methods. He told me that they consist in visualizing "chakras," the seven centers of energy situated along the spine. His meditation aimed at establishing contact with his spiritual guides, who are, in fact, "a group of pale blue angels" and who "come to help him with his social achievements." Mr. T. refers to his savoir, which has a precise "healing" function. How can the analyst introduce a gap in this savoir? In the name of what can the analyst question its truth? Meditation, of course, is a practice now accepted as part of our culture, and it is precisely from the place of *cultural* practice that the analytic question will come. In asking Mr. T. whether he has himself invented his meditative method or whether, on the other hand, he learned it from book or from a collective practice in a social group, a crucial third party is introduced into Mr. T.'s relation to the savoir that he has set up. The inscription of a third party in the cultural, symbolic, or social space now acts to limit the omnipotence of Mr. T.'s imaginary. Mr. T. is thus led to distinguish what he has read elsewhere ("The Xeda Angels" and the method of visualizing the "chakras"), from the elements that he himself introduced in the system (the "pale blue angels").

At the next session, Mr. T. reports that he may have dreamed the previous night, but he cannot remember for certain. He does, however, remember perfectly the end of the last session. He therefore resumes speaking, as I have requested, about the "pale blue angels." "I was telling myself that in my previous lives and in my spiritual progression, I had developed the possibility to channel beings like that, to let them speak through me." I ask, "The angels speak through you?" He answers, "I had thought so, but now I don't know anymore. It is because of what you said the last time. You put a doubt in me, it is as if I had imagined that." I intervene with a question about the meaning of the expression "To be an angel." He laughs and tells me that people have often told him that he was an angel. He always did what was asked of him, what society was asking. The idiomatic expression, "to be an angel," which refers him to his position as a subject in his history, has the effect, as a metaphor, to break the closed meaning given by delusion. The metaphor empties the signifier of its imaginary consistency and refers it to another signifier. That ceaseless referral undermines the fixity of meaning that delusion aims at.

At the two next sessions, Mr. T. reports dreams that we can at last call real dreams, with a sequence of signifiers that encircle a hole, a point of unassimilable real. The first dream is a dream that has been recurring for many years. He recognizes its form, which is always identical despite the varying elements it contains each time.

> He has some homework, a work to finish, for a specific deadline.
> He has not worked and therefore is not ready and he panics.

More than any other type of dream, recurring dreams show the insistence of the real being treated. The anxiety associated with the recurring dream shows both that the dream is processing that anxiety and that the dream is failing in its attempt to process that anxiety completely. Something insists and constantly restarts the formation of the dream, and so the signifiers of the dream turn around an irreducible opening point. This is what one sees mobilized in the case of Mr. T., when his delusional certainty is giving way. Mr. T.'s second dream stages this collapse:

> There is some scaffolding for construction at the Château Frontenac, in Québec City. Someone is taking a picture. At one point, the scaffolding collapses and some people die.

After that dream, Mr. T. simply says: "The scaffolding may be my imaginary."[9]

The appearance of the first real dream implies that there has been a gap introduced in the savoir of the psychotic subject. The position of the analyst supports and maintains that opening. The dream comes as an answer to the hole introduced in the closed system of delusion. The dream questions the savoir of the psychotic as it proposes a completely different logic—a logic taken from the signifiers, which, when picked up by the analyst, bring back memories and events that have remained "out of meaning," events that are failing points in the psychotic's history that the delusion had tried to plug. Signifiers that to that point had been detached and invasive find possible links in the associations of the dream and are thus referred to events in the subject's history, and render obsolete the meaning set up by delusion. Through that work, the psychotic accedes to the logic of language that regulates the production of dreams and their interpretation. Dreams undermine the delusional certitude and establish a new savoir where the consistency of the persecuting Other of jouissance gradually vanishes.

Notes

1. Sigmund Freud, *The Standard Edition of the Complete Psychological Works, Volume 5: The Interpretation of Dreams*, ed. James Strachey (London: The Hogarth Press, 1958), 541.
2. ———, *The Interpretation of Dreams*, 561.
3. ———, *The Interpretation of Dreams*, 562–563.

4. ———, *The Interpretation of Dreams*, 614–615.

5. ———, *The Interpretation of Dreams*, 525.

6. ———, *The Interpretation of Dreams*, 111.

7. ———, *The Interpretation of Dreams*, 578.

8. ———, *The Interpretation of Dreams*, 529.

9. The phrasing here, that the scaffolding of the dream "may be my imaginary," has an oddly technical ring to it in English translation. Such is not the case in French, where the noun "imaginary" has more common usages. For the patient (who really did use the term), "imaginary" was not necessarily a therapeutic term.

Chapter 6

The Letter of the Body

WILLY APOLLON

Under the rubric of the "letter of the body," we have developed in our clinical work with psychotics a psychoanalytic conception of the body as, precisely, the writing of a lost jouissance in the speaking being. Such a concept of the body is latent in Freud's own writing, but Lacanian theory brings it to a fuller articulation, proposing the theoretical conditions of its limit and its clinical action. Such a conceptualization may find its greatest clinical urgency in the treatment of psychosis, but it remains—even if unacknowledged—a fundamental one in any properly Freudian psychoanalytic treatment.

The present chapter shall propose a clinical exposition of this concept of the body through the questions of the letter of the body, of the symptom as a writing of jouissance, and of the aesthetic field of the object that causes the subject's desire from the fantasy. If the signifier, the dream and its interpretation were the touchstones of the first period of analytic treatment, these new questions may be thought to bear more on the second period of analytic treatment, dealing with the real of jouissance through the symptom and the fantasy.

Transference and the Trauma of Language: the Subject, Jouissance, and the Signifier

In chapter 1, Lucie Cantin described the human subject as one who speaks as the effect of a trauma. This insight is generated out of the clinical experience of psychoanalysis, as well as out of a specific conception of human being. It contradicts, to some degree, Freud's early position on

---

This chapter is based on an essay that was first drafted in February 1989.

a biological and genetic development of the human psyche. We can see Freud's theory as relevant to the social and scientific milieu in which it emerged. Lacan, who recasts Freud's theory as a structural outgrowth of the action of language on the living being, simultaneously recontextualizes Freud's discovery within French culture and modern science. Following Lacan's position, we in Québec have posited the work of language on the subject as, precisely, a *traumatic* event. The question of the truth status of such a trauma—whether one hypothesizes it as a real historical event or as an imaginary one—is an academic question and of no consequence within the ethical act of psychoanalysis. What is significant and of great practical consequence, however, is the very fact of that hypothesis as such: it stands as an unpredictable basis of analytic discourse, and as a scientific myth which frames the work of the analysis. As such a starting point, this hypothesis is not, in principle, subject to falsifiability. So Lacan radically transforms the metapsychology that was founded on Freud's desire; and the new frontier Lacan delineates serves as the basis of the ethical action of the psychoanalyst in assuring the conditions of that action.

Thus, the trauma of language emerges as an axis in the ethical action of the analysis. An initial approach to this peculiar and central hypothesis might be made by way of anthropology. Anthropology, as a science of culture, highlights the dominant role of language and the symbolic order in shifting the regulation of the whole existence of a human life away from the logic of its own animal satisfactions to the necessities and exigencies of the group. Amazingly, psychologists tend to ignore this fact to pursue their research from a hypothesis of human development as some complex neuropsychological maturation. As a matter of fact, at first glance, the living being seems to look for satisfaction of need in the immediate natural neighborhood and expects objects of satisfaction from these first efforts. The consuming of those natural objects, to the extent that their access may be immediate and free of obstacle, is an act of jouissance in terms of right as well as in terms of enjoyment.

For the human being, however, such conditions of living are pure fantasy. Anthropologists cannot provide any credible example of a society—whatever degree of freedom of behavior is accepted or promoted—that would suffer such access to the objects of satisfaction without any rules or myths to both justify and prohibit. It is a fundamental fact of the social relations of speaking beings that satisfaction of need must, unquestionably, be negotiated through rules of coexistence. Lacan stresses the effect of that symbolic order on the human being as one of *castration*. As a matter of fact, Lacan posits the constitution of human subjectivity in Freud's discovery of that fundamental and mythical point of rupture brought by language and the symbolic order to the animal, organismic conditions of life. This mythical point, which cannot be located as an historical event in the life of a given society or individual, nevertheless constitutes the specific and true "trauma" that institutes the living being *as human* through the wound of language.

The idea of the symbolic order of language as a wound leads us to the way the human child has to face that order. As Lucie Cantin wrote in chapter 1, children are, even prior to birth, subject to a host of discourses—those of parents, society, medical science, and so forth—which prescribe the place they are expected to occupy, the anticipated trajectory of their life, and so forth. These discourses are endorsed or rejected by the parents' own discourses and fantasies concerning their child. The child, then, encounters the symbolic order as a structure of the discourses of others. There are two obvious effects of this enmeshment, two primary cuts bearing on the satisfaction of need and on self-representation. First, the symbolic order encloses the satisfaction of need within the Other's desire and discourse. That is, needs are decided by others through medical and psychological knowledge, through social and cultural conditions and exigencies, through parental desire, frustration or failure, and so forth, and are partially satisfied through the demands of others. The human being is cut, then, and must assume a loss of jouissance with respect to the total and immediate satisfaction of needs accorded to a free physiological development. Second, the symbolic order severs the speaking being from self-representation. The primary identification of the subject comes rather out of the capture within the signifiers of the Other's discourse, as well as within the unconscious representations of parental desires.

Admittedly, such facts have a peculiar epistemological status: they may be inferred from an analysis of the actual conditions of social and cultural life, but they escape us as facts of history. Their status as *logical but non-factual* inferences constitute the trauma as a fundamental fantasy for all subjects. The structure of such a fantasy institutes the subject as "the subject of the unconscious," and highlights the relation of the subject to jouissance as *lost,* and to the signifier as failing to symbolize the subject's truth. So the trauma, as a wound from the symbolic order, has no other representation than that primary fantasy where the subject is expelled from animal life, despoiled of the jouissance of animal satisfactions, and overwhelmed in the signifiers of the Other. That exile and that bewitchment constitute the subject as a ravished one in the site of the Other.

In the analytic field, the Oedipus complex operates as the mythical structure of that trauma which underlines the domination of the Law over the satisfaction of the drive. The Oedipus complex is the time when the actualization of the power of the symbolic order is at stake in the dramatization of the father's role as representing the author of the Law.

By this time, the father is the signifier of the loss which attends subjectivity and which establishes the child as a subject in language, and a subject of the Law. From this position, the subject's discourse will find its unconscious support in the possible chaining of the signifiers—as if the father, the signifier of the Law, sustains the chaining and thereby acts as a barrier against jouissance. This point is crucial to the relevance of the Lacanian stress on the foreclosure of the signifier of the Name-of-the-father in psychosis. Psychosis suggests something is jeopardized in the chaining of the signifier, a jeopardy which ultimately bears on the emergence of the delusion, and which cripples the psychotic's barrier against jouissance (in the psychotic break). Nor is this point to be forgotten in the handling of the transference.

One fundamental dimension of the transference is to restore the phallic effects of the closing of the Oedipus complex. The structure at stake here serves to sanction the traumatic effects of the symbolic order of language, guarantees the consequences of the Law in terms of exclusion of the jouissance, and furthers the desire of something else. The challenge of the action of the Oedipal structure in the transformation of the jouissance returning in the drive into a *desire* for something else, is what brings any neurotic subject to the analyst. Hence, the transference might be thought of as the focal point in the ethical action of the analysis for the maintenance or restoration of a barrier to the jouissance. In other words, the analyst's desire under the transference elicits various materials—such as the signifier in the dream, the letter in the symptom, and the object in the fantasy—in order to convert the return of the forbidden jouissance in the drive into some unlimited desire for anything else that could stand for that lost jouissance. The analyst, in treating the transference as an ethical fulcrum that converts lost jouissance into an actual desire, sustains the emerging subject of the unconscious as, precisely, a subject of desire.

So then, in the connection from the trauma to the Oedipal complex, the analyst infers a structure which will determine the way the transference is handled. Such a structure circumscribes the status of the subject as constituted by the trauma, and indicates to the analyst the position of the subject with regard to jouissance in the drive, and in relation to the signifier that fails to represent the subject. The ethical action of the analyst handling the transference is itself, therefore, circumscribed by the three possible positions of the subject in the structure according to the relations to jouissance and the signifier. In *neurosis*, the signifying chain in the dream allows the passing of the drive to the signifier in a structure of desire, when the barrier against jouissance has the guarantee of the father as a representative of the Law. In *psychosis*, the unchaining of the signifier essential to the structure of the delusion, exposes the subject to being overwhelmed by the jouissance returning in the drive and jeopardizes the physiological functions and structures of the organism through the disturbances that this unchaining introduces in the logic of the body. So under the process of the transference, the action of the "letters of the body," as hints and traces of the jouissance from the trauma to the symptom, underlies the work of the psychosis to fend off the Other's jouissance. In *perversion* the relation of the subject to the signifier is mediated by a scenario whose structure is a pact that bonds both parties to an enigmatic localization of the jouissance. The bond of the subject to the jouissance in that structure is signified in a fetish object. In those two facets of the perverse structure, the denial of the effects of the Law and the symbolic order highlights the position of the subject while informing the ethical axis for the analyst's desire. These structures will be explored in greater detail in later chapters.

The Parceled Body as a Writing of Jouissance by the Agency of the Letter

In our view, one of the most important and clinically relevant elements brought into relief by the recasting of Freudian metapsychology in terms of jouissance and castration as effects of the symbolic order is the psychoanalytic conception of the *body* and its implications for the clinical handling of the symptom. Work with psychotics in psychoanalysis only sharpens this perception. Moreover, clinical work in the treatment of perversion and psychosis passes through the treatment of the symptom as a writing of jouissance, and requires a reconsideration of the distinction and the linkage between the *body* as constituted by the signifier and the symbolic order and the *organism* structured as physiological entity.

The traumatic action of the symbolic order upon the living being necessarily and undoubtedly produces traces. One might well question the *status* of such traces, but clinical experience reveals them to be documents from a lost history of the subject, monuments of an insisting and mysterious past. Freud's discovery of the fantasy as more important than any actual event, was a break from his earlier biological and mechanistic position regarding the status of the psyche. It thereafter became much easier for Freud to imagine tracks, prints, marks, and trails for the repressed and returning jouissance. Nevertheless, clinical facts underline the choice of the organs, or the pieces of body, or the physiological function, in the outline and shape of the symptom, and they confirm the connection of the body part to the signifiers extracted from the discourse and the history of the subject. In much the same way, common everyday life experiences demonstrate the way any peculiar part of the being may be invested as if it were the whole body—if it is wounded, for example, or if it is the object of an other's desire. So, Freud's discoveries in the clinic and in the psychopathology of everyday life bring to light differences in the knowledge of the body and knowledge referring to the organism.

Furthermore, it is necessary to distinguish the individual subject as a whole (referring to the personality and so forth) from the unconscious subject established by the signifiers as effect of the symbolic order—indeed we must differentiate between three schemata of the body. The *organism*, the object of medical science, remains the basic meaning and the structural limit for the living being. The *individual body*, a representative of the self and the personality in the social linkage, includes the relationship the subject sustains to the organism as source of the rejected jouissance resulting from cultural exigencies and the others' demands. The *parceled body*, whose parts are related to the jouissance the signifier has repudiated, is the third schema. In the work of analysis, the analyst's desire deals precisely with the assumption of that body as parcels, whose organization is impossible except in terms of the imaginary or as symptom or as fantasy. Moreover, the analyst works under the hypothesis of the parceled body as the site of the subject of enunciation in speech, the place when the analyst must face or request the subject's truth, the ground of the subject's ethical answer in the analysis. Truth therefore doesn't have to do with conformity to historical reality, but rather with the relation of the subject to the content of the structure, that is, to the signifier and the excluded jouissance as conditions of desire.

Thenceforth, it becomes impossible to separate the logical and clinical inference of the parceled body from the trauma that has instituted the subject as such, and from the structure that defines the subject's position regarding jouissance and the signifier. In the clinical work aiming to convert the return of jouissance in the drive, the body is the script of the exclusion of the jouissance from the living being. It reflects the loss in the organism; and its partitioning, emphasized by the symptoms, delineates the erotogenic cartography of the seizure of the organism in the symbolic order of language through the trauma and the structure of the signifier. In Québec, we call the "letter," any segment, mark, or unit of that capture as an indefinable parcel of the body: a border, an opening, the outline of a hole, a stroke, or even a gesture or a glance as a referential mark and the like. . . . As inscription of a lost jouissance, the letter doesn't take precedence over the language which caused the trauma and which gives the letter its consistency. It cannot be identified *as such* as a part of the body; notwithstanding that fact, it is always delimited in the signifier or in the symptom as apart from meaning and heterogeneous to knowledge. It becomes linked to the hole the signifier surrounds, and traces a path, on the edge of the organism in the symptom, for the death drive where jouissance returns to challenge the effects of the Law. The "letter" acts as an edge outside the signifier toward the exteriority of the jouissance as real.

Linked to the constitution of the body, the letter inscribes the body in the field of desire that restrains jouissance within the signifiers of the Law. The letter implies that parceling out of a body for which the ego as a covering image stands for unity. Moreover, the letter perverts the living being, vitiating the physiological function of the organs from their specialized uses (as mouth, anus, in relation to the penis, etc.) to divert them within the drive in a relentless quest for jouissance. The letter marks the external fringe where desire splits the signifying chain of unconscious knowledge to open out a way to the real. It divides and parcels the body, divorcing the body from the organism without giving up the energetic supply the one provides to the other. The letter backs up and settles the signifiers that articulate the subject's discourse to the truth of the subject's desire or position regarding jouissance. Its exteriority with regard to the signifier, initiates in the psychoanalytic treatment the possibility of the analytic maneuver, when interpretation reaches its internal limit in the signifying chain. This fact is crucial in the psychoanalytic treatment of psychosis. Nevertheless, in any analytical and ethical process, when the ethical answer of the subject is required as an action, at the place where knowledge of the causes or the structures is of any help, the letter founds the choice and the action of the subject. So the letter relates the analysis to an ethical action toward the object that the fantasy sets apart for the desiring subject. It doesn't require interpretation nor does it sustain it, like the signifying chain in the dream does. Rather, the letter commands the maneuver in which the analyst's desire undertakes to divide the remaining jouissance in the symptom toward the production of an object through the fantasy.

The Clinic of the Symptom and the Ethical Action of Analysis

The conception of the parceled body as a writing of jouissance by the agency of the letter introduces the primary concern of psychoanalysis in the clinic of the symptom. The medical concept of the symptom is specific and deals with whatever is going wrong in a structure or a function, in the organism. It concerns the physician as long as the health and well being of the individual body is grounded in the organism. The medical symptom answers a logic that is proper to the organism responding to its physical and cultural surroundings. At stake in the symptom considered by the analyst, on the other hand, is basically something else. The analytic symptom refers to the letter and the parceling of the body. It obeys the logic of the signifier, but appears as a failure in that logic. As it was first assumed under the transference, the analysand's demand encounters, through the analyst's desire, an obstacle in the lack of any signifier adequate to identify such a desire or to open the way to satisfy it. The obstacle of the lack comes in the process as a failure of the signifier and thus opens the way to something else. That opening is what urges the drive to express the forbidden jouissance. Such an operation is a jeopardy for the chaining of meaning in the individual subject (the ego, and by some way, the self), and for the individual's social linkage to the other. That rupture in meaning and the social link confronts the individual subject with the unbearable emptiness that meaning and the social link have to fill.

In the process of analytic treatment, the dream arises as a spontaneous handling of that rupture by the chaining of the signifiers. Up to a limit point, which is a knot and the "navel" of the dream, the dream assures the passage of the drive to the signifiers as representatives of a wish or fear. So the dream, as a spontaneous chaining of signifiers, handles and divides the driving back of jouissance into both an imaginary display of desire, as well as a remainder—the leftover jouissance—as an off limits point in the dream. This much, even in the dream, the signifier fails to enclose, and the jouissance remains. The remaining knot of jouissance may turn the dream into the nightmare that awakens the dreamer. To some extent, it might be said that the dream marks the limit of the signifier. The analyst's interpretation and the analysand's association reinforce the abutment of the signifier against that limit, that "external intruder," so to speak. And an other moment within the process begins. On behalf of the jouissance at work in that outburst of the signifier, the letter draws a breaking point toward the action of the knowledge. The psychoanalytic symptom outlines the action of the jouissance on the trail of the letter and obeys the logic of the letter in the break opened up in the signifier. Such a logic is sustained by the fantasy. Therefore one must conceive a sort of double map in the clinic of the symptom. This double map relates in the first instance to the signifier that opposes its logic to the external action of jouissance throughout the drive. In the second instance, its way out between the body and the organism is the letter that escapes any taking up in the signifier. At this point the symptom requires a maneuver from the analyst.

As a matter of fact, acting as the driving back of jouissance in the paths of the letter which parcels the body and adulterates the functioning of the organism, the analytic symptom doesn't submit to physical (physiological or biochemical) intervention from the physician. To be sure, the effects of the symptom in the organism are—and must be—alleviated by such an accurate intervention. But the logic of the analytic symptom answers the ethical confrontation of a *desire*, namely, the analyst's desire acting in the transference. The mainspring of the disturbance in the analytic symptom isn't to be found in the organism. The cause lies in the *lack* of the Other that the signifier fails to represent and handle whenever the *letter*, which limits the signifier and unlocks the site of the real, makes its way out to the jouissance inhabiting that site. There isn't any physical way of reaching such a cause ruled by the structure of the trauma that brings about the logic of the letter. Under the transference, the clinic of the symptom demands an other kind of hindrance. Only the analyst's desire, coming in the place of supporting the Law of the signifier as surrounding the lack in the Other, may offer the letter in the symptom a basis toward the partitioning of jouissance. In the same way the signifier in the dream succeeds in apportioning the jouissance in the representation of desire and in a remaining knot of real, the analyst aims to attain in the symptom an allocation of jouissance by the letter in the body.

Partitioning jouissance in the symptom assumes that the remainder of that division will be not a segment of the symptom, in its effects of disturbance and destruction, but rather something else transforming the process to precondition the emergence of the subject's desire. Such is the hypothesis at work in the maneuver that handles the symptom through the logic of the letter. The symptom is the spontaneous answer of the drive to the lack in the Other and to the jouissance challenging the signifier in the interpretations within the dreams, the analysand's associations, and the analyst's knowledge. How does the analyst oppose and restrain that spontaneous response? The parceling of the body in the symptom enforces the traumatic choice of the letter. Moreover, the attack on the organism follows the logic of that choice, and illuminates the connection between the scientific name of the symptom and the chaining of the signifier. But that connection which sustains an interpretation as possible is useless if it fails to bring to light what is unfamiliar and strange in the symptom. The letter and parcels of body involved in the symptom indicate random knots of jouissance expelled from the meaning and the social life of the individual subject. The analyst must relate these letters to any writing in language that may be representative of the Law and its effect regarding the seizure of the subject in the symbolic order. That is, the process of the treatment requires a limit to framing the wandering of the jouissance. For that sake, the analyst brings the letter of the body underlined by the symptom into a confrontation with the writing that rules language.

In the first part of the process, the dream refers the action of the analyst to the interpretation through the signifier. But another dimension of analytic action emerges through the symptom. Symptom refers the process to the writing, first in the inscription of jouissance on a piece of the body elected from the organism, and second in the writing of the technical or medical name of the symptom. These two levels of writing are distinct. The letter is ruled by the logic of the trauma and the structure of the loss of jouissance, while the name of the symptom refers to the rules and logic of the language. The writing of the symptom through the register of language corresponds with those parts of the language that secure the drifting of meaning in any given culture. Like scientific discourses, language in this instance guarantees the stability of common meanings and connotations in spite of the diachronic nature of discourse. Through language, this writing limits the wandering of the signifier surrounding the unfixable hole of the desire. Writing in language creates units of cultural meaning through rhetorical figures, idioms, metaphors, double entendres, slanders, as well as stylistic devices and turns of phrase that determine the emergence of meaning in a given culture. This dimension does *not* refer to the field of the letter or jouissance. To the contrary, it represents the independence of language and the effects of language as a frontier against the action of jouissance.

As the arena in which the analytic process connects the traces of jouissance in the body to a writing in language, the symptom guides the analyst's ethical act toward a partitioning of the jouissance at work in the symptom. What is at stake in the symptom is the failure of the signifier of the Law to contain jouissance. At this point, the mechanism of the dream is no longer useful in converting jouissance into a representation of desire that might serve as an alternative to the symptom. The abutment of the signifier against the tragic lack of the Other reveals the weakness of the installation of the Law as a barrier to jouissance in the Oedipus complex. It is as if the secondary process of the Oedipus failed to delimit the primary process of the trauma. Under the transference acting as an alternative to the default of the Oedipus, the analyst's desire sets up the acknowledgement of the Law as the instigator of the lack and as the barrier to the jouissance in the drive. The symptom, though, works in the other direction, seeking jouissance through the default of the signifier, and repeating, on the side of the letter, the suffering and injury in the organism that stands in for the desired limit.

The analyst's action in relation to the symptom will not be of an *interpretation*, but rather a *maneuver* by which the analyst appeals for an ethical position from the analysand. This ethical position reflects the subjectivity at stake. It is well known that the benefit the analysand takes from the symptom counterbalances the suffering of the sickness; this benefit defeats many efforts to solve the symptom through medical procedures. By contrast, the analyst's desire maintains the priority of the lack in the Other as an effect of the Law. Such a position asks for an answer from the analysand. The difficult point lays in the fact that the analysand's answer itself has to enter an ethical position regarding the signifier of the Law as foundation of the lack.

In the first part of the analysis, the extraction of the signifier through the analysand's associations circumscribes the subject's position regarding the lack in the Other. The emergence of the symptom reveals a failure in the ethical assumption of the Other's lack. The analyst's use of the writing and the inscription must rectify this position as the answer to that lack that the analyst's desire represents and maintains in the process of the treatment. At this moment, the encounter with the analyst's desire is crucial. Its issue cannot be reduced to the results of some technique or procedure. One's interventions at the level of the signifiers, the script, the interpretation, or any other technical strategy are irrelevant without the ethical ground where the analysand must answer to the analyst's lack.

The clinic of the symptom entails the ethical character of the analytic process, based upon the necessary meeting between the analysand as a subject and the signifier of the Law that founds both the letter where the subject stands, and the lack that causes the subject's desire. The analysand's ethical position is a key element in inducing a shift in subjective positions. One moves *from* the position of an individual subject defined in relation to cultural exigencies and the demands of others, *to* the assumption of a subjective position as that position is determined by the signifier and erupts from the letter in the symptom insofar as that symptom is connected to a forbidden jouissance. Thus, the analysand faces an acknowledgement of his or her status in the symptom as a response to some unidentified quest attempted in relation to the analyst and the analytic process. The analysand can no longer persist in the pursuit of that quest and of the analyst's desire. The signifying chain and the knowledge gleaned from the first phase of the process, as well as the recent persistence of the letter in the symptom helps to extricate the analysand from this misattribution within the analytic process. But, in the last instance, it is a question of an ethical choice.

The psychoanalytic treatment of the symptom situates the subject with respect to the jouissance rejected from the chaining of the signifier. In turn, that subjective position circumscribes the basis of an ethical answer. The subject is asked to answer on his or her own, that is, from the letters that *support* the site of enunciation, and not in terms of the signifiers through which the subject is *effaced*. To reach this moment, the analyst aims to obtain a shift in the position of the subject in the symptom regarding the letters. The ethical answer the analyst requests from the subject opposes the working of the jouissance through the letters. The acknowledgement in the letters of a truth leftover in the symptom becomes the starting point of the subject's answer. The letters are no longer only the paths that mark the driving back of the repelled jouissance; they begin to support the subject's speech as a gap in the meaning, conveying the desire in the failure of the signifier.

Out of this process, the clinic of the symptom makes an opening to the object of the fantasy. The maneuver, which the ethical position of the subject authorizes through the writing, partitions the jouissance. Thus, it organizes the way out for the real of the subject, a real as expelled from the site of the signifier, without any adequate mode of representation. One part of that real is shaped into the fantasy, through the working of the letter as restrained by the framing of the signifier. In the symptom, that framing of the working-through of the letter was lacking. Earlier, the jouissance only elicited the working of the letters, as a "driving back," so to speak. As such, that working of the letters had no other form and frame than the very body of the individual subject, a frame limited by the functioning of the organism. During the clinic of the symptom and within the limit of the analyst's desire, the analysand's ethical answer sustains the framing of the letter's work by the signifier as author of lack. The issue of that ethical confrontation is the emergence of the object in the fantasy, opening the process to a new challenge: the clinic of the fantasy.

The changes in the analysand's life and body at the end of this part of the treatment bring about a closing off of the analytic process. But the analysis hasn't reached its aim yet. The clinic of the symptom illuminates the concept of a body that is constituted by the letters the trauma left as traces, marks, and trails of a jouissance, that the signifier has repelled from the organism, and that witnesses of the lack of any self-representation for the subject in the field of the signifier. Moreover, the clinic of the symptom reveals within its ethical exigencies, beyond that loss of jouissance and that lack in the signifier, that the parceled body refers the subject to the lack in the Other, to a failure to justify the Law with respect to any foundation of the symbolic order. That failure will be the core of the next part of the process. The subject confronting the Other's lack through the ethical choice, has no other ground to sustain the ethical assumptions than the letters acknowledged by the subject in the symptom. And the subject is about to graft the writing of language, as aesthetics, to the signifier, in order to cultivate a border for the work of the jouissance in the letters. Opening the way to the fantasy, the clinic of the symptom brings the process to that specific abutment of an ethical exigency without any credible ground, outside of the relation of the subject to the writing of the jouissance. The clinic of the fantasy offers the way out of that dead end through the varied logical and grammatical arrangements of the fantasy. The analyst's desire restrains the numerous variations in the fantasy by the ethical exigency to bypass the imaginary work of the jouissance to the articulation of plain speech, speech that confesses the subject's lack.

At the very end, it is obvious that the process of the psychoanalytic treatment is based upon the possibility of an ethical encounter between the failure of a demand on the side of the analysand, and the lack that sustains desire on the side of the analyst. Such a ground for the analytic process of the treatment assumes that the body isn't just a biological organism answering only to the rules of physiological development in a given set of surroundings. Rather, it requires the concept of a body that reflects the logic of the signifier in terms of the working-through of the repressed jouissance in the letters. The Freudian concept of the trauma is a central one here, bringing to light the constitution of the body as partitioning of the organism. As the above suggests, the analytic process entails an ethical exigency for the practitioner as well, that any clinical approach has to articulate the concepts that ultimately sustain its action and establish their theoretical links. Insofar as the clinic has to deal with human beings, the ethics that guide human choice must form the central reference of any clinical theory. This theoretical articulation of such an ethical basis indicates Lacan's contribution to the clinic.

Chapter 7

The Symptom

WILLY APOLLON

The premise of the present chapter is that Freudian clinical practice reveals the symptom to be the writing of a jouissance, a writing which is inscribed in rebellion against the action of the signifier, and whose only solution is to be found in the construction of the fantasy and its traversal.

Let us begin, therefore, with the question of the precise jouissance at stake in the writing of the symptom. Within the writing of the symptom, we find, there is a jouissance which resists complete inscription in such a way as to become the central element of the fantasy and regulate the future of desire. The structure of this jouissance determines both the ethical axis of an analysis and the logic that organizes the unfolding of its specific term. The importance of understanding this particular jouissance, then, cannot be overstated.

According to Lacan, in his seminar on ethics, it is this jouissance that traces the paths that lead most surely to one's death.[1] Moreover, we recall from chapter 2 that jouissance in its very constitution presents an obstacle to the satisfaction of needs, in so far as it is introduced by the Other. This chapter shall proceed from these two remarks to allow us to form generalizations on the basis of particular cases, and to move, for example, from child to adult and from woman to man while still underscoring the singularities of each of their relations to the general logic of a clinical praxis. The singularities of any given case can not be used as the sole reference by analysts, who must establish for their clinical praxis the basis of generalization upon which those singularities can be seen as clinical references in the first place.

This piece was first presented in an earlier version in February 1995 for a workshop on "Lacanian Psychoanalysis: Jouissance: A Concept at the Core of Lacanian Clinical Practice" at the Center for Psychoanalytic Study, Chicago, Ill.

Jouissance, the Object, and the Problem of Satisfaction

The problem of the satisfaction of individual needs will help us enter into this logic of clinical praxis, which is determined on the one hand by the subject's relation to the *Other*, as the framework for the introduction of jouissance and, on the other hand, by the subject's relation to *jouissance*, as the primary obstacle to the satisfaction of need.

An animal is equipped with instincts for the satisfaction of its own needs and for the needs of its species in reproduction. But these instincts, as physiological automatisms, must be triggered and directed toward their aims by specific environmental stimuli, and in spite of individual variants, the satisfaction of an instinct cannot be considered a matter of autonomous individual decision. However, for the human, as subject of speech, things go rather differently. Humans depend upon a social companion for satisfaction, to such an extent that the malfunctioning of this dependence could jeopardize the survival of the social group, as well as the individual life. So, for the human subject, the satisfaction of need passes through the demand addressed to the Other.

Right from the outset, language is at the heart of the problem of satisfaction for the human being, but so, too, is the *politics* concerning the Other's jouissance. The demand addressed to the Other gives to the Other a power of refusal, in which the subject sees the principle of its jouissance. This is precisely what causes the obsessional to stop short in the face of any demand. The obsessional fears that the Other is using him to get jouissance. Jouissance is not only imputed to the Other in the structure of the demand, it is also deduced and legitimately presupposed. The obsessional is not wrong when he despairs of being able to escape this jouissance that the power to refuse signifies. The fact is that the Other has its own demands and will not respond to the individual's demand for satisfaction unless certain rules are first observed, certain conditions fulfilled.

The nature of these rules and conditions, however, is not the concern of the present chapter. We have, in any case, already indicated that Freud categorized them in terms of three basic concepts: the *Superego*, from which the subject deduces the Other's jouissance on the basis of its power to set conditions, and thus to refuse; the *Ideal Ego*, which gathers together the cultural and sociohistorical imperatives that overdetermine the response to the demand of the Other; and finally the Ego Ideal, in which the subject's self-perception is conceived in terms of the fickleness of the Other's will to satisfy, in order to inflect the Other's response. For the purposes of the present chapter, what matters is that these conditions imposed by the Other are there and that they come from beyond need, from much further away, such that they surpass even the stakes of their satisfaction. In other words, in the structure of the demand, the signifier of the Other's jouissance overtakes the object that was reckoned upon for the satisfaction of need. This object is therefore lost even before it has been obtained, and *as* lost becomes the remainder of the processes of the demand, the lost remainder of the introduction of the Other's signifier. This irrecoverable loss, both logical and structural, becomes the object of a singular theoretical elaboration in the work of Lacan, who makes of it the object *a*, the object-cause of desire.

This object is anticipated by the signifiers of the subject's demand, but is at the same time barred, or forbidden, by the signifiers of the Other's demands and requirements. As such, the object *a* already symbolizes the impossible as that which can only ever be desired. Crucially, because it is repressed in the unconscious, this object also becomes the symbolic and imaginary support for whatever jouissance the subject might manage to extract as his or her due from the Other. The jouissance this object supports has to do more with the relationship that the signifier institutes between the subject and the Other than with any hypothetical satisfaction that might be drawn from this object—if at last it turned out to be accessible. To the contrary, the approach of this object is all the more a source of anxiety for the subject in that it does not relate to any sort of satisfaction. What such an object evokes is something that surpasses any problematic of satisfaction: a jouissance that comes from elsewhere with regard to need and its satisfaction, and that relates, as we explain later, more to collective history than to individual concern.

Symptom as an Inscription and Division of Jouissance: An Anorexic in Love

The signifier thus places the subject in an elsewhere outside of individuality, and this other place is regulated by jouissance. This displacement is what accounts for the ambiguity, and sometimes the horror, that often mark the subject's relation to the signifier. The signifier necessarily precipitates the subject into a universe where individual interests are of secondary importance in relation to what is being played out in the elsewhere regulated by jouissance. This is what the symptom comes to mark: the symptom inscribes in the individual's life the insistence of an other jouissance, a jouissance amenable neither to the satisfaction of needs nor to the structuring of coexistence—that is to say, amenable with neither of the two realms that define the individual's vital dual needs to be satisfied and to coexist with others.

Thus, that which the symptom inscribes introduces the subject to the real; but the repetition and insistence of this inscription have to do with something else. As was suggested at the start of this chapter, the inscription of the letter of the symptom fails to inscribe all of the jouissance at stake in the symptom. In fact, the symptom inscribes something that, within the demand itself, is *opposed* to the satisfaction demanded. Most simply, this very specific opposition is what we are dealing with in anorexia, as we see in the case of a certain girl, in love with her neighbor, a happily married man who is fully fourteen years her senior and also a friend of her father's. The girl suffers an attack of anorexia when she discovers that her idol has been seeing a mistress in private. And yet this young lady has never declared her passion to him nor to anyone else. So, from the onset of her anorexia, everyone in her circle is extremely uneasy. The psychiatrists who are consulted cannot discover anything unusual that might have provoked the situation, because she never confides to them the object of her love. A depression is diagnosed, requiring a long rest period, with appropriate medications. In effect, the young lady is delivered over to her fantasies.

What is interesting about this clinical anecdote is what it teaches us about the functioning of the symptom. It emerges in her analysis that the discovery of the other woman came precisely in response to a demand that this young lady had addressed to the gentleman upon whom she lavished her unavowed love. His car was in the shop and he needed to pick it up, so the young lady offered to drive him. He accepted the offer, though, it seemed to her, only halfheartedly. She thought at first that his discomfort was on account of her audacity, since she had a reputation for discreet modesty—even self-effacement—when faced with men and their advances. As they arrived at the shop, she noticed that someone else, an older woman, seemed to be expecting the gentleman there. The young lady dropped him off discreetly, and then left. But as she turned the corner, she slowed to observe them from a distance. The woman, she saw, was nibbling on some sort of treat, which she held to her companion's lips with a gesture that was too familiar not to be a sign of intimacy. The young lady's world turned upside down.

That evening after dinner, the young lady vomited. Then for the eight or ten months that followed, she was unable to develop an appetite for any food, "whether poorly or well prepared," as she put it. During the same period, all the details of their brief conversation in the car returned with astonishing precision. In sum, she recalled him asking about her apparent lack of interest in love, in seeming contrast to other young people her age—to which the young lady responded that she was, quite the contrary, very much interested, but that she was waiting for the right person to come along. The neighbor failed to understand—and no wonder!—that by offering her car, the young lady was giving him the chance to declare himself.

Even though it could not be avowed, and remained unspoken, the signifier of the young lady's demand plunged her into a universe in which the encounter with the jouissance of the Other (here, the other woman as well) deprived her forever of the benefit of knowing how the Other (here, the gentleman) might have responded to her desire. In effect, the demand is dictated from the place of the Other. The subject can only demand what the Other offers, or what she thinks the Other can offer. This is a fundamental failing of the Other, and thus, for the speaking subject, a failing in the very structure of language itself, concerning what she is able to tell the Other of her desire. For this young lady, therefore, something becomes inscribed in the symptom, while something else is left behind. The jouissance of the Other, inscribed in the symptom of the "indigestible" and unassimilable treat, eclipses and condemns to silence, even to vomiting, the desire to express her love. A certain jouissance thus remains uninscribed and comes back as the cause of the repetition of the inscription of that other disallowed jouissance. The jouissance that fails to be inscribed in the symptom, that is, insists and returns, endlessly seeking out and failing to find its own new modality of inscription with each repetition of the symptom.

This repetition is so inevitable that if we manage to isolate its structure, it may enlighten us as to the nature of that jouissance that is forever failing to attain its own inscription in the repetition of the symptom. In analysis, therefore, the very structure of the symptom's repetition becomes the scene of the maneuver in which the analyst's desire for savoir interrogates the repetition in its failure, in order to grasp that remainder that resists inscription within the symptom. In the treatment, the analyst offers him- or herself as a semblance of the object a, in order to obtain the repetition of the symptom through the analysand's demand. The analysand's demand to the analyst encounters the "absence of response" that is motivated by the lack of the Other (here, the analyst), but that the analysand imputes to another cause altogether—a misrecognition that repeats the structure of the repetition of the symptom. For the patient, the absence of a response from the analyst represents the Other's failure to guarantee the satisfaction of the subject's demand. Hence, the analysand quickly encounters in the analyst both the signifier's failure to respond to desire and the jouissance at stake in the demand.

We must therefore underscore the clinical fact that the symptom appears precisely when the Other's failure is discovered, as though its writing on the letter of the body were making up for the signifier's failure to represent the desire betrayed by the demand. What I am designating here as betrayal is the fact that the demand both discloses *and* hides the desire, because the subject is ignorant of the Other's position with regard to her desire. The symptom thus inscribes the Other's failing within the jouissance that it contains. But at the same time, the symptom also draws attention to another jouissance left hanging by the failure of the signifier for which the letter of the symptom serves to compensate.

These then are the two dimensions of the symptom. On the one hand, the act of inscribing the signifier in order to close in on its failing is both what fuels the patient's complaint and what unconsciously dictates the patient's demand to the analyst upon deciding to undergo treatment. This is the signifying dimension of the symptom, which allows interpretation to get a certain take on the structure. But, on the other hand, there is a jouissance which escapes the action of the letter of the symptom, returns with insistence, and thereby determines the repetition of the symptom. Here we see the real dimension of the symptom, from which only the analyst's maneuvering can disengage the fantasy. This stranded jouissance, that insists in order to find its own path and that never manages to express itself in the terms of the signifier, is what interests the analyst, in that it is the source of the misunderstanding that gives rise to the transference in the repetition of the symptom's structure. The object of the patient's demand is not the same as that of the analyst's desire for savoir. Inevitably, the experience for which the symptom was supposed to offer a solution is repeated for the subject: the encounter with the Other's failure to respond to the demand.

The Passage to the Fantasy as a Structuration of Leftover Jouissance

For the analyst, the leftover jouissance that comes back with the repetition of the symptom is, paradoxically, the very object that causes the repetition. Therefore, the analyst's aim in analyzing and interpreting the symptom is to disengage the structure of its repetition. Through the clinical work on the symptom, the analyst hopes to draw out the structure of its repetition and thereby question and elucidate the subject's singular relation to this jouissance that the signifier has failed to account for and that has also eluded the writing of the symptom. As the clinical work progresses, the scenario of the fantasy reveals the subject's relation to a singular jouissance.

Returning, then, to the case we considered earlier, of the young lady with the indigestible treats, a few comments and clinical indications should help refine our problematic. The young lady produced, in addition to the anorexia, a whole set of symptoms, more or less benign, which I won't go into. Since the anorexia encapsulates so neatly the repetition structure of *all* these symptoms, we might confine our observations to it alone. But it is striking, even so, to consider the common thread in each of the symptoms she recollected or complained of. Each symptom—whether her frequent and long headaches, or her insomnia at certain periods of her life, or what she called her "light depressions" at the end of the school year when she was in college—operated as the conclusion of some specific juncture. Though the context of the repetition eluded her, she had an expression that came back to her again and again as a kind of refrain, which captured rather well the stakes of the structure. She would say, "So there you have it! Once again I missed the train!"

What the repetition of the symptom calls attention to in this particular case is a certain relation the subject has developed to a jouissance that has been taken away from her by a third party. In a sense, the symptom comes along to sign a self-accusation. She always makes herself responsible for once again missing the train, imagining that she is neither good enough or beautiful enough for a man who courts her, nor intelligent enough or competent enough for a promotion. But in spite of this declaration of inadequacy, a suffering invariably comes along to simultaneously both sanction this judgment and annihilate it.

One day the young lady recollected an event that finally dissipated the void that the analysis of her symptom had been circling around. Her father, who traveled quite a bit, always came back with gifts for each of his three children, whom he adored. For her brother, he always returned with a new toy. For her sister, he most often brought a book or a piece of clothing. But for the young lady herself, the gift was almost invariably some edible treat—often a new kind of chocolate. Her more beautiful sister, who was considered their father's favorite, envied our young lady the treats she received. Our young lady felt, however, that she would have been glad to get dresses or a book. But every time, when her father would ask before leaving whether she would like to get something else, the young lady never dared to express her desire to have the same thing as her sister. Each time, that is, she would again "miss the train."

Progressively, a particular modality of lack came to define for her her relation to jouissance and to the Other's failing. When she saw the Other, to whom she dared not address her demand, hand the object of her desire over to a third party, she found she was obliged to content herself with a jouissance mediated by another person. From this she concluded that, no matter what, she would always "miss the train." One can see, then, that the fantasy comes to formulate the subject's relation to the lost object that gives rise to her desire. Initially, fantasy is staged as an imaginary scenario that attempts to lend a space and a meaning to the jouissance left hanging for the subject as a result of the Other's failing. In clinical treatment, we must never lose sight of the fact that if fantasy serves to stage the subject's relation to a jouissance, it is because this jouissance has resisted the anchoring of the signifier and has failed to inscribe itself within the writing of the symptom.

The analyst's desire requires that there be some coherence between the dream and the symptom, and between the symptom and the fantasy, in which a cause can be articulated beyond the particularities of the phenomena. This desire dictates a strategy that assumes the *fantasy* to be at the foundation of the formal envelope of the *symptom*. In other words, the fantasy determines the logic of the symptom and the form of its presentation, its phenomenology. What is at work in the symptom—the jouissance that the dream has passed over, always failing to check or contain it, either within the forms of dream representation or within the signifiers that constitute those representations—is the same jouissance that began to insist with the very first forms and scenarios of the fantasy.

It is important to note that the *symptom* has more to do with *the failure of the signifier* than with the loss that signifies the subject's castration. It is the *jouissance at stake in the symptom* that relates more radically to the *Other's castration*, in that the Other's castration is the mode in which the failing of language is verified. In the case of the young lady, the Other's castration assumes a form that she is able to bear only at the price of the symptom—namely, that the Other seems in advance to be ill-disposed or incapable of responding to the demand in which she ventures the signifiers of her desire. Faced with the impotence of all possible demands, she retreats into a silence, in which the jouissance that is now left hanging must devise a new fate for itself, even while she persists in attributing it to the Other. In this singular position, the young lady is all the more inclined to attribute what happens to her to the malice or the will of the Other, rather than to something inherent in the structure. Hence, we say that the writing of the symptom calculates this articulation of the singular to the structural, in which jouissance is evacuated from the subject.

For the subject, this evacuation of jouissance designates the place where the fantasy appears in order to take over the writing of the symptom. By lending an imaginary form to the jouissance that exceeds the power of the signifier and the phallus, the fantasy makes its operation bearable at less expense to the subject. Hence, it is that the fantasy becomes the support for the real of the drive and comes to guide *desire*, which remains beyond all (un)satisfaction. The drive that manifests this jouissance, in excess with regard to need and its satisfaction, actually comes from *further away* than the sphere of the individual life of the subject. It responds to a jouissance that comes from the Other, and, even beyond the Other, from whatever it is that the Other represents: the species, society, even history. In fact, the life and the signifier that the Other (real or symbolic) incarnates actually *preceded* the subject, and will survive her as well. They divide the subject and subject her to modalities of jouissance (real jouissance, that of life and phallic jouissance, that of the signifier) that overflow and exceed the sphere of individual needs, demands, satisfactions, or frustrations. This unbreachable gap, which renders jouissance irreducible to satisfaction, is a structural fact. It is the very substance of the fantasy, which articulates the subject's relation to this gap, that Lacan identifies as the structural lack at the core of the analytic process.

The Traversal of the Fantasy

In the logical progression of the analytic experience, in which the subject's demand encounters the ethical obstacle of the analyst's desire in the transference, the traversal of the fantasy confronts the subject with the different forms that the fantasy may take in the course of this experience. We will not explore this fully in the present chapter, but a few brief remarks will give some indication of the direction that the logical development of the analytic experience takes from this point onwards. The internal logic of the experience must be deduced by the analyst. This deduction isn't really a guide to some chronology of events. Rather, the supervision or the "pass"—or both—have allowed the analyst to identify the logical developments of the structure of the fantasy, in its different forms, through the analyst's training analysis. The savoir derived from it is a precise aid when the time comes to take responsibility for the direction of an analysis.

As the analysis unfolds, the analyst's desire forces the subject to encounter the real of this jouissance that exceeds the signifier. As a result, the structure of the fantasy gradually undergoes a series of formal transformations concerning its modes of representation. The *originary fantasy* in a sense stages the subject's first encounter with a jouissance that defies meaning. Jouissance is at this point the jouissance of the Other, sometimes taking the superegoic form of commands addressed to the subject, or perhaps even the more traumatic form of an unbearable truth that breaks in on being—for example, a word overheard about parental jouissance, or the witnessing of a love scene between the parents in special circumstances, from the viewpoint of the subject's position in relation to the event. The *seduction fantasy* signals a change in the subject's position in relation to this jouissance. The fantasy here positions the subject as the object of the Other's desire. Besides the defensive character of the transition from *jouissance* to *desire*, the seduction fantasy introduces the subject as an active agent, whereas in the originary fantasy the subject is passive. The subject's position in this form of the fantasy hinges upon the illusion that the Other is in possession of the object that might reduce the anxiety linked to jouissance through individual satisfaction. Love becomes the means of obtaining this object from the Other.

The *castration fantasy* appears in the treatment as the logical consequence of the Other's fall from its position as the agent of seduction. The dropping of the subject's illusions in relation to the Other leaves the subject on a tightrope, with excess on one side, and the Other's absence on the other. The limitlessness and the real of a lack suspended between void and excess mark for the subject the logical entry into castration. What the subject experiences at this point—even more than the loss effected by the interdiction that submitted the quest for satisfaction to the signifier's imperative—is the structural lack that the seduction fantasy for a time overshadowed. At the same time, castration consecrates the collapse of the vain hope that the Other might be the guarantee of an object that would insure satisfaction against the Other's jouissance. At this stage in the analysis, the analyst's strategy consists in maintaining the ethical imperative of the savoir that alone enables the subject to traverse the stage of castration by reconstructing the structure that sustains each of the transformations of the fantasy. Under this ethical imperative, the analysand takes over from the analyst in the position of the subject-supposed-to-know, the *sujet supposé savoir* that Lacan speaks of, and engages in elaborating a relation to the signifier's failure to apprehend that errant jouissance in excess of individual life.

Notes

1. Jacques Lacan, *The Seminar of Jacques Lacan, Book VII: The Ethics of Psychoanalysis, 1959–1960*, ed. Jacques-Alain Miller, trans. Dennis Porter (New York: W. W. Norton and Co., 1992), 191–217. Original edition (Paris: Éditions du Seuil, 1986), 225–256.

Chapter 8

From Symptom to Fantasy

WILLY APOLLON

In our clinical teaching in Québec, we frequently make the comment, inspired by the position of Jacques Lacan, that for Freud, the process of analytic treatment moves from symptom to fantasy. One might add that for Lacan, the end of analysis presupposes that the fantasy has been worked through. The intent here is not to delve into the details of the process in terms of clinical hypotheses made possible by Lacan, nor to provoke a debate about the stages of psychoanalytic treatment. Rather, the present chapter will simply attempt to outline the main points of this process as it moves from symptom to fantasy, and thereby explicate the stakes of the Lacanian clinic.

It must be stressed that our clinical positions are highly tributary of our daily practices in the Québec clinic, even if these positions may be informed by theoretical debates flowing from Lacan's method of proceeding. After all, we do work from within a North American problematics, and our particular clinical experience remains deeply marked by our daily relationship with the stakes of psychosis. These parameters clearly distinguish our approach from classical psychoanalysis as understood in North America. As well, it should become evident that many of the reigning North American prejudices against Lacanian theory have no relevance to an understanding of our psychoanalytic concepts or practices.

This chapter was presented, in different form, at a workshop entitled "Lacanian Psychoanalysis: The Process of Working Through and Dreams," at the Center for Psychoanalytic Study in Chicago, February 1993.

Marguerite's Dreams: The Symptom as a Writing
of Fatal Jouissance

To begin with, the symptom in psychoanalysis is a specific disorder whose insistence causes a person to seek consultation. It is not the equivalent of the medical symptom for which the patient may seek a cure. Indeed, a patient engaging in analysis knows, even if not consciously, that what is suffered is more than something that can simply be healed or cured. Should the patient be in doubt, we strongly recommend seeing a physician. The source of the psychoanalytic symptom—and its cause—is not biological. The psychoanalytic symptom concerns the unique relationship the subject of the unconscious has with a jouissance which should have remained repressed or censured, and which is in any case impossible.

The question of the symptom cannot be understood outside of its relationship to the dream. Both must be understood as bearing upon the subject's encounter with its position as a response to the jouissance of the Other. What is insistent in the unconscious, as is the case in the return of the repressed, leads the subject to confront a jouissance that the dream has failed to reduce. The symptom is the evidence of this in the chaining of the signifier. What exactly happens in the dream? Freud explains that the dream represents a wish. For Lacan, that wish is *desire*. In French psychoanalysis, desire is a far more radical term that involves the subject of the unconscious. Desire in Lacanian terms designates the indestructible insistence of an unachievable jouissance, arising either from the prohibited or from the imposition of language itself. The role of the dream in the treatment is therefore to open a space in the signifier to accommodate the insistent jouissance. In the dream, a chain of signifiers delimits this lack of satisfaction symbolized by the navel through the absurdity of its nature.

A patient, Marguerite, repeatedly dreams that she is in the water and that a huge wave bowls her over. In her dream, she can't swim, and the water tries to force itself down her throat. Drowning appears imminent but she wakes up, without knowing whether she drowns or whether someone saves her. Her dream, which monopolizes the entire first part of her treatment, accompanies a specific symptom that brought Marguerite to analysis. She experiences the feeling that, in her words, her "whole body is getting away from her" and that, for instance, she "could faint" while making love. That feeling reappears in the treatment when she speaks of her desire, and in circumstances in which a man shows interest in her and courts her. In such situations, she finds herself with her back to the wall; she can no longer sustain the cat and mouse game. She is excited, but flees at the last moment. And if she feels that no escape is possible, her whole world falls apart.

The repetitive dream that Marguerite brings to her treatment is grounded in something that, for her, would represent a fatal satisfaction, were it achievable. In the dream, Marguerite meets some part of the real that is, in a way, her limit. Thus, her dream is in fact a nightmare. Usually a dream interprets a desire in producing signifiers that reduce jouissance to a level that is bearable, if not acceptable, for the sleeper's consciousness. In contrast, a nightmare is the meeting with a jouissance that cannot be reduced by signifiers to a desire; through the navel of the dream a nightmare marks the impossible nature of the jouissance. As we shall see, the difference between a dream and a nightmare is significant within the psychoanalytic process.

In Marguerite's case, another dream of this period in her analysis provides the interpretive scope of this presence of the navel in the dream, in contrast to the nightmare where the symptom serves as the clinical counterpart of this uninterpretable knot.

> A little girl goes out to pick up a small and cherished spoon that has fallen on the ground. A knight on a huge horse suddenly rides up in full armor, brandishing a long sword. The little girl lies face down on the ground and plays dead.

One is struck by the anachronistic presence of a knight in full armor in a modern city of Québec, and the knight's objection to the little girl picking up the tiny spoon is especially strange. The very oddness of this scene, a tie to the unknown navel, clearly ruptures the chain of signifiers in the dream and forces us to consider a jouissance "aimed at" the signifier so as to be reduced to the insistence of a desire. By contrast, in the dream-nightmare of the unachieved drowning, nothing interrupts the chaining of the signifier except the sleeper's awakening. Nothing replaces the drowning to stand as the navel, and anguish awakens the dreamer. Such a dream is like a direct encounter of the dreamer with a real. Jouissance is not reduced to knowledge through representation. The symptom responds to such dream-nightmares or substitutes itself for them. The symptom appears because it is the inscription, in the body, of a jouissance that the dream was unable to reduce so that it could be represented.

The dream's role of reducing jouissance to a desire by containing the impossibility of any satisfaction in pursuing the desire sheds some light on the double stakes of the psychoanalytic symptom. Something insists and is repetitive in the dreams, as we see in the case of Marguerite. The stakes of the psychoanalytic symptom are decided at the heart of the repetition. The symptom inscribes in the subject's body or behavior a jouissance irreducible by the signifier. In other words, it inscribes, in the relationship to the Other and as an obstacle to that relationship, a defect or lack that derives its justification in the subject's relationship to jouissance. What the dream is incapable of representing as desire in Marguerite's relationship to a certain jouissance returns as an obstacle in the real of her relationship to others. Consequently, even though the symptom takes the form of a physical disorder or physical dysfunction in Marguerite (a rash and an ulcer of the duodenum), the symptom is in fact the writing, in the real of the relationship to the Other, of the fatal jouissance in its realization. Its counterpart, in the dream, is evidenced in the dream-nightmare of the failed drowning. While the dream attempts to reduce jouissance to its failure, the symptom attempts to limit jouissance by inscribing it as a failing of the relationship to the Other in the real of the body.

The psychoanalytic symptom in this perspective differs fundamentally from the medical symptom, even when its action on the body is not without biological consequences which, as such, may require medical attention. The resulting consequences from the biological standpoint do not in any way alter the meaning of the psychoanalytic symptom and what its cause may be. Analysis is not intended to cure the consequences, but to learn something of their source. What is in fact at play in the psychoanalytic symptom concerns the truth of what is repetitive for the subject of the unconscious in relation to undue jouissance. For the patient in treatment, that is the question to be clearly understood. It is not a case of simply seeking a cure for a physical symptom. That would only cause it to move around at the mercy of the repetitions of what in the unconscious is so insistent. After a time of repetitions of the signifier and its failure to reduce jouissance, the subject must confront the ethical demand of a truth where, beyond satisfaction, what is at stake is her very being, if not sometimes her very existence. At the mercy of the symptom, Marguerite comes face-to-face with an unbearable truth. As we shall see, she is returned headlong to something uncontrollable whose limits had already been traced out in her childhood by the stories of her mother.

What the dream cannot reduce for Marguerite comes back in the real of her life, always at the same spot, and imposes itself as something unbearable. It may destroy her, but still she cannot shake it, and she becomes attached to it as if it were an essential part of her being. Interpretation runs up against this work of jouissance in the symptom, as if against a rock. Both the analyst and Marguerite learn that this truth cannot be reduced—it returns. There is no valid treatment for the psychoanalytic symptom. What it requires is an ethics, a *savoir faire* with truth. On this point where Freud encounters the work of jouissance, where the truth at work in the subject's unconscious insists, Freud locates the function of the death drive. Faced with this clinical discovery, Freud introduced the clinical concept of negative therapeutic reaction. Lacan, commenting on this rather deceptive formulation by Freud, points to what he calls the "double-sided symptom." On one side is the analyzable, where interpretation by the signifier reduces and segments the symptom. On the other side, mirroring the pertinence of Freud's clinical encounter with jouissance, is the uninterpretable side of the symptom—a veritable rock oblivious of any attempts by the signifier to reduce it. Lacan then poses the clinical question of what is required so that the jouissance at stake in the symptom, the work of the death drive, can be reduced through analysis in the situation of transference. In truth, what the symptom turns into an obstacle by covering it over is the lost truth that would enable the subject to learn the cause of his or her desire.

The Clinic of the Symptom, or the Freudian Passage from Symptom to Fantasy

The clinic of the psychoanalytic symptom turns on the ethical question of a truth hidden for the subject by a prohibited jouissance. But what truth and what jouissance? Something in the psychoanalytic symptom repeats itself unceasingly, and refuses to let itself be reduced during transference. It is important at this point in the discussion to underscore the clinical relevance of Lacan's reconsideration of the question of transference. The way in which the analyst conceives of the transference and sustains it within the analysis is determinative in the fate of the psychoanalytic symptom. For Lacan, transference does not consist in corrective repetition, with the analyst in treatment defined by what is reenacted in terms of Oedipus and the prohibitions in childhood with the parents. With Lacan, the fundamental element in the clinical experience of transference is that the analysand presupposes a knowledge, a savoir, in the analyst. The analyst is supposed to know something about what is unceasingly repetitive for the analysand, something about the truth at stake in the symptom. The analysand's position of presupposing that the analyst possesses a savoir that could offer reprieve from the symptom is a clear indication that the analysand has no doubts about the ethical nature of the symptom. It is acknowledged that a savoir is at stake.

In the transference process, this supposition of savoir triggers the power and action of the signifier in the dream. The realm of the process thus triggered is that of the ethical. It is ethical because the subject knows at once, despite the body's objections, that what the entire process involves is a confrontation with the jouissance at work that pushes to the limits of the truth of being, where one must assume the lack in which desire finds its source and its relation to death. The clinic of the symptom, as generated within the transference, thus begins under the sign of a particular ethics. Both the analysand and the analyst must find a foundation for this ethics in the elements of truth at stake in the symptom because as analysis progresses, it will become increasingly apparent that the symptom itself is an ethical choice. The subject takes a position in the symptom, even without being conscious of doing so. This position is taken on the side of the prohibited, either for the jouissance that cannot be, in terms of the impossible, or for the jouissance that language makes impossible, and as such, because it is lost in advance, is the lack causing the desire. In this sense, the symptom is an ethical choice, a choice against desire.

The symptom inscribes in the body the mark of insistence. But what is recurrent in the insistence is not what is inscribed. There is something that does not succeed in imposing itself as truth in the subject, short of what is written for the subject's suffering. Marguerite's complaint of frigidity, as a consequence of her fear of fainting while making love, seems to maintain for her a firm distance from any masculine sexual approach implying commitment, while at the same time nourishing a unique jouissance that Marguerite accepts as satisfying. Freud is correct in insisting upon the importance for the economy of the psyche of the secondary gain of the symptom despite its apparent contradiction. Through this jouissance, the clinic of the symptom meets the limit of the action of interpretation on the symptom. The analyst's maneuver must require the removal of the jouissance so that the subject comes face-to-face with the real truth it is hiding. But, one must ask, just what is involved in such a maneuver toward truth?

What Marguerite tells us of what we may call her first meeting with jouissance will serve as a guide. In her childhood, her mother, a very Christian person, would tell her "stories of young girls kidnapped to be sold in far away countries or else used as prostitutes in the big cities." Whatever the reality of such stories attributed to her mother, this is what comes out in treatment as an association. She specifies that the mother told her such "terrifying stories" for the purposes of her education. Her mother wanted to reinforce a prohibition against "being free with strangers." Marguerite admits that she wondered for a long time what "being free with strangers" really meant. It must have been something quite bad for it to be so strongly prohibited. That was probably what the jouissance was.

It is interesting to point out here that Marguerite's encounter with something that would later impose itself on her as the real (in Lacan's terms), or as a psychic reality (in Freud's terms), is an encounter provoked by the Other. Whether fantasy or reality matters little, the crucial thing here is that something was imposed upon the child that would, some twenty-five years later, be attributed by the adult to the maternal Other. Marguerite's first meeting with what Lacan designates as the real is a jouissance introduced by stories attributed to her mother. And the mother here is not the woman who in reality is her mother, even if, as a historical figure, she does give consistency to the Other of the story. This Other is constituted by language as the place of speech. In this case, it is the mother who, in Marguerite's imaginary, told frightening stories to prohibit the specific form of jouissance consisting in "being free with strangers." And when for Marguerite, it became evident that this was what in fact jouissance was, what she encountered was clearly the jouissance of the Other. The prohibited in the form of the narrative opened up a world for Marguerite, one where jouissance was to be free or in other words, to be "accessible and available" to men who would take you far away to be used as a prostitute. It was no doubt the fantasy of being accessible and available sustained by the dream that was so important for Marguerite. There she lies, face down on the ground before a knight in armor on horseback. Did she faint? Available as fantasy would have it, but innocent as required by the prohibited?

The analyst's interpretation of the dream will introduce ambiguity and equivocation—especially in terms of the dreamer's situation—and it may raise a question. The point remains that what Marguerite meets in the real is the jouissance of the Other, a jouissance prohibited but designated by the Other. Marguerite is in the grips of a fantasy that re-creates the very story that she attributes to her mother. Is that her way of obtaining access to her mother's fantasy? That is the question we are proposing in focusing on the jouissance of the Other. In reality, the structure through which she has access to the prohibited is rather particular. What is prohibited to her as jouissance is what she infers from the Other's story. Marguerite arrives, through pathways that escape us, at the conclusion that what is prohibited for little girls is accessible to mothers, and that "a girl must not enjoy more than her mother." That formulation came out as an afterthought following a voluntary and innocent remark from the analyst on the fact that, inevitably, she had become an adult. Everything points to the idea that the prohibited jouissance, within the fantasy that sustains Marguerite's story, is a jouissance reserved for her mother. And it is something that her mother takes away from her.

Marguerite's complaints against her mother are numerous, but never initially focus on sexuality. She readily admits on this point that she was well-raised by her mother and that her upbringing enabled her to go through adolescence without ever having to experience the unfortunate adventures typical of her generation. Every once in a while she felt, in her words, "an anguishing surge of hate" against her mother that she never could explain. Nevertheless, she maintains that her mother is "too controlling." Her mother devotes a great deal of attention, too much according to Marguerite, to each of her new male acquaintances. "She organizes my life too much, as if I were a little girl that people tell stories to."

What repeats itself here for Marguerite through dreams and symptoms progressively confronts her in treatment with an unbearable truth about what jouissance is for her, and about the place held by her mother in the stakes of her jouissance. The analyst's maneuver is to sustain an ethical approach rather than remitting the subject indefinitely back to the Oedipal situation by imposing himself as a third party through force. It is important that the subject escape from the trap of the false prohibition. As long as Marguerite continues to impute responsibility for the prohibited onto her mother, she will never gain access to the savoir of the impossible, where the very fact of language directly affects jouissance. For Marguerite, jouissance is prohibited for her solely because it is reserved for her mother. There is a level of satisfaction forever out of her reach because a young girl must never enjoy more than her mother. And because she cannot know when she is enjoying as much as her mother, nor when it is on the verge of overstepping that limit, she does just as well to faint before reaching such a point. Of course, the fainting is in itself a jouissance, but the choice she makes removes any responsibility for it.

The analyst's precise exigency in treatment is clear; it is an ethical requirement to remain within the prohibited. Marguerite cannot indefinitely refer to this maternal Ideal of jouissance as a substitute for the imposition of the phallus as a signifier of what the Law, as represented by the father's specific demands, prohibits. For Marguerite, as for any little girl, the phallus marks that jouissance, which devolves through the fact of the father, just as it functions for the mother. This fact of the father, the phallic fact par excellence, is to a certain extent a problem for us in North America, as a required passage for feminine jouissance. When I say us, I refer not only to patients in analysis, but also to the analysts, from both the theoretical and practical standpoints. The point to be made here in the particular case of Marguerite, is that the prohibited is set up to reside in her, so to speak, by a passage through the *mother's fantasy*, rather than through the *father's phallus*. Marguerite's mother does not resort to the authority of the father as support for the Law of language in initiating her daughter to what cannot be done and must remain prohibited. In any case, if she did do so, it certainly did not have the same impact on Marguerite as the terrifying stories of kidnapping and child "trade."

Marguerite nonetheless was enormously proud of and had great admiration for her father. She spoke of him as having great physical and moral strength. She readily faults her mother for sexually denigrating her father. She even holds a grudge against her mother for various unflattering remarks she made concerning the sexuality of the couple, such as blaming her husband for not being able to satisfy her, for looking at other women's breasts, and for waiting for her to die to be able to go and live with someone else. It is only during analysis that Marguerite comes to realize the love she has for her father, and the more she discovers it, the more she develops a hatred for her mother which eventually turns into a hatred for certain other women.

These other women all have the characteristic of coming between Marguerite and a man, but only in a peculiar way. During analysis, she described several typical cases of conflict between herself and a cousin close to her mother or between female colleagues, either at university or in the workplace. The women include childhood friends of the man with whom she is living. In every case, the scenario is the same. In some specific fashion, the women impose their viewpoint on what for her was a relationship of seduction with a man. It is as if the women assumed the very role that the terrifying stories had played in her childhood—that of barring her access to her father's love. The women meant that for Marguerite, a meeting with love would indefinitely continue to be a missed encounter. At the same time, she had a feeling of.supporting in those women a jouissance that is the object of her hate. With each woman, each time under a different form but always with the same purpose, she once again played out the scene under the imperative that a daughter must not enjoy more than her mother.

As Marguerite gained access to these formulations through her dreams, associations, and memories, she began to take control of her treatment. She showed great interest in the knowledge made accessible through the treatment because, as she says, she is less fearful of men and can stand up to her cousin and to certain of her colleagues at work without being paralyzed by hatred. In the treatment sessions she also complains less frequently about her boyfriend. No doubt she realizes that the sexual complaints about him were only copied on the complaints her mother made against her father. One specific point became central for Marguerite: in her words: "she must come to terms with the truth about her life, which is more important than sex." She had not at that point realized that sex was inseparable from that truth.

The Master and Marguerite: The Lacanian Clinic and the Working Through of Fantasy

The question may be asked: How did Marguerite benefit from the clinic of the symptom? Without a doubt, the feeling of frigidity that led her to seek consultation so that she could enjoy as much as other women, gave way to access to the ethical requirement of a savoir about what, beyond the subject's suffering, constituted the knot of her being as a woman. What had continually repeated itself in her life took on a new dimension as a truth imposing itself on her. A specific relationship to jouissance, where the maternal Ideal hid the paternal phallus, was altered for her. The truth, hidden up to then because it was unbearable for her, finally emerged. Marguerite realized that the prohibition of jouissance did not derive from her mother's special privileges. The symptom revealed itself to her for what it was: a particular form of knowledge about jouissance, or the inscription of a failing of jouissance on the subject's body or in the subject's relationship to the Other. The knowledge concerning the failing of jouissance confronts Marguerite with the maternal Ideal, which sustains, as Superego, a prohibition which limits access to jouissance, that is, to the phallus of the father, which would indicate something lost, if not impossible for the mother. Prohibition is distinguished from the impossible. What did her mother have to complain about because jouissance for her was not prohibited? Would the paternal phallus situate her mother in an impasse other than the impasse within which the maternal Ideal was situating Marguerite?

The clinic of the symptom thus led Marguerite to a division of what—for her—had been joined by the symptom. The castration of the mother was hidden within the fantasy of a jouissance that was reserved for her. The truth of the symptom lifts the veil on that castration. What her mother complains of lacking and of not receiving from her father is represented by the phallus of the father. It is now on her father's side that Marguerite will attempt to discover what her mother is lacking and what is causing in her the desire that her complaint refuses to acknowledge.

Marguerite perceives in her mother's complaint a lack of ethics, but continues for herself to wonder how a woman's jouissance is created by giving in to desire. The dream of the small girl trying to retrieve her little spoon at the foot of a knight on horseback collects decisive signifiers in Marguerite's story. These signifiers mark a turning point in her treatment, not unlike the answer to a question, or the passage, so to speak, from symptom to fantasy. The removal of the maternal ideal marking as an Ego Ideal the limit she may in no circumstances overstep, opens for Marguerite an other space where the real of the jouissance is set into a framework by a formula inferred by the dream of the knight on horseback. The deduction is made possible both by the chain of signifiers staged by the dream *and* by the ethical requirement sustained by the analyst that consists in not yielding on what is causing the impossible.

The time at which the signifier most seriously confronts its limits is during this point of the treatment. The analyst's ethical demand underlies the discovery of the lack founding the desire against any imaginary constructions of meaning. These emergency constructions operate to maintain the illusion of a specific object able to foil the lack in fantasy. The removal of the symptom reveals fantasy at the point where the signifier fails, because the object imagined in the fantasy is substituted for the lack delimited by the signifier. Everything in the dream of the knight on horseback and in the concurrent water and wave dream refers to a series of decisive events and memories in Marguerite's subjective story. From the knight, the *chevalier*, which in French contains a pun (*lier*) for being bound and tied, to the phallic sword, to the little girl who cherishes her little spoon, *sa petite cuillière*, which in French contains a pun (*son petit cou*) for her small neck, to the return of the waves which threaten to "swallow her up," what sets itself up is a fantasy of availability to be possessed by the "Despotic Prince," as she put it. One may parody Lacan in saying that "Marguerite is looking for a Master." But the matter of what now haunts Marguerite's desire to know still remains.

As the various forms and imaginable representations of this situation in which a woman must be possessed by a despot are set into place and worked through, three changes throw Marguerite's life into turmoil. She experiences what she calls a "series of losses." On several occasions, she loses cherished objects of value, generally pieces of jewelry, whose shape in every case evokes a hole. Not only do the lost objects by their shape evoke lack introduced by loss, the analyst notes that "family jewels" are also the sexual organs of the father. At the same time, Marguerite speaks of significant change in her sex life. For the first time it consists in something other than masturbation—she discovers that she has a partner and that there isn't only what she calls her "fantasy." She does not notice, however, that the change takes place after a long period of contesting the maternal position and the mother's complaints against the father as a lack of ethics on the mother's part. She also begins to wonder about the knight on horseback, the master and the despot, on the basis of what soon appears to her as an inadequacy between sexual satisfaction of the orgasm and what she calls "the rest." "There is always something else," she says, "that is never it."

With these various transformations of the fantasy, Marguerite realizes that in the second part of the treatment she was demanding a variety of possibilities for transgressing the prohibited. Beyond the initial complaint, she thus continued to identify with her mother, refusing to lack, in reference to what she believed to be the phallus. Each new time and with each new form of fantasy, her demand failed. She finally began to realize that whatever the despot's powers, there was always something which seemed to be beyond her grasp, and of which the fantasy was only an empty frame. But she couldn't bear the emptiness. In anxiety, she discovered that the prohibited offered no space beyond; it only defined a space for what was still unknown to her. It could not be transgressed. Every form of transgression apparently sustained by the multiple possibilities in fantasy only opened onto a "that is not it" which brought her back to what she initially called emptiness. To designate the meeting with the fundamental lack that was to terminate her treatment, she eventually found a homonym of her first name that she construed with the very signifiers that reoccurred time and time again in her treatment.

She was unaware that she was to leave analysis with such a revealing knowledge that would take the place of the jouissance that she had come to demand. She had come to psychoanalysis with a demand for what she believed to be a jouissance, and subsequently found herself caught in a desire to know. What she left with said a lot about what she had always desired without knowing, and about the surprising forms in her that such an irreducible quest could take. She no longer had any illusions about what was continuing to take her outside herself, yet she seemed to understand both the personal impact brought about by the knowledge of herself as well as what it is to be a woman in her case, as something more essential than the love and jouissance that brought her to analysis at the outset.

In this last part of the treatment, what prevails in the work of analyzing the fantasy is a consequence of the fact that the outcome of the clinic of the symptom consists in the subject assuming personal responsibility for the treatment. The subject is cornered, owing to the analyst's silence, a silence seen in the abstention and distance maintained vis-à-vis the subject's demand, and in the management of treatment time through a strategy determining the beginning and end of the session. The patient is now guided by the discovery and truth of that which is at stake in each session and at each encounter with the real of desire and of castration. Such a manner of proceeding is a sort of prerequisite for the clinic of fantasy, because what the symptom hides at the same time it writes, is properly the function of the impossible, thus of castration, in the subject's meeting with the failing of jouissance on which the subject's unconscious truth depends.

In the Lacanian clinic, the subject requesting treatment confronts an ethics that Lacan defines as the requirement of not giving in to what is causing the desire. Far from sustaining some object offered up by fantasy as a support for the passage of desire, the Lacanian clinic makes the ethical requirement that the focus remain on the particular working of the impossible, where deficient jouissance creates lack where the subject's desire finds its cause. A knowledge, therefore, of the nature of the failing of jouissance in terms of the signifier, and of the ethics that may underlie it, are required in the place of a jouissance for which the subject must elucidate the very means of extinction in both the subject's own history and in the experience of the treatment. The search for a subjective truth, enabling desire to find its justification and the subject to find a place to be lost in, signals the end of any identificatory adventure obscuring the subject's relation to truth. Such identification simply allows the ego to find substantial support against death where the subject is guided irrepressibly by drive.

The reduction of jouissance, due to a failing of the chaining of the signifier in the dream, was effected in three stages in the clinic of the fantasy. We shall briefly outline them in Marguerite's treatment. First, under various forms, the bridging of a fantasy of jouissance reserved for the mother drove Marguerite to the foot of the wall of the paternal phallus as the sole representation of what the prohibition returns as something else that would lie beyond the whims of the parental Other. The father would be only the carrier of the phallus, which is an effect of language, a limit that conditions human socialization and the coexistence of the sexes. Every form of seduction is then reviewed, with the fantasy of the knight on horseback, where for Marguerite it is a question of transgression or of a jouissance that would be accessible and beyond the prohibited. Even if for Marguerite, such a fantasy marked a final abandonment of identification with the maternal ideal, it was not without the sustained ambiguity that the transgression was possible while sustaining the paternal phallus. Lastly, there is the fantasmatic quest for the power of the "Despotic Prince," which affords Marguerite the occasion to realize that there is no Other to sustain her quest for such jouissance, and that there is a lack of ethics presupposed by her mother's complaint against the failing to which the paternal phallus refers. The sexual jouissance she enjoys with her partner over and above her fantasy then finds its beyond in the analysis of the impossible jouissance with the Despotic Prince. There is, however, a remnant, one that Marguerite recognizes as essential and that no satisfaction reduces. Here she finally recognizes the source of all her misfortune and of her greatest madness. She hangs on to this remnant in the same way that the little girl in the dream clings to her spoon. And to do that, she will take any risk. In not wanting to make any concession on this remnant, her life may now take an unpredictable turn. But that is precisely what she seems to want and what takes away any usefulness in pursuing treatment. She is happy with this knowledge that takes the place of all the objects and lost jewelry.

The Lacanian clinic favors an ethics where savoir is substituted for the quest for a jouissance that the treatment experience reveals as lapsed and thus impossible. The knowledge at stake at the end of the process concerns the cause of the lapsing. The savoir that concludes the experience is unlike the knowledge that the analysand in transference supposed the analyst knew at the outset of the experience. The analyst refers the analysand to an ethics where desire feeds on the failing of jouissance, and where the analysand takes that cause and the risks of desire as the only determinative realities for one's story, and as a source from which the analysand will draw principles of action, as the necessary support to assume one's sex and one's relationship to jouissance. The principle of Lacanian analysis is predicated on this failing of jouissance, this lack that pierces a hole in the chain of signifiers and that is signified in the object which Lacan calls object *a*. This is why the signifier is only a means and not the object of the process. It is a means that, in a way, fails to serve its purpose. And it is this failing of the signifier to reduce the jouissance it delimits as a real that enables us to link the dual bridging underlying the logic and ethics of the treatment: from the symptom to fantasy, and from fantasy to object *a*. In time, after the subject's encounters with whatever is the anguishing knot of the real in the unconscious, the desire to be cured yields to the ethical requirement of a truth that is incommensurable with the knowledge of science or psychology. The false need of belonging within which the stakes of ego identifications justify themselves, disappears with the return and recognition of a desire bearing its own markers with no other regard for the demands of the Other than the symbolic limits of social or citizen coexistence.

Chapter 9

Perverse Features and the Future of the Drive in Obsessional Neurosis

DANIELLE BERGERON

Some have read Freud to say that homosexuality is a perversion of the sexual drive. But a Lacanian, for whom clinical interest is aimed at *structure*, rather than at diagnoses based on phenomenological features, must ask whether homosexual fantasies or behaviors necessarily suggest a *perverse structure*. That is, do such phenomena necessarily serve to negate the symbolic phallic function of the Father and the Law of language? To what extent does one see in such fantasies or behaviors a structure where the logic of the organs and the return "to nature" perversely negate the logic of the signifier? In the clinic, one sees rather that many gay men present instead a hysterical or obsessional *neurotic* structure, and that it is simply the shift in social mores that has made it easier for these neurotics to act out their fantasy in a quest for satisfaction.

The Case of Mr. Beauregard

Mr. Beauregard, a middle-aged father, leaves his job, his wife, and his young children in order to "explore his homosexuality." As a teenager, he had been excited by the sight of nude boys at summer camp; since that time, his sexual fantasies have continued to revolve around masculine

This material was first presented, in different form, at The Eighth Annual Interdisciplinary Conference of the International Federation for Psychoanalytic Education, October 1997, Ann Arbor Michigan.

characters. His wife had guessed as much even prior their marriage, but they both wanted to raise a family, and for many years they found a sort of satisfaction there. After having moved to another country, he begins to go to gay bars looking for relief, thinking that he has at last the right to be happy. He then starts to live with a young man, hoping to find happiness by no longer denying what he felt to be a cornerstone of his identity.

It is at this time that Mr. Beauregard comes to analysis to consult about a long-standing social inhibition that has recently become unbearable. He says that he has lived a solitary life since childhood and that he had always felt a panic when obliged to communicate with others in a group. This anxiety and his efforts to avoid such situations also forced him to quit a job as a librarian he'd held for many years. Moreover, having believed that assuming his homosexuality in sharing a daily and sexual life with another man would improve his relationships with others and bring him the satisfaction he expected from life, Mr. Beauregard now fears that these hopes are not to be fulfilled. Ironically, while he remains overcome by haunting homosexual fantasies (and some consequent guilt), what the man fears most and what he constantly avoids is having sex with his boyfriend. Indeed, he now finds all kinds of excuses to escape it and instead takes to compulsive activities that consume his nights, such as masturbating while looking at gay magazines or sitting alone in bars and looking at young men. On the one occasion where he went so far as fondling someone in a men's restroom, he caught genital herpes and "was punished," he says, "for having tried to materialize my fantasies." All of which makes him feel sad, unsatisfied, and powerless.

During the analysis, Mr. Beauregard discovers that his mother wished him to be polite, obedient, mild-mannered and kind, and she hoped he would become a priest. Now, in his adulthood, he finds himself insecure, sensitive to remarks, "femininely" emotional, and perfectionist. He lacks self-confidence, feels socially isolated, is anxious in love, and experiences a constant guilt. He recalls that his mother used to confide in him. She described his father as violent, and the boy felt specially loved by her— that she was not treating him as she did her other son. Nevertheless, he always sought his father's approval, though his father preferred the boy's more virile brother. Yet, until he turned five, Mr. Beauregard says he was "as aggressive as his father." He adds:

> I then decided to become serious, to be on my mother's side, to emulate her virtues, and to stop being aggressive. My father began to complain about my squeamishness. I often stayed at home with my mother instead of playing sports with other boys; I loved reading and was sex-oriented from my earliest years.

Childhood Identifications: Ego-Ideal, Ideal Ego, and the Movement of Desire

To enter the realm of language is to take a loss. In his "graphs of desire," from the essay "The Subversion of the Subject and the Dialectic of Desire in the Freudian Unconscious," Lacan shows how the effect of language on the living being is *the* determining factor in the loss that forms the human subject (see Figure 9.1). As was discussed in the early chapters of the present book, this loss resulting from the capture by the signifier is the loss of biological logic aimed at the satisfaction of needs. The satisfaction of needs is thus permanently diverted from its objects by another logic, the logic of the signifier, which is introduced when the foundational cut takes place. The introduction of the signifier diverts biological energy from the immediate satisfaction of needs towards the parental Other who has inscribed the child in language and who supports the child in the name of society. The future of the newborn child in quest of satisfaction is then irremediably linked to the availability and goodwill of the Other. The object of the foundational loss (which Freud related to an hallucination, since it was always already lost with the establishment of language in the human species) will be the source of the drive, defined by Lacan as the response to Other's demand. This drive will be life bearing if it finds its expression in the imaginary forms of desire we call "dreams" or "fantasies" or in

Figure 9.1
The Graphs of Desire, Graph I

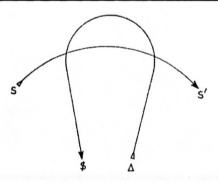

else in "creations in the social sphere"; otherwise, it will be a fatal form of energy, a death drive in a symptom of the body where it will follow the erogenous path of its exclusion by the Other.

A first circuit of Lacan's "graph of desire"[1] determines the level of the identifications as they are oriented by parental demands, where the subject identifies with the demand heard coming from the parents (see Figure 9.2). Thus, the subject is marked by a first feature, a unary trait, in Lacan's formulation, an Ego Ideal written into the parents' and the family's discourse about the child. This first tale, these first words spoken "stand as a decree, a law, an aphorism, an oracle; they confer their obscure authority upon the real other,"[2] that is, upon the parent. From this moment, the subject is captive, alienated, as was seen with Mr. Beauregard, offered at birth the future of a priest. His mother had said to her family that if she had children, she wanted at least one girl. Could this be why, at a certain moment during the treatment, Mr. Beauregard felt devastated and resentful, and came to feel, "I have been used as an object?"

To the symbolic demand inscribed by the Ego Ideal, the subject responds through the imaginary construction of the Ideal Ego, which is the "channel taken by the transfusion of the body's libido towards the object,"[3] to build the body image according to the object that one imagines one hears in the Other's demand, and thus according to the perception one has of the object that the Other lacks and requires in order to be satisfied. The Ideal Ego is the imaginary perception of what the

Figure 9.2
The Graphs of Desire, Graph II

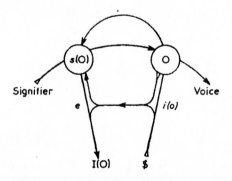

parental Other wants; it is the specular image to which the mother's smile is directed. For example, when Mr. Beauregard's mother asked the boy to accompany her to church, he was struck by the smile he saw on her face during the homily as the priest enumerated various ways of becoming a saint. Then, he adopted his mother's virtues, he says, and repressed his aggressivity to the point that what thereafter characterized his relationships with others was a squeamishness and a certain feminization in the form of social passivity. He then also began to avoid any competitive situation.

The subject is thus determined by the Other; the ego, on which one relies to assert one's existence and claim one's conscience, is also trapped inasmuch as it is the product of the unary trait, the meaning of which was defined by the Other. "It is not part of my values to do that, to make love with men," says Mr. Beauregard in a moment of exasperation. He is not wrong. From the Ego Ideal defined by the Other to his response through the Ideal Ego and the setting up of the seduction fantasy in a context of phallic deficiency, it will be seen that his future path depended in large measure on his unconscious relation to the parental Other.

Even if "it is insofar as the subject is situated and is constituted with relation to the signifier that the break, splitting or ambivalence is produced in him, at the point where the tension of desire is located,"[4] the passage *from* the circuit of the response to the *Other's demand* as a predetermined path for the drive *to* the path of the *subject's desire* is only possible if the capricious and arbitrary demand of the Other is kept "in check" by the Law[5] (see Figure 9.3). The Law makes possible and frees the subject's desire from the demand of the Other by offering other means of expression for the energy of the drive: dreams, fantasy, artistic creation. Law restrains parental demand and marks out its path by introducing a lack in that demand, both through interdiction under the form of sociocultural rules which expose abuse by supporting a meaning for life and through the impossible, now represented by the phallus as a signifier for the irremediable and irreversible effects of language on the regulation of the physiological functioning of the human body. Through the Law, the parental Other introduces the child into the realm of symbolic castration and desire.

The Obsessional, as the Imaginary Phallus of the Mother, Looking for the Father

The child who first forms an ideal ego in conformity with what, through the mother's demand was imagined to be her lack or her desire, later sees that any response to that demand leaves the mother unsatisfied,

Figure 9.3
The Graphs of Desire, Graph III

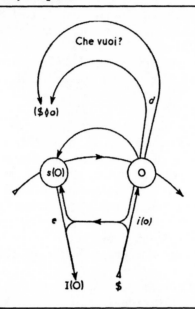

since it fails to stop her from turning to the father to express her desire, which they both recognize as impossible to fulfill. It is to support this impossible desire that she turns to the father, who also bears a lack that his own desire keeps reminding him of. The signifier humanizes the living being through a traumatic break from the "natural" satisfaction of physiological needs. From then on, only words, despite the misunderstandings that they weave, can alleviate the gaping hole thus created and from which originates the life of the drives. This is how the symbolic phallus is established for the child: it signifies the effects of the definitive loss due to language and its incompleteness, and it represents the motion of desire. The phallus, as signifier of the effects of the signifier, introduces the child to lack and desire.

But rather than the desire of the mother for the desire of the father, it is the dissatisfaction of the mother in relation to that father that the boy who will later suffer from obsessional neurosis perceives at a second stage. This marks a certain failure in the setting up of the symbolic phallus. Mr. Beauregard's oldest memory reveals how he became preco-ciously sensitive to his mother's complaint: "I was very little. It was dur-ing summer vacation at my grandparents' cottage. Through the thin wall behind my bed, I heard my parents making love, and then my mother cried. I thought she had been injured by my father."

On the other hand, Mr. Beauregard's mother's excessive investment in him put him in the position of an imaginary phallus—that of the one who could give satisfaction when the father seemed unsatisfactory. The obses-sional subject then begins to try to respond to the mother's unrelenting and ever-unsatisfied demand. "I have always tried to fulfill my mother's dreams," says Mr. Beauregard, adding "I had to be perfect, only my par-ents were allowed to make mistakes; this outrageousness was assaulting me." Confusing the mother's lack with her demand, the obsessional child then *represses his or her own desire*, which would have been easily accessed, if only the setting up of the phallus had been clear. The mother forces herself on her obsessional son through her continual demand and her son will become the object of her own desire. This will be revealed, during the treatment, by the formulation of his seduction fantasy.

"My mother was often catching me out," says he. "At five, I had a girlfriend—we 'planned' to be married one day. My mother refused to allow her into our house. She was afraid I could become attached to her. She also refused to let us play alone in the fields behind the house. One day she found us lying in the tall grass, fascinated by the movement of the clouds in the sky. She became furious." For Mr. Beauregard, to be-come a priest would have meant to be consecrated to his mother, since after her, there would have been no other woman. It must be pointed out that the arrangement he had made with his wife before they got mar-ried—he had told her of his fantasies about men—also preserved Mr. Beauregard from desiring a woman who was not his mother. Thus, to re-spond to his mother's complaints, he gave up his desire, something not achieved without symptomatic manifestations.

But while the phallus (the representation of the impossible) is hesitant and unsteady and poorly established in the obsessional's unconscious, the other side of the symbolic Law, which dictates the submission of the child and of other family members to cultural prohibitions, is faultless. The ob-sessional child may be the object of an excessive love on the part of the mother, but it is the father's recognition that is sought and it is from the father that the obsessional waits for an intervention which would separate the child from the mother's desire and allow access to the subject's own desire. "I have always sought my father's approval," says Mr. Beauregard. "If he had loved my mother, I could perhaps have got closer to him." Freud, noting homosexual fantasies in obsessional men, suggested that they are an attempt to get closer to the father and gain his love. As for Mr. Beauregard, he identifies with his father, saying that he has always thought that his father was "an unavowed homosexual." These words and many others of a similar nature heard during the treatment of obsessionals, lead us to conclude that the Father is established for the obsessional and not denied—in contrast to the case of the pervert—since the obsessional hopes for the father's recognition and support.

Even if the father has been devalued in his symbolic function as phallic representative, the father retains his function as the representative of the authority of the Law and has managed to transmit the social prohibition to his obsessional son. This is attested by the fear of retaliation that dominates the obsessional's psychic life. But, loved to excess by the mother whose demanding love loads him down and who is always asking for more, the obsessional is nevertheless fascinated by the imaginary proximity of the mother's desire, which is toyed with in the secrecy of fantasy. This fascination is inversely proportional to the terror that overcomes the obsessional when considering the magnitude of the father's vengeance for having taken (imaginarily) his place in the mother's desire and for having indulged in death wishes and aggressive intentions against him. This is why obsessionals often depict their fathers as violent men.

The obsessional is aware of the prohibition against incest, and will transgress only imaginarily and with feelings of guilt and anxiety that are dealt with by forcing desire for the mother through rituals and compulsions whose repressed and hidden connection with the fantasy can only be unveiled in analysis. Thus, unable to break away from the mother and fearing the father's wrath, the obsessional strives to *make desire impossible*—the desire which realizes, through fantasy, incest with the mother. To make desire impossible—both the obsessional's and the Other's, since they are confused in the imaginary—is the unconscious motive which conditions all of life for that subject. Guilty in the eyes of the Law, anguished due to the prohibition of desire, the obsessional gives up desire by giving up genitality, says Freud, by regressing to the anal stage. In the best of cases, this solution explains the production of certain workers who, while constantly struggling with their mother's desire, manage to become good citizens who dedicate themselves to producing for society (which represents the Father), and who gain, through a form of sublimation, a recognition that satisfies them and compensates for giving up their own desire.

However, the neurotic who consults an analyst is at an impasse. Because the neurotic has found no way to respond to the Other's demand in the social sphere, a conflict is harbored between the parental demand

and the stifled expression of a forbidden desire. This is the conflict staged by the symptoms: guilt, anguish, fear, isolation, obsessional rituals, and compulsive actions. In neurosis, symptoms are the deadly reversal on the body of the energy of the drive, the jouissance striving for satisfaction in the body when the conflict between demand and desire cannot be resolved in favor of the latter.

Perverse Features in the Obsessional's Family and the Acting Out of Fantasy

When the analysis of men who suffer from obsessional neurosis reveals features of perversion in the family, we see, on one hand, that the symptoms specifically related to the neurosis, including social isolation, are worsened due to an acting out of the fantasy. Indeed, when a weakness of the symbolic phallus is combined with a possible transgression by the mother, in real life, of the Law prohibiting incest, it seems that the neurotic pathology gets complicated by the idea that an actualization of the seduction fantasy could provide, in organ pleasure, the satisfaction expected from life, where the sublimation of desire has failed. Such, for example, were the extravagant hopes of Mr. Beauregard in leaving everything "to live his homosexuality." What aspect does this take in the analysis? Mr. Beauregard remembers:

> One afternoon, when I was five, I went into the bathroom. My mother was undressing. She made a motion as if to cover herself, let out a little cry, and then continued to undress without asking me to leave the room. I think this happened a few times and then, one day, she told me to stop coming in the bathroom when she was undressing. But as she usually left the door ajar, I kept peering at her. I think that she knew I was doing it and that it excited her.

Another event comes to his mind:

> I must have been three or four. My mother was taking a shower. I was seated on the toilet, trying to defecate. I touched my anus and felt pleasant sensations. She began to dry herself, with her back to me. I got hold of my glasses to play in my rectum. When she turned around, I think she guessed what I was doing. She said nothing.

In the first memory, the child becomes aware that the body of his mother is accessible to his eyes in reality and that she gains a drive satisfaction, a jouissance in the real of her body which she indulges in, in her ambiguous relation to her young son. Here, we are not anymore in the realm of desire: it is his mother's jouissance that Mr. Beauregard approaches. This is why, after being startled and having had a reaction of modesty, she then allows his look as she undresses—as if acknowledging that "it excited her" and that this jouissance was so intense it overcame the prohibition she would have had to enforce. As for the second memory, one must question the silence of the mother about her son's gesture: how, after all, can a mother let her son insert the shaft of his eyeglasses into his rectum without warning him against the danger of such an action? In saying nothing, she reveals her ravishment for something that blinds and silences her: the sexual excitement she has caused in her son. This is confirmed by Mr. Beauregard when he says: "I felt there was a complicity between us, she was secretly talking to me, I was always afraid that my father would appear." Through her gestures, her looks, her silences, and her abstention, the perverse-featured mother has let her obsessional son suppose that an incestuous acting-out was possible, that the prohibition could be transgressed, that jouissance from the body of the mother was not impossible.

These scenes provide the basis for the forming of Mr. Beauregard's seduction fantasy, which could read: *A child takes his eyeglasses to more clearly look at his rectum, where he feels the excitement caused by his mother.* It could yield the following fantasy formulation: *The rectum of a child is excited by the mother's look* and the following imaginary about the mother's jouissance: *a mother takes jouissance from knowing that her son watches her nudity from behind.* From his rectum to the smooth buttocks of his mother which he watched through the door left ajar, to the asexual buttocks of young boys at summer camp, his fantasy evolves until it "materializes," to use his word, in its disguised version where his sexual drive is triggered by the sight of young adult men's buttocks. The scenario then stages a key element of his memories: the gaze. From his mother's look on his sexual excitement to his own look at her nudity, he has eroticized both *rectum* and *the look.* When Mr. Beauregard analyses his compulsive habit of masturbating while looking at gay magazines or sitting alone in bars, he calls himself a voyeur since he gets excited by looking at men's buttocks and concludes with a sense of humor: "It's funny, I have long believed that it was the buttocks and not the penis one had to hide to be decent." At a younger age, not only had his own buttocks, his rectum, been eroticized, but they were also marked by a forbidden jouissance through his mother's silence. In the seduction fantasy, the subject becomes the object of the imaginary Other's desire; as for Mr. Beauregard, his sexual practices with men take the form of the first memory with his mother.

In short, by implying a refusal of the phallus as signifier for lack and a denial of castration by the Law of language, the perverse features on the parent's side unsettle the symbolic function of the Father. A putting into question of that function then follows, both as the force that imposes the prohibition against incest and parricide, and as the assumption of the impossible under the phallic signifier.

As we see, the acting-out of the fantasy at a mature age, under the guise of overt homosexuality, doesn't make the obsessional a pervert. Mr. Beauregard's feeling of guilt testifies to that. In the nostalgic quest for satisfaction outlined by the mother in the proximity of her body, it is the very glimpse at the possibility of an incestuous act with her that interferes with the obsessional's desiring relationships with any other. The Other's desire, in a relationship based on true words or in a sexual intercourse supported by desire, yields feelings of anxiety and guilt, which are increased tenfold by the close proximity of the forbidden jouissance, resulting from the subject's relation to the mother.

With the mother of his own children, Mr. Beauregard had settled that question. By telling her of his fantasies about men, he also told her that he did not desire her, but rather wanted children. Later, with his boyfriend, things were different. Due to the framework established by Mr. Beauregard's fantasy (from his mother to young men), sexual intercourse with his boyfriend—something that was not supposed to be merely occasional, but rather something that was supposed to be part of a daily relation based on words and desire—collapsed, "rotted," under the imaginary of an incestuous act with his mother. This panic caused by the prohibition clearly describes Mr. Beauregard as a neurotic. The pervert, by contrast, would enjoy the scene staged in the contract with the partner, a scene in which, desire being entirely excluded, it would be crude drive that was pursued, without any guilt or anxiety, in the relation to jouissance and death. Basing the relation to others on the Law of nature, the pervert excludes desire by demonstrating the absurdity of the prohibition based on the laws of language, which have no foundation. However, if the laws formulated by men and society are arbitrary, the symbolic castration that they repress remains unavoidable for any speaking subject, whatever the pervert might say to deny it.

For Mr. Beauregard, living with a man implied that sexual satisfaction was at the heart of this cohabitation, since children could no longer be used as a pretext to refuse sex. But the unconscious link with his mother made this project unfeasible: his lover, the object causing his desire, was confused with the partner of a forbidden jouissance. In that context, the drive is at an impasse. Unable to find a solution in fantasy or in social production through creation, the drive is reversed: on Mr. Beauregard's thoughts through obsessive ideas that consume his energy, on his behavior through compulsions that take up his time, and on his body. The genital herpes caught in the men's room is a sign of self-punishment, something frequent among obsessionals. And this symptom also has a secondary benefit: having caught contagious herpes, Mr. Beauregard need no longer justify his refusal to have sex with his boyfriend.

Passage From Seduction to Castration and the Ethical Act of the Obsessional's Analysis

The pervert extols the supremacy of nature and the logic of organs over the phallic function and the logic of the signifier, which the pervert equates with garbage and works to expose as false and arbitrary in order to demonstrate their uselessness. Since words cannot say everything, reasons the pervert, doesn't the essential lie in the act and the acting out of the drive? In imagination, the obsessional has been formed as the mother's phallus; for this subject, the mother has also, in discrete gestures or manifest actions, maintained the illusion of a complicity in satisfaction, a satisfaction which would set the father aside and avoid castration. It is therefore very difficult for the obsessional to enter the castration problematics during analytic treatment. The mother has promised so much that the obsessional simply cannot abandon the hope of one day finding this "lost paradise." It is as if, despite a hatred he discovers for the mother (whom the obsessional blames for many of his own setbacks), the obsessional could not separate from the jouissance glimpsed within her. The acknowledgment of the fact that there is no Other, which should bring down the fantasy of seduction that was repressing the symbolic castration by language, is not enough to make the obsessional relinquish the maternal Other and stop surrendering imaginarily to a desire full of a forbidden jouissance whose spell can be measured by the intensity of the anxiety it causes.

To assume, alone, "the irreparable," the devastating effect of the signifier on biological logic—without expecting anything from the Other—in order to enter into a relation with others on the sole basis of one's desire, such is the step that the obsessional will have to take. Difficult and pained is this ethical choice which conditions the end of the analysis for the obsessional, to whom the acting-out of the fantasy was offered as solution. It amounts to leaving everything to board a ship with only the blue emptiness of the horizon as a future, and with only those that desire and chance will put across one's path for companions.

Notes

1. Jacques Lacan, *Écrits: A Selection*, trans. Alan Sheridan (New York: W. W. Norton and Co., 1977), 306. Original edition (Paris: Éditions du Seuil, 1966), 808.

2. ——, *Écrits: A Selection*, trans. Alan Sheridan (New York: W. W. Norton and Co., 1977), 306. Original edition (Paris: Éditions du Seuil, 1966), 808.

3. ——, *Écrits: A Selection*, trans. Alan Sheridan (New York: W. W. Norton and Co., 1977), 319. Original edition (Paris: Éditions du Seuil, 1966), 822.

4. ——, *The Seminar of Jacques Lacan, Book VII: The Ethics of Psychoanalysis*, trans. Dennis Porter (New York: W. W. Norton and Co., 1992), 317. Original edition (Paris: Éditions du Seuil, 1986), 366.

5. ——, *Écrits: A Selection*, trans. Alan Sheridan (New York: W. W. Norton and Co., 1977), 311. Original edition (Paris: Éditions du Seuil, 1966), 814.

Chapter 10

Perversion and Hysteria

LUCIE CANTIN

There are two ways to approach perversion: through the clinical or subjective experience, or through the writings and cultural works of perverts
who have marked history with their singular contribution to philosophy,
literature, and the arts in general. The study of these texts seems essential since it broadens the perspective on perversion by displacing it out
of the narrow field of sexual deviation or psychopathology to which it
has too easily been reduced and confined. In such writings, one can dis-
cern what is really at stake in what might be called "the politics of perversion." They also attest to the necessity of establishing a radical
distinction between structure and illness.

Moreover, whereas perverts don't easily enter into analysis unless
they have met with serious obstacles in maintaining the solution they
have devised, the patient populations of hospitals and public institutions
sometimes include perverts whom psychiatry, diagnosing from the phenomenology of apparent symptoms, has been treating as psychotics or
else as "personality disorders." In such cases, the distinction between
phenomenology and structure becomes essential to dissipate the diagnostic confusion not only between psychosis and perversion, but also between a perverse structure and the mere acting-out of perverse fantasies
by neurotics—a topic already visited in chapter 9 with regard to obsessional neurosis. The present chapter explores a certain structural complicity between perversion and hysterical neurosis.

This material was presented, in different form, at the 8th Annual Interdisciplinary Conference of the International Federation for Psychoanalytic Education, on The Future of
Psychoanalysis and Psychoanalytic Education, Ann Arbor, Michigan, October 1997.

The Choice and Solution of the Subject in Perversion: Jouissance, Signifier, and the Other

A number of elements delineate the perverse solution as the pervert makes certain subjective choices in relation to jouissance, the logic of the signifier, and the Other. First in relation to jouissance, that is to the real of the death drive, which Freud defined as the free energy of the drive produced by the effect of the signifier in the subject's relation to the Other, the pervert's position consists in *denying* the effect of the signifier as the source of the drive. The perverse denial seeks to equate the energy of the drive with that of the organism or the instinct, and thus to reduce the effect of the signifier to the logic of the organ. Hence, perversion maintains the treatment of the drive outside of the relation to the Other; the Other (and the signifiers of the desire of the Other) efface themselves in favor of the features that the Other bears and that are all constituted as possible objects offered to the drive. What matters is not so much the fact that the drive is confused with the instinct. Freud defines perversion in terms of the signifier's diversion of goal and object from the logic of the organism, a diversion which forms and produces the erogenous body by electing and parceling it out in a series of pieces. In perversion, this process is not only recognized, but also overinvested, exploited, and even pushed to its limit; one thinks, by way of example, of the fetishized object. What matters is rather the fact that the subject's way of handling the drive reveals the pervert's will to obscure the logic of the drive's functioning by imposing the logic of instinct, in an attempt to veil—or maintain the veil on—the necessary submission and articulation of the subject to the Law of the Other's desire. This denial, which Freud considered central to the perverse position, implies a twofold movement—a simultaneous affirmation and denial. Indeed the affirmation is essential to making the denial possible. This fact is confirmed in many ways in clinical practice, where the pervert's attempt to deny any articulation of the subject's desire to the Other's desire demonstrates in fact a constant reaffirmation of the pervert's position precisely as a captive object of the law of the Mother's desire, where the pervert remains.

A second determining factor of the perverse solution concerns the position of the subject in relation to the *empire of the signifier*, where the effects of language create the symbolic human universe and the effects of speech articulate the relation of the subject to the Other. The perverse subject has a particular knowledge, a *savoir*, about the arbitrary dimension and ungroundedness of the symbolic. This *savoir* is attested by the pervert's relation to the Father, to the Father's function, whose role is precisely to introduce and represent the symbolic dimension for the child. The pervert questions the necessity of the Father myth and seeks to demonstrate its uselessness. Here again the double movement of denial is essential, since the Father, the signifier of the Name-of-the Father, must first be *stated* in order for the subject to then be able to neutralize, devaluate, and "make nothing" of it. On this ground, as will be seen, the pervert invites the hysterical subject's fascination, since the hysteric is caught up in the contestation of the signifier's authority and the elusive quest for a word, a signifier of love coming from the Father.

Perhaps more essentially than this position in relation to the Father, the relation of the pervert to the signifier radically concerns the effect of the signifier on what is at stake in *speech*; that is, it bears upon what speech, and therefore the address, establish as an inevitably political *relation to the Other*, who (as discussed in chap. 2) is constituted by that very address and given the power of refusal and abuse in the subject's very demand. The relation to the Other is unavoidable for human beings, since the subject is caught up in it even prior to birth; for beings subjected to speech, it accounts for the primacy of the law and of the logic of the signifier over the law of nature and over the logic of organs and instinct. In attempting to refuse the split from the order of nature, the pervert targets precisely the relation to the Other, the stage for the inevitable encounter with castration.

The third determining element of the choice of the perverse subject, then, might be called the "eradication of desire." In fact, what must be bypassed here is still the submission of the subject to the signifier of the Other, but in the specific field of desire. The goal is to eradicate desire inasmuch as desire is always for human beings "the desire of the Other's desire,"[1] articulated to the signifiers of the Other's desire, which it seeks more than any satisfaction. In the staging of the "contract" binding the perverse subject to a partner, this eradication appears in its stereotypical aspect. One might think, for example, of the Sacher-Masoch contract which will be discussed more fully in the next chapter. The implicit or explicit contract immediately states, with infallible precision, the framework of the relation to the other, the positions of each partner, and the rules of the game, while perfectly delimiting the realm of the possible as well as whatever would terminate the contract. In short, once it has been stated or even signed, the contract becomes the very mode of evacuation of the Other, since the contract suppresses the need to go through demand (demand *of* the other and demand *to* the other) and since it determines in advance the effacement of desire. The scenario defined by the contract and staged in reality demonstrates that the Other is reduced to the features it supports and to the role it is given. This strategy corresponds to what we previously referred to as the subject's handling of the drive, one which attempts to escape the effects of the signifier of the Other, and function instead according to an organic logic of a mechanical action—reaction type. The scenario's formula is determined and reducible to the features, pieces or partial objects that the other, the partner, offers. In fact, the "staging in reality" dimension is crucial, since it is also the mode which maintains the ignorance of the subject concerning the overdetermination and control of this staging *by* the Other, who is absent from the scene but to whom it is nevertheless addressed. This absent Other, who nevertheless witnesses the scene, is most often the imaginary position of the untouched, untouchable—uncastrated, Freud would say—Mother. Thus, the staging of the scene by which the subject attempts to avoid the Other's desire is determined through and through by what has been put in place for the subject in relation to the maternal Other, to whose desire the pervert remains attached and devoted, as a slave to a master. This uncastrated Other's position is in fact *included* in the scenario which, by conserving this archaic and imaginary figure of an Other, who has escaped castration, maintains the subject's pretense of having escaped his or her own castration.

Whether it is by the "cultivated" confusion of the drive with the instincts, the veiling of the effects of the signifier under the logic of the organs, the demonstration of the uselessness of the Father, or the eradication of desire, the logic of the subject's endeavor in perversion always leads to the same point: the relation of the subject to the effects of the signifier or to the Other's desire, but inasmuch as in that relation, the subject is reduced to a *submission* to the effects of the signifier. One might faithfully follow Freud by saying that perversion is essentially concerned with the denial of castration, if, as Lacan would say, castration is truly the result of the effects of the signifier in the speaking subject. Lacan defines the phallus not only as the signifier of "the whole of the effects of the signifier" (as constitutive of the signified as such), but also as "the signifier of the desire of the Other," or again as "the signifier of lack."[2] Through perversion, in its diverse modalities of questioning the effects of the signifier, one can see how thoroughgoing indeed are the interrelations of lack, the desire of the Other, and the effects of the signifier. The "denial of castration," as Freud calls it, can just as well be described as the denial of the phallus and the phallic effects.

The Clinical Experience of Perversion: The Case of Mr. Buckold

Clinical practice, inasmuch as it tends to concern perverts for whom the denial of the phallus and castration has met the conditions of its failure as a solution, allows one to see the framework, the historical ele-

ments, and the subjective position that have determined the perverse solution and that have conditioned its setting up and failure. The case of
Mr. Buckold should help outline the main elements determining the
structure of perversion as experienced in clinical practice.

The pervert tends to claim a central and particular relationship to the
mother, a relation of complicity that supports the setting aside of the father's desire in the maternal universe. It is in fact a genuine contract that
binds the subject to the mother, and it has a double import. Under its
terms, the subject is first bound to the jouissance and/or suffering of the
mother, to her will, to her *bon plaisir* (jouissance is taken here in its
clearer legal sense, where it in fact concerns a power of use and abuse).
Whereas the psychotic is in the position of an object handed to the
Other's jouissance, the pervert is linked to the Mother's jouissance, but
not without complicity, not without a tacit consent or an active, albeit
unconscious, participation which leaves the pervert in the position of a
subject. This mother-child contract conspires to stage and demonstrate
the uselessness of the paternal phallus for the mother. There is another
important distinction to be made between perversion and psychosis. In
perversion, the Father, its function and authority, is well-established and
stated, and then, in a staged production, is invalidated, devaluated, reduced to nothing. This double movement, whereby, for example, a certain discourse takes place and is then invalidated by actions, or by a
scene that signifies the opposite of what was said, is very often how the
pervert radically experiences the defect of the signifier. The pervert is all
too acutely aware that the signifier of the Name-of-the-Father is based
on nothing and that the Law of the symbolic it represents is riddled with
holes, since the subject *experiences* a possible way to avoid castration
through the link with jouissance, which secretly unites the pervert with
the mother, outside of the sanctioned realm of the social link.

Mr. Buckold tells his analyst: "There was only my mother in the couple. My father was a weak man. He had failed in his career as a professional singer. He was going out with another woman while my mother
was sick and my mother was lacing his food with sleeping pills to keep
him at home." He brings the following dream to his analysis:

> A two-year-old child is running all over the place; his mother buck-
> les him [*l'attache*] into a harness.

These words and this dream account for the link that exists between
Buckold and his mother, for his servile "attachment." Ten years younger
than his only sister, young Buckold is *the* mother's child. She confides in
him and tells him details of her intimate life; she takes him everywhere,

keeps him with her at an age when he should go to school. Once he asked his mother why he was not going to the school; Mr. Buckold still remembers her answer: "Because you are different from the others." These are not uncomfortable memories, but they confirm his privileged status. When he came home from school one day at the age of nine, she told him she had sclerosis. From that moment and until she died nine years later, he lived as a recluse, staying at home, caring for his mother, with school as his only social life. In fact, the description he gives of that period of his life is quite typical. On the one hand, he trivially describes his relationship with his mother who complains to him about her marital dissatisfactions, demands his help getting dressed, and talks disdainfully about his father's penis; on the other hand, he is full of reproach, contempt, and hatred for his egoistic and cowardly father, an unfaithful husband and a torturer, who is to blame for the illness and unhappiness of his mother, who is herself a victim he alone can console and support.

Mr. Buckold cannot see what is so obvious for the analyst who listens, namely, that his deprecating discourse about his father is somehow directed from an other place, that it is not his complaint, but rather that of his mother speaking through him. Buckold nevertheless has made her complaint his own and has adopted the position of a witness who fully adheres to this story, in which his mother is the victim of a heartless torturer. Buckold has also become an accomplice in the maternal attempt to retaliate and undermine the paternal phallus, and has somehow complied with the tacit contract that binds him to his mother and of which he bears the brunt without knowing it. The position in which he complies with the scenario that is tacitly dictated by the contract was to take grotesque and tragic proportions in what Mr. Buckold calls his "attempted parricide." Here are his words:

> The idea to kill my father came to me when I was about ten, while we were swimming together. The day after, I asked for my mother's permission; I said: "Do you want me to kill him?" She told me: "Don't do that," but she never said why. I had a plan, I wanted to drown him.

Many years later, Mr. Buckold, now an adult, was to act this out in an "attempted parricide." His mother had died one year earlier, and his father had long suffered from cardiopulmonary weakness and was very ill. Mr. Buckold himself had been psychologically ill for some time.

> As it seemed my father would live forever, I thought to myself "Is there a way to kill him?" I pondered my plan for several months: I

was going to take the barbiturates I had saved since my mother's death and dump them in his food. The day I decided to do it, I put the pills in my father's teacup and then took them out again right away. I will tell you something that I never told anyone. I behaved as if I had left the barbiturates in the tea, but I knew that I had not done it, that I had only done it in my rehearsals. I always knew that. But I set out and went to the hospital, continuing to claim that I had killed my father by poisoning his food.

I wanted to be interned for my intent, because it was now certain that he was going to die. My father did not lodge any complaint when he heard about it, but I was not allowed to see him or to call him. I never saw him again. It has been in my head ever since. I am telling it for the first time, and I say it very coldly—I feel completely insensitive.

Mr. Buckold's plan tragically illustrates what is fundamentally at stake in the devaluation of the paternal phallus central to perversion. In this case, the devaluation is fully staged as a parricide scene which is commanded in the unconscious of the subject and by the maternal Other's discourse. As a child, young Buckold asked his mother if she wanted him to kill his father and she answered him only trivially. The fact that the question is *thinkable*, that it is actually asked to the mother and that she answered it, thus granting, it the status of a *possibility*, reveals how the acting-out, its staging ten years later, was complying with a prescription of the maternal Other as it was formed in the child's unconscious.

Mr. Buckold has in fact been ill since the age of 18; his mother died at that time. But the event he regards as the cause of his illness is not in fact his mother's death, but rather the realization that his mother deprived him of his adolescence. A year before she died, the adolescent Buckold started having friends and wished to go out more often. At this, he says, mother told him that he was "more and more becoming like *him*," referring, of course, to his father. For his mother, Buckold was becoming like his father and was thus perturbing the balance of the contract binding him to her for the devaluation of the paternal figure, to which she was now conflating the adolescent Buckold.

A few years later, Mr. Buckold was hospitalized, for the first time, for a serious nervous breakdown that followed the collapse of a love relationship he couldn't get over. For eight months, Mr. Buckold remained in the hospital, where he received a series of treatments, including several sessions of electrotherapy, all of which proved ineffective. Since then, Mr. Buckold has been unable to get on with his life and has been hospitalized about ten more times at ever more frequent intervals since that first "fall." It is in this context that he began his analysis.

Mr. Buckold's breakdown was occasioned not simply by a romantic split, but also by the restaging in his adult life of the scenario that had determined his subjective position. Mr. Buckold was in a masochist position. He describes himself as "dependent" on the woman with whom he had been living and who was constantly "bickering" and had violent fits when he answered. She not only engaged in affairs with other men, but told him about her exploits while at the same time demanding his continued fidelity. Mr. Buckold said a curious thing in the analysis, which clearly suggests how his apparently masochistic position nevertheless left the other with the impression that *he* controlled the situation: "She was jealous of the things that were not happening because I was faithful." This woman was Mr. Buckold's partner in a new alliance that was replicating the exact same scenario from his boyhood, except that now he was the *agent*, whereas before, with his mother, he had only been the conniving and willing *witness*. In this new contract, Mr. Buckold was masochistically both taking up the role of the victim previously played by his *mother* and restaging, in his own role of the scorned husband who is tortured by the sexual exploits of his unfaithful wife, the position of his scorned *father*. The way the reproduction of the devaluation of the father was restaged (the father was cuckolded) is obviously not trivial, since the mother had always complained about the unfaithfulness of her husband who, according to Mr. Buckold, had a mistress. It is important to emphasize the staging dimension which is a determining factor here. Indeed, one can't understand what was at stake in this relationship for Mr. Buckold if one does not literally take him off the stage where the actors play their role. As a subject, Mr. Buckold is excluded from that stage. Instead, he is directing the production, which is itself programmed from elsewhere by an absent Other, the Mother, the invisible witness for whom the scene is meant and whom it serves to avenge. Mr. Buckold's masochist position testifies to his devotion for his mother, whom he continued to serve even after her death.

The Hysteric with the Pervert

For present purposes, one might describe the structure of hysteria by first saying that the hysterical subject struggles with maternal demand. In one way or another, the hysteric is confronted with what has been interpreted as a maternal dissatisfaction and complaint, which have not been referred to *lack*, to the inevitable castration that the mother experiences like any human being, but which instead refer to the failure and insufficiency of the paternal phallus. But contrary to what is found in perversion, the mother has *not* staged, from the viewpoint of the hysterical subject, the *denial* of her articulation to the signifier of the father's desire; the mother's complaint instead bears on her unsatisfied demand for a signifier of the father's love that would put to an end the jouissance (death drive) at work in her. Thus, the hysteric is in turn addressed and mobilized by the mother's unsatisfied demand to which the subject tries to respond. In that context, the hysteric's "response" can only be an effort to consolidate the father, a quest for the phallic ideal or the Master, whose double purpose is to satisfy the mother while repairing the inadequacy of the father. Such is obviously the role taken by the pervert, who is always in the position of the master offering the solution of this double injunction of the hysteric's superego.

But more fundamentally, this structure reveals a number of the problems that the hysteric faces. There is first the problem of abandoning a perspective where lack and castration are attributable to someone. This is where the accusation of the Other in hysteria and the victim's stance (in which the hysteric finds a way to justify the reproduction of the maternal complaint, in the relation to the other) find both their logic and their impasse. There is also the problem of the unending quest for the father's signifier of love, that the hysteric still vainly expects, an identificatory signifier which would both constitute the hysteric as the object of the Other's desire as well as rescue the subject from the empire of the maternal realm. In the hysteric's unconscious, the father is insufficient, and efforts to consolidate him serve to repress and hide the fact that the problem is not due to the failure of any particular father, but rather to the inadequacy and the defect of the signifier itself regarding the work of the death drive. In short, the hysteric represses castration by giving to the Other of the unconscious a real consistency through an other who, in real life, is made accountable. Whether it involves an Other to be *seduced* who will allow the hysteric to constitute him- or herself as the object of the Other's desire and love, or an Other to *accuse* when the aim is to repress the lack of the Other as the subject's own, the "presence" of a responsible Other is the very mode under which the hysteric avoids and represses castration.

It is then clear that the pervert who offers to be the Master takes the place of this Other who will make it possible for the hysteric to avoid castration. The pervert takes on responsibility for the jouissance at work in the hysteric (such as that from the hysteric's mother), by promising a total satisfaction and the occlusion of any encounter with lack. The pervert offers to be the phallic ideal in the place of a weak father and thus, embodying the Father-Master, the pervert supports and maintains in the hysteric the misunderstanding which uses the father's failure to hide the lack and the defect of the signifier as such.

The pervert's effort to erase the signifier's castrating effects (those achieved through the diversion of the organic functioning in the constitution of the body) obeys the same logic as the subject's handling of the drive outside of the primacy of the phallus, where the drive's multiplicity governs and maintains the lack of differentiation of the object. This effort to deconstruct the phallic effect ends up being an effort to deconstruct the body that the signifier has snatched away from a logic and jouissance of the organ and that the signifier of the Other's desire has unified. Finally, the aim is always to deny castration, the prototype of which is the submission of the subject's desire to the signifier of the Other's desire. This effort by the pervert finds an echo in the hysteric. When ill, the hysteric is often struggling in the body with the faulty establishment of the phallic effects. Moreover, the hysteric is left to the workings of the death drive which capture the body through symptoms whose multiplicity precisely accounts for the fragmentation of the body submitted to the random movement of the free energy of the drive. It is as if the faulty establishment of the (father's) phallus were indicated by the absence of a signifier for the desire which could have organized the fate of the drive, and tied up its energy around an object supporting and articulating itself to the signifier of the Other's desire. The pervert also offers an economical solution to the hysteric searching for the signifier which would make of the hysteric the object of the Other's desire. From the viewpoint of the hysteric, the hysteric is somehow "consecrated" by the pervert as the object of desire. But in fact, the pervert supports the treatment of the drive outside of the phallic effects by proposing to the hysteric a limitation in the real instead of a limitation through the signifier. The pervert offers to be the master in order to force the disorganized work of the drive, something accomplished by working on the body until the jouissance of the organ is summoned to propose a limit in the real.

The inadequacy of the signifier which the hysteric encounters and must keep repressed in an attempt to avoid castration accounts for the hysteric's relation to the frailty of the signifier. The experience of an overwhelming jouissance, which is not stopped by the signifier, finds an economical solution in the pervert—a solution which, however, always fails and tends to prove catastrophic. The perverse promise is always sooner or later exposed, because it feeds instead the disorganized workings of the drive which is maintained outside of the only place (the realm of the signifier) where it could find calm. The perverse promise reinforces the dissatisfaction attributed to the Other and keeps alive the accusation, even if there is nearly always a misunderstanding as to the identity of the accused. Even so, this misunderstanding is supported for a time and somehow responds to the hysteric's attempt to avoid castration, by reducing the stakes of desire and of the lack that causes it in the universe of the drive, where the illusion of a possible object is maintained.

Notes

1. Jacques Lacan, *Écrits: A Selection*, trans. Alan Sheridan (New York: W. W. Norton and Co., 1977), 312. Original edition (Paris: Éditions du Seuil, 1966), 814.

2. Definitions of the phallus appear throughout Lacan's seminars. These are derived from "The Signification of the Phallus." Jacques Lacan, *Écrits: A Selection*, trans. Alan Sheridan (New York: W. W. Norton and Co., 1977), 285, and 290. Original edition (Paris: Éditions du Seuil, 1966), 690, and 694.

Chapter 11

The Fate of Jouissance in the Pervert-Hysteric Couple

LUCIE CANTIN

The Drive as an Effect of Language

A woman under analysis had long complained of her frigidity. One day, she related with both astonishment and anxiety that she had experienced "jouissance" while reading a seemingly banal passage from a book she had casually plucked from a friend's library. In her powerful bodily response to mere words on a page, one can see how in human beings, something in the language- and word-based relationship of the subject to the Other mobilizes an energy that follows not the laws of nature, but instead a logic of the signifier. Freud was right to describe the death drive as an unbounded, unmarked, and unchanneled energy, unrestricted by an economics of satisfaction and pleasure. With the drive, one is no longer in the realm of the instincts. Rather, the drive is introduced by the Other and responds to the signifier. This is what Lacan wanted to stress when he formalized the matheme of the drive ($\$ \Diamond D$) as, precisely, the response of the subject to the Demand of the Other.[1]

In fact it is the drive which shows most clearly that the Other is primarily language itself, the result of the signifier whose effect and defect mark the subject's body and history and mobilize a new energy, which

This material was presented, in different form, on a panel called "Jouissance: The Roots of Violence," at the Third Annual Conference of the Association for the Psychoanalysis of Culture and Society, on the theme of Aggressivity and Violence, George Washington University, Washington DC, November 1997.

is no longer oriented around the conservation and survival of the living organism (or species) per se. The literal other, who in reality embodies the effects of the signifier, also bears the stakes of speech and the dimension of address therein. The relationship of the subject to the Other is initiated by this encounter. The subject's interpretation of the Other's request (or demand) solicits a response from the subject. Thus, the drive is an effect of the signifier, the effect of the real, resulting from the defect of language; but it is spontaneously processed in the realm of the *response* to the Other, where drive finds its axis and perhaps even the illusion of a possible object.

The signifiers of the Other's discourse not only divert the body from a logic of the organ, but also parcel it up into the pieces that collectively compose the psychoanalytic body as such. These selected pieces, invested and animated by an energy that is the effect of the Other, produce the body as a nexus of drive multiplicities (*multiplicités pulsionelles*) which function autonomously as traces left by the encounter with the Other. It is here that the free energy of the death drive described by Freud takes its full meaning. The energy is at once free, that is, unbound, separated from the logic of the organism, but it also remains unchanneled and can therefore circulate freely. One must therefore ask what happens to this unbridled energy of the drive, which is still nothing other than the death drive. The drive takes its source in the letter and the mark of the body, which are the effects of the signifier. From the moment the energy is released, the drive's aim becomes to link up that free energy with an object, which can be anything, according to Freud, so far as it links up and channels the energy by offering it the imaginary of an illusory object.

Seduction as Refuge From Castration: The Letter of the Body, the Insufficiency of the Signifier

Clinical practice shows that, whereas the drive is produced by the signifier and by the encounter with the Other and its defect, it is also in the field regulated by the logic of the signifier that the drive finds paths other than the symptom, the *acte manqué* or the "passage to the act." In other words, drive can find there (in the realm of the signifier) an aim other than the one which closes itself on the letter of the body or inscribes itself in the outside of the relation to the other. In the history of the body's formation, it is the signifier of the Other's desire that makes possible the regrouping of the drive multiplicities and their ordering, by allowing for the building up of the body image, of the *ego* as the imaginary of the object offered to the Other's desire.

Thus, the hysteric is precisely someone for whom the signifier of the Other—the signifier of the Father's desire—has been insufficient to allow the subject to assume a position as a possible object of desire. Hence, the endless, hysterical appeal addressed to the Other, for points of reference that would allow the subject to measure and construct an ego *as* an object of desire. The hysteric is essentially caught up in the seduction—a solution destined to fail, because whereas the hysteric is in quest of a *signifier*, it is in the realm of the *letter of the body* that the hysteric stands, waiting for the response. The signifier of the Other will always be insufficient, baseless, and devoid of the guaranteed truth that the letter of the body would offer. Incapable of trusting the signifier, the hysteric lays in wait for the letter of the body where the word of the other is based and verified, the letter of the body being *that without which the signifier remains unbelievable.*[2] It is as if each time, the hysteric has to constitute—and verify—the adequation of ego and body image with the object of the other's fantasy. In this operation, the idea of verification is central. The other doesn't give anything; the other is seduced and offers, in a consent more or less extracted, the manifest proof of imaginary irresistibility which consolidates the identification of the subject with the object that causes the other's desire. One can also view in that same logic the importance for the hysteric of maintaining a lack of satisfaction in the other, something Lacan calls the "hysteric's desire for an unsatisfied desire." It is as if the tension maintained in the other could give visibility to the real of the letter of the body, a letter written by the desire of the other, in which the imaginary adequation of the ego to the object of desire is suspended and maintained. The relation of the hysterical subject to another woman reveals that essentially narcissistic goal: the other woman, who is either an object of admiration or hatred, of love or envy, is the standard against which the ideal object is measured in the imaginary.

What is primarily at stake for the hysteric in fact appears *outside of* the realm of the Other and the signifier of the desire of the Other, and is rather caught up in the quest for an object of imaginary identification which would support the illusion of a possible object for the drive. It is the very access to desire and the impossibility of its object, which must be repressed as well as its wandering form, and thereby also the void and subject's solitude that the desire opens up.

Thus, the hysteric seems to be subjected to a passionate confusion of the ego and the object of the Other's fantasy. It is undoubtedly there that one must situate the trial of identification in the hysteric, a proceeding which always takes a somewhat paranoid dimension. The inevitable failure of the hysteric's attempt at seduction logically leads to accusations against the other, whose victim the hysteric then becomes. In the way the failure is processed, in the accusation against the other which is the negative side of seduction, one sees what lies at the heart of the hysterical solution. To the last, even when the imaginary identification with the object of the other's desire becomes impossible and the illusion fails, the Other is maintained in place. The responsibility of the Other—literally the ability to respond—is maintained. The Other should have or could have, the Other did not want or else deceived: amid these accusations, the request addressed to the Other remains intact. One might say that the accusation becomes the desperate expression of the necessity of maintaining the Other. Thus, beyond the phenomenology of seduction or accusation, it is the very maintenance of the address to the Other which is central. The hysteric endlessly addresses the Father, whether in the form of an authority figure or in the form of an abusive, seductive, defaulting, weak, or despotic father. The Father thus addressed is the Other of neurosis, an Other who is asked to take charge of the drive's workings, who is *made accountable* for the unbridled and disorganizing jouissance which the hysteric attempts in vain to process in the realm of the imaginary and in the real of the letter of the body—without jumping into the void and losing the imaginary, as the hysteric would under the logic of the signifier.

When one reconsiders the hysteric's solution in the treatment of the drive—the quest for sensible proof, for the truth of sensation, for a basis for the Other's word in the real of the letter of the body, which is mobilized by that word, the maintenance of the dissatisfaction which gives the other substance and guarantees that the other is put to work, the passion that feeds the confusion of the ego and the object of the other's fantasy— one finds that all of these dynamics reveal a treatment of the drive that takes place *outside* the phallic effects and outside the realm of the Other of language. What the hysteric tries to occlude is the Other's desire, insofar as the hysteric is not the object causing it. But what this spontaneous solution organizes is the repression of the defect of the Other and the occultation of castration. Anxiety appears with the unveiling of the hysteric's self-delusion concerning the object of the other's desire or with the subject's awareness of the Other as incapable or unwilling to take charge of what is at work in the hysteric's body.

The hysteric has difficulty accessing desire. When faced with the Other's desire, the hysteric can no longer maintain the illusion of being the object of it and is then forced to rely—without guarantee or grounding—on the signifier. The encounter with the defect of language, with the gap of fundamental incompatibility introduced by the signifier between the word and the thing, leaves the drive orphaned and the ego without the imaginary landmarks which until then had marked out the construction of the identification. This is precisely what must then be repressed. The assumption of castration, beyond the collapse of the illusory possibility of an object for the drive and for desire, would force the hysteric to face the impossibility of appealing to the Other to process and take charge of the "thing" and the lack that are at work in the hysteric's body and being. What is in question here is the whole relationship of the hysteric to the loss and castration that result from the entrance into the logic of the signifier, in other words, from the hysteric's relation to the phallus. This relation lies hidden under what passes, in hysterics, for a resistance or a contestation of the arbitrary dimension of speech and of the signifier.

The Pervert's Response to the Hysteric

The pervert responds to the hysteric's call for an Other who would be accountable in the processing of jouissance, and promises the hysteric to do away with the necessity of encountering the defect of the Other. Whereas the hysteric's Other was constantly faltering and insufficient, the pervert *knows*. It is the perverse exemption from castration which is at stake in this mode of processing jouissance and which establishes a complicity between the pervert and the hysteric. And indeed the pervert responds in the realm of the letter by limiting the drive in the real of the body, beyond the phallic effects, where the castrating effects of the signifier's logic can be bypassed and considered useless.

The example of Sacher-Masoch and the woman who was his wife for ten years will serve as a basis for the analysis of the stakes which, in perverts, fascinates the hysteric and sustains the complicity of the hysteric with the pervert. Sacher-Masoch had already written *Venus in Furs* and was famous when he met his wife-to-be, Aurore Rümelin. This relationship, which started mysteriously through anonymous letters, led to a marital union and a genuine *contract* in which Aurore became "Wanda," the main character in *Venus,* whom she was to embody in reality. After a bitter divorce, Rümelin published her memoirs in a book entitled *Confessions of my Life,* under the penname Wanda von Sacher-Masoch. These confessions are structured as a real plea that has a double objective: to take revenge by giving her version of the story and some intimate details of her relation with Sacher-Masoch (thus attacking the reputation of a famous man) and to position herself as an innocent victim in a trial supporting an accusation against the other.

The Pervert and the Effects of the Signifier

We can certainly say that the pervert has a special relationship to the Law of the symbolic, to the order and the logic of the signifier. The pervert questions the necessity of the Father myth, and seeks to demonstrate its uselessness; the pervert also exhibits a particular knowledge, a "savoir" in relation to the arbitrary and baseless dimension of the symbolic universe that, as the pervert shows, produces its own truth. As for a relation to the signifier, the pervert's efforts seem, at first sight, to organize a revamping of the effects of the signifier on the body's "organ logic" with the aim of negating the break caused by language in the natural order and the logic of instincts. In fact, though, the perverse goal is rather more subtle than just this.

If one starts precisely from what fundamentally distinguishes the instincts from the drive, namely, that instincts are governed by organ logic whereas the drive essentially and strictly responds to the logic of the signifier, it becomes impossible to hold that, in perversion, the instincts and the drive are confused. The pervert knows better than anyone that the signifier diverts the logic of the organism from its goal and creates the body as a collection of pieces that are elected, invested, and parceled out from the organism. Indeed, in perversion, the effect of the signifier is exploited and pushed to its limit—for example, in the fetishized object. Thus, it is not the effect of the signifier that is negated in perversion, any more than the drive is reduced to the instincts—that would be a mistake a neurotic would make. Faced with anxiety resulting from an experience of the relative autonomy of the signifier and the drive, the neurotic attributes to *instinct* what is at work in the body against one's will, in order to deny responsibility and soothe guilt.

Thus, the pervert accentuates the effects of the signifier by triggering the drive; but at the same time—and this is what is primarily at stake— the treatment of the drive must essentially stay outside of the relation to the Other, as the Other, who, along with the signifier of desire of the Other, withdraws in favor of the features that the Other bears and that are all possible objects offered to the drive. This operation aims at negating the necessary articulation of the drive and desire to the Law and the signifier of the Other. These two stages are essential: first, to affirm of the effects of the signifier and, second, to take hold on these effects of the signifier in order to evacuate the Other and the hazards of the desire of the Other. Sacher-Masoch provides wonderful examples of this. As Gilles Deleuze emphasizes, "It would appear that both for Sade and for Masoch language reaches its full significance when it acts directly on the senses."[3] The pervert knows the power of words and knows that the drive responds to the signifier ruling over it. As Deleuze remarked, "In Masoch's life as well as in his fiction, love affairs are always set in motion by anonymous letters, by the use of pseudonyms or by advertisements in newspapers."[4] The other may be absent, but the words of the other—or rather what they evoke—suffice. Sacher-Masoch is attentively on the lookout, and offers himself to the effects of capture and jouissance caused by the signifier. Prior to their first meeting, in an early letter dated 23 December 1871, Leopold von Sacher-Masoch wrote to Rümelin, his future Wanda:

> I can only be in love with your letters and not with your charms. . . . I am in love with the way you are, with the way you talk of my *Venus in Furs*. I feel attracted by that. If I had the chance to find a woman who could embody this *Venus in Furs*, I could love her madly, I could become her slave.[5]

The hysteric dashes headlong in the belief that she is causing the pervert's desire, but she is deceived. On Sacher-Masoch's part, the anonymity of the letters is a caricature of the evacuation of the other, who is then reduced to the characteristics required to trigger the repetition of the scenario.

The Contract and the Eradication of the Other

While Sacher-Masoch's love is triggered by anonymous letters, it is afterward regulated by genuine, written and signed, *contracts*. The contract which bound Wanda and Sacher-Masoch is exemplary:

> *CONTRACT BETWEEN WANDA AND SACHER-MASOCH*
> My Slave,
>   The conditions under which I accept you as my slave and tolerate you at my side are as follows:
>   You shall renounce your identity completely. You shall submit totally to my will.
>   In my hands you are a blind instrument that carries out all my orders without discussion. If ever you should forget that you are my slave and do not obey me implicitly in all matters, I shall have the right to punish and correct you as I please, without your daring to complain.
>   Anything pleasant and enjoyable that I shall grant you will be a favor on my part which you must acknowledge with gratitude. I shall always behave faultlessly toward you but shall have no obligations to do so.
>   You shall be neither a son nor a brother nor a friend; you shall be no more than my slave groveling in the dust.
>   Your body and your soul, too, shall belong to me, and even if this causes you great suffering, you shall submit your feelings and sentiments to my authority.
>   I shall be allowed to exercise the greatest cruelty, and if I should mutilate you, you shall bear it without complaint. You shall work for

me like a slave and although I may wallow in luxury whilst leaving you in privation and treading you underfoot, you shall kiss the foot that tramples you without a murmur. I shall have the right to dismiss you at any time, but you shall not be allowed to leave me against my will, and if you should escape, you hereby recognize that I have the power and the right to torture you to death by the most horrible methods imaginable.

You have nothing save me; for you I am everything, your life, your future, your happiness, your unhappiness, your torment and your joy.

You shall carry out everything I ask of you, whether it is good or evil, and if I should demand that you commit a crime, you shall turn criminal to obey my will.

Your honor belongs to me, as does your blood, your mind and your ability to work.

Should you ever find my domination unendurable and should your chains ever become too heavy, you will be obliged to kill yourself, for I will never set you free.

"I undertake, on my word of honor, to be the slave of Frau Wanda von Dunajew, in the exact way that she demands, and to submit myself without resistance to everything she will impose on me."—*Dr. Leopold, Knight of Sacher-Masoch*[6]

In the contract one sees clearly the pregnant character of the perverse relation to the signifier and the effacement of the other's desire. The contract regulates, defines, and formalizes the relation to the other. Things are said before they are done. The signifier compels and one must abide by it. At the same time, however, in this very situation, the other is evacuated. The contract effectively erases both Demand and the subjection to the Law of the other implied in it. The pact replaces the Demand. It renders useless the passage through the demand, just as it regulates—with the other's complicity and free consent—the evacuation of the other. Once the contract is signed, the other as a subject is abolished, along with his desire and freedom. As Georges Bataille very appropriately wrote of the Marquis de Sade, "It is a language which repudiates any relationship between speaker and audience."[7] The contract per se and the scenario it defines demonstrate that the other is reduced to the mere traits the other supports and to the role given in the scenario. Thus, the contract responds to the processing of the drive beyond the phallic effects, in a mechanical, action-reaction organ logic set in motion by the trait, the piece, or the partial object that the other then supports.

Violence resides in that reduction of the Other to the status of pure object. But it is also from that position that the pervert complies so perfectly with the demand addressed by the hysteric. It is in that position that the pervert takes charge of the hysteric's jouissance and gives to the hysteric the dedicated status of an object. By reducing the other to mere traits possessed, the pervert works on the letter of the body, in the hysteric, and pushes it to the limit where jouissance becomes confused with anxiety. The pervert thus becomes the master of this, of the disorganizing, unbridled drive, by forcing it and framing it through the rites of the scenario. The hysteric is thus spared the effects of castration linked to the passage through the signifier, and finds in the pervert the master who embodies an accountable other. The hysteric's position as the innocent victim is structurally determining, since it is what allows the hysteric both to consolidate an imaginary identification with the object of the other's desire and to keep seeing in the other the one who takes charge of jouissance and spares the hysteric both anxiety and guilt.

Desire Leads Back to the Drive

By staying as close as possible to the real of the letter of the body, the pervert clings to the drive and keeps desire in check. The workings of the letter in the staging, in the real of the body, in the scenario, make it possible to do away with the passage through the signifier and therefore also to do away with the various forms of address to the Other, where the subject's words necessarily become a request for recognition by the other. The staging is not a request. It is a demonstration; it wrests the consent or complicity from the other who, knowingly or not, becomes solely responsible for the meaning given to the action. The scenario claims no interpretation, no recognition of desire from the other; in that sense, it abolishes the other as a subject. The pervert has no access to desire, inasmuch as desire is always fundamentally the desire for the Other's desire. Indeed, the pervert demonstrates the uselessness of *desire* by giving access to *jouissance*, the emergence of which no longer requires the participation of the object that brought it about.

In that falling back on the drive, the signifiers which have marked the history of the subject and determined the subject's relation to jouissance, are somehow emptied, cut off from their articulation to the Other's desire; they become pure letters, pure traits, traces, fetishes. A childhood memory of Sacher-Masoch reveals the signifiers and the structure that regulate the essence of the perverse subject's relation to jouissance. The memory, as is often the case in perversion, concerns precisely a *scene*, a sort of picture where gestures and acts have the advantage over what could have been said. Then ten years old, Sacher-Masoch was visiting a woman remotely related to his father, and with whom the

ten-year-old boy was in love. The woman, the countess Zenobia, asked
Sacher-Masoch to help her take off her sable-lined coat. This moved the
child, who rushed to obey and followed her into her bedroom to help her
remove her heavy fur coat and put on her green velvet coat adorned with
gray squirrel. He then knelt to help her put on her slippers and, feeling
her feet move slightly, he kissed them passionately. The countess was
first astounded, then burst out laughing, and gently kicked him.

Sacher-Masoch proceeds with his story. As he was later playing hide
and seek with the countess's children, he hid in her room, behind a coat
stand and witnessed a scene. The countess walked in the room followed
by a beautiful young man, whom she pulled close to her. Still hiding, the
child saw the husband suddenly enter the room. The countess rushed forward, violently punched her husband and, brandishing her riding whip,
showed him the door. At that moment, the coat stand fell and the countess turned all her fury against the child. She grabbed him by his hair,
forced him to lie on the rug and, keeping him down with her knee pressed
on his shoulder, she violently whipped him. Sacher-Masoch adds:

> But I must recognize that, while I was squirming under her cruel
> blows, I was experiencing a sort of jouissance. Her husband must
> have often experienced such sensations, because he soon came up to
> his wife's room, not as an avenger, but as a humble slave, and kneel-
> ing before this perfidious woman, he begged her pardon while she
> pushed him back with her foot. The door was then locked. This
> time, I felt no shame, I did not cover my ears and I listened carefully
> through the door, perhaps out of revenge, perhaps out of childish
> jealousy, and I heard again the cracking of the whip of which I had
> just been offered a taste.[8]

Whereas the psychotic does not invest the signifiers that mark one's
body and history (and that pass through the psychotic as pure, faceless
voices) to build his or her subjectivity, the pervert disincarnates the signifier, detaches it from the Other to keep only its effect, its mark, on the letter of the body. The pervert makes the signifier of the Other's desire fall
back on the letter of the body and on the Other's trait, where the effect
of the signifier has managed to register. The memory, or rather what is
made to pass for it, gives a refined version of the scenario which will be
replayed with each new partner, adding each time the presence of a third
party required for the remake. The "memory" precisely brings back the
whole series of objects and traits to which the other will have to be reduced in order for the scenario to be launched again: the despotic authority, the cruel look, the kick, the furs, the whip, the green velvet coat,

the gray squirrel fur. The "memory" also reveals the structure of the scene, by determining a series of positions (and the very precise links between these positions) and above all, by predetermining the progression of the scenario. The signifiers which, coming from the Other, wrote the matrix of the scenario—probably signifiers provided by the parents, by the Ukrainian nurse's folktales of cruel women, or by books of the sufferings of saints and martyrs (which put young Sacher-Masoch in "feverish states")—all lose their articulation to the Other when they are re-used in the staging that they nevertheless determine. It is as if what must be erased is the signifiers' initial determination by the Other, inasmuch as that determination stresses the subjection of the subject. The signifiers must be reduced to a series of traces of jouissance that must be discovered, revived, or embodied in anyone who proposes to occupy one of the possible positions in the scenario. The demonstration will always aim at proving that one can do without the signifier of the Other's desire, which only hinders jouissance.

Violence and Aggressivity: The Violence of the Demonstration

The pervert's *demonstration* is a form of violence insofar as it abolishes the other as a desiring subject. The aggressivity fundamentally implies, however, the maintenance of the address. It marks the failure of seduction, on the negative but nevertheless active side of passion, where the other must respond and even justify its incompatibility with the object of the fantasy. The aggressivity maintains the other, to preserve the illusion of a possible object for its desire, where the ego imaginarily takes its bearings. It is the aggression of the other who *could have revealed* the mistake, leaving the ego in the anxiety of the void, confronting the absence of an object for desire.

The pervert's demonstration is a form of violence in its very staging. An event in Vancouver in the mid-1990s offers a perfect example of the violent character of the perverse demonstration. A man who had been sentenced to more than twenty years in prison for the murder of several children asked the court to reduce the period after which he would become eligible for parole. New hearings took place, in which he was naturally present, together with the families of the victims, who were thus obliged to relive yet again painful events and wait anxiously for a jury's decision. During the days of the hearings, lawyers and psychiatrists testified that the man was still dangerous. In return for a reduced waiting period, the murderer proposed to give information that would solve a series of unexplained murders. His request was, of course, rejected. After the judge delivered the verdict, the murderer turned to the family members of the victims and, smiling, told them he had made his request *only be-cause the law allowed it*. What the murderer wished to demonstrate was, precisely, the absurdity of that law and of this symbolic order, which he could use and turn against precisely that which it was intended to protect and guarantee. But it is mainly in the staging of the demonstration that the violence resides. After a week of hesitations, during which court experts had to take great care to remain within the bounds of the law and to base their decision on it, the smile of the murderer clearly revealed the meaning of the demonstration *and* emphasized the active participation of everyone involved—including, of course, the journalists who had brought the proceedings so much media attention.

What had been interpreted as a request addressed by the murderer to the other, is abolished and retroactively canceled when the game is set and the partner is sufficiently committed (and made accomplice by his or her response to the request) to render any accusation against the pervert unbelievable. Maintaining the treatment of jouissance in the domain of the letter of the body, beyond the stakes of the signifier and the relation to the Other, when this treatment finds a complicity on the part of a partner, is in itself a demonstration of the uselessness of the phallus, of the logic, and the law of the signifier for the treatment of jouissance. The fact that what is signified does not use words, but rather actions and is thus *staged* instead of *said*, gives the demonstration its violent dimension. The other is abolished in that which makes the partner a subject, and the partner's capacity and power to respond are thus negated and made useless. Moreover, the other is the unknowing tool and accomplice of that demonstration. A negative response or the absence of any response on the part of the other to the subject's request for recognition would be in the realm of aggressivity. Violence implies not only the evacuation of the response, but the cancellation or effacement of the demand, in a realm and under a form not regulated by the signifier.

Hysterics are not the only ones summoned by the pervert's solution. Neurotics in general are distressed, worried, fascinated, and involved as accomplices by it. Neurosis is in fact the organization of the repression of desire and castration. Perverts and neurotics share a common hatred for desire, about which they wish to know nothing. Perverts demonstrate that jouissance is fundamentally incompatible with the Other's desire; neurotics stick close to the fantasy and to the jouissance that the fantasy stages in the imaginary without the other's knowing. The fantasy and the illusory object it offers and supports are like the machinery with which neurotics also pretend to do away with castration and the solitude of desire.

Notes

1. Jacques Lacan, *Écrits: A Selection*, trans. Alan Sheridan (New York: W. W. Norton and Co., 1977), 314. Original edition (Paris: Éditions du Seuil, 1966), 817.

2. Readers are referred to Willy Apollon's chapter in this collection, "The Letter of the Body," for a fuller discussion of this concept.

3. Gilles Deleuze, *Coldness and Cruelty* (New York: Zone Books, 1991), 17.

4. Deleuze, *Coldness and Cruelty*, 18.

5. Leopold von Sacher-Masoch, *La Vénus à la fourrure* (Paris: Presses Pocket), 31–32.

6. Gilles Deleuze, *Coldness and Cruelty* (New York: Zone Books, 1991), 278–279.

7. Deleuze, *Coldness and Cruelty*, 19.

8. Gilles Deleuze, *Présentation de Sacher-Masoch* (Paris: Les Éditions de Minuit), 253.

Chapter 12

Violence in Works of Art, or, Mishima, from the Pen to the Sword

DANIELLE BERGERON

Violence in Works of Art

Some works of art so profoundly move the spectator that they arouse a sort of vertiginous fascination, a kind of insidious anxiety, or else seize the spectator in the shock of true horror. In such instances, the aesthetic impression is registered with a violence that is all the more powerfully felt in that it is impossible to describe or to represent at the moment of its greatest force. Something unspeakably alien is glimpsed in these paintings, sculpture, stories, films, and plays, something that cannot be expressed in words, so that the full impact of the work of art is experienced only in the body, which expresses its turmoil along paths traced in the early unconscious history of the subject. In distinction from those works of art that feed fantasies of a reunification with the neurotic's narcissistic object, or those that reflect the cultural values of a society, the works we are concerned with in the present chapter do not meet with popular assent and must be defended for a long time by avant-garde or critical circles before they are finally found tolerable.

This chapter was presented, in different form, at the conference for the Association for the Psychoanalysis of Culture and Society, at George Washington University, in Washington DC, November 1997.

One might say that the artist of such a work has found an original way
to process the real and has approached what Freud called "*das Ding*,"
the Thing. From the various histories of the letters of the artist's own
body, a radically new mode of apprehension of *das Ding* is created. One
thinks, by way of example, of Hieronymus Bosch, Frida Kahlo, René
Magritte, or Egon Schiele. Anyone who is faced with such works must
learn to tame them by linking the overwhelming emotion, the alarm
which signals the entrance into the field of *das Ding*, with words that
evoke what had, until that moment, remained in the sphere of the un-
suspected.

Mishima's Specific Violence

Yukio Mishima, novelist, screenwriter, actor, and sportsman, is for
many among the most famous Japanese of his day.[1] Flamboyant, original, and prolific, he left an impressive collection of works and was a
likely candidate for the Nobel Prize, had he not "prematurely" put an
end to his life in 1970 by committing public suicide through seppuku, at
the age of forty-five. It is generally said of his writings and of his tragic
death that they give an impression of inordinate violence. Some find
them provocative in their staging of scenarios that are seen as perverse,
intriguing or strange, while some others find in them a senseless aggression. The uncomprehending westerner may be inclined to see manifested in Mishima's writing—as in the theatrical radicalism of the
samurai's seppuku, in the unwavering determination of the kamikaze, or
in the practices of the yakuza—Orientalist clichés of a Japanese predis-
position to gratuitous cruelty said to lurk beneath that nation's refinement and courtesy. What shocks westerners is that these manifestations
make no sense for them. Having studied Japanese culture for many
years, we have learned to recognize in these positions the form taken by
the ethics of Japanese masculinity, according to which each man is the
only person responsible for his debt and the only conceivable bearer of
his obligations, of his *giri* or *bushido*.

But beyond such cultural traits, one must ask where the violence
comes from in Mishima's life and works. What was it that structured his
unconscious and that found its solutions—at least in part—in the memory of his culture? To address this question, the present chapter will look
at some well-known historical elements of his life and at two of his au-
tobiographical novels: *Confessions of a Mask*, published when he was
twenty-our, and *Sun and Steel*, published at age forty-three, just two
years before the tragic death whose ritual he had been planning and
rehearsing for so long.

The Production of the Thing in Language

> In the average person . . . the body precedes language. In my case, words came first of all. Then . . . came the flesh. It was already, as goes without saying, sadly wasted by words . . . Any art that relies on words makes use of their ability to eat away—of their corrosive function—just as etching depends on the corrosive power of nitric acid. Yet the simile is not accurate enough; for the copper and the nitric acid used in etching are on a par with each other, both being extracted from nature, while the relation of words to reality is not that of the acid to the plate. Words are a medium that reduces reality to abstraction for transmission to our reason.[2]

Mishima, the writer, by indicating the absence of any necessary relationship between words and the reality of nature, and by highlighting the corrosive power that words have over the flesh of human biology, effectively expresses the traumatic aspect of that experience unknown by the subject, the violent event which creates the human condition: the capture of the subject in the signifying chain.

Human being is indeed the result of a trauma—namely, the irreversible and traumatic diverting of instinctual functioning and of the neurophysiology of the organism that is effected by language. Language, when it traverses human being, excludes a certain jouissance, whose knowledge or *savoir* is carried by the instincts, and which Freud called "*das Ding*" and Lacan the "primordial real." At the same time, the exclusion of the jouissance of the real of *das Ding* by the signifier leaves marks on the organism which it has *de-natured*. These "elected points" or "gaping points,"[3] these openings on the surface of the body, replace the physiological mechanism which served to satisfy the instinctual needs and attest to the introduction of an other jouissance which gives form to the erogenous body. This invisible tattooing of flesh by word/law henceforth becomes the source of the drive, the inexhaustible energy and the constant force which will endlessly aim at a reunion with the lost object causing the energy, in the mad hope that the energy created by the signifier corroding the organism, the death drive, will at last be exhausted.

But the object of this primordial loss is the object of an impossibility. While *das Ding* is created by the signifier—as the part of the primordial real which "suffers from the signifier"[4]—it cannot be reduced by the signifier. It is, in other words, impossible to represent *das Ding*. This defect of language, this incapacity to express the real of the Thing, this "fundamental incompatibility between language and the real,"[5] which is the defect of the Other of language, creates a void at the very heart of the subject, and generates, in consequence, an energy that endlessly seeks a mode of expression. But since it cannot be represented, the Thing, inasmuch as it is the "absolute Other of the subject,"[6] must be *re-presented* by the subject under the guise of a so-called reuniting object, an inadequate hallucination of *das Ding*. The object *a*, an impostor representative of the impossible representation, and, in its wake, the series of substitute objects (oral, anal, urethral . . .), will cause the irrepressible tendency of the subject to recover this loss induced by the failure of language, precipitating some violent inner tension that will be directed at the parental Other. The drive, an inexhaustible energy fed by *das Ding*, aims to recover what has never existed. The drive threatens the homeostasis of the subject and can fatally devour a human being if the subject of the unconscious cannot invent a way to channel the drive by linking it via the signifier into fantasies, dreams, or creations in the social sphere.

The "letters of the body" and the Return of *das Ding*

Besides the superficial "scandal" (at the time) of Mishima's homosexuality—which upon closer examination rather appears as the building up of an identification to homosexuality as a symptom, in brilliant literary form—*Confessions of a Mask* primarily introduces the reader into a peculiar childhood and adolescence. The narrator, Kimitake Hiraoka writing under his pen name of Yukio Mishima, seems a frail and powerless boy who suffers from strange life threatening illnesses and whose body is overtaken by brutal and tenacious sensations, strong emotions, nauseating smells, bloody images, murderous and cruel fantasies. Also striking are the narrator's powerlessness against the forces that batter his body and his constant surprise when he is confronted with "bizarre images" and particular characteristics of others' bodies that trigger in him a "violent, sensuous craving." Violence seizes hold of his body; he feels there an intense emotion that, for the psychoanalyst, has its origin in his childhood.

Wrenched away from his parents at an early age by his paternal grandmother, who claimed to be protecting him, Mishima became the obedient and devoted hostage of that "extravagant" woman who came from an illustrious samurai family[7] and who scorned her proletarian husband, a former colonial governor who had resigned his position. The interest she showed for her still very young grandson seems to have been concerned very narrowly with the preservation of his physical integrity. After the one-year-old child tumbled down the stairs and cut his forehead, she intensified her supervision. Fearing the child might catch cold if he went outside, she kept him in her room, amid the stifling odors of sickness and old age. Shortly before Mishima turned four, she was there,

inquiring about his death, when he had the first of a strange series of au-
tointoxication crises during which he received so many shots that he
looked "like a pincushion." For two hours, he was thought dead. "They
stood looking down at my corpse," Mishima wrote, but when suddenly
urine appeared, the doctor declared, "He's alive!": He urinates, therefore
he lives! But what kind of life was this? They watched and treated his
body but no one talked to him. Alone with each subsequent crises, he
was lying in wait for death: "By the sound of the disease's footsteps as it
drew near," he wrote, "I came to be able to sense whether an attack was
likely to approach death or not."[8] On account of his frail health, his
grandmother strictly controlled the boy's diet. For example, she forbade
him to eat blue-skinned fish. She would not allow him to stand in the
sun. If he caught the slightest cold, she kept him from school. He suffered too from anemia. From his earliest years, it seems that only his
physical problems mobilized the attention of his grandmother, who
seemed to care for him only inasmuch as she could not bear the thought
of losing the physical presence of her grandson's body.

Moreover, the directives and the constraints imposed by Mishima's
grandmother showed no educational purpose whatsoever, but rather
seemed to arise out of her personal caprice. For example, it is because
she feared that loud noises would give her neuralgia that she allowed
only girls to play with the boy. Whether it was for the risk of him catching a disease or for the desire to preserve her peace and quiet, or any
other such pretext, all seemed to conspire toward the same end: the removal of her grandson from the normal competitive social life that boys
lead. In short, this woman, who exploited him openly and freely—at
least according to the account of Himitake—misused her power over the
child for the sake of her own jouissance.

Was it due to this seizure of Mishima's life for the jouissance of the
maternal Other that the child felt a "grief at being eternally excluded?"[9]
As with other children, Mishima had been subjected to language by his
very birth: each life experience inscribed a vivid letter on his body, as
witness to the return of *das Ding* in the drive. But maintained outside of
the social link and outside of discourse by his grandmother, the excessive jouissance, which invaded his body in disorganizing multiplicities,
could not be articulated to the order of the Law, which would have given
this invasion a meaning in social life. As his illnesses expressed, the jouissance of the Other which invaded him was a death drive ceaselessly setting traps for the well-being of his organism. His grandmother's
capricious refusal to submit to the phallus as signifier of lack, her devaluation of the Name-of-the-Father (i.e., her husband's, which she
scorned) which would have supported a symbolic meaning for the loss,

as well as her occultation of Mishima's filiation to a father whose authority she defied by appropriating his son, left the boy with a body parceled out by the searing return of the death drive through the letters that bore the marks and the persistent open wounds of the imaginary Other's jouissance. Mishima was left alone to face the void without words. His illnesses testify to this fact. At twenty-four, while writing *Confessions of a Mask*, Mishima found signifiers for childhood events that could not be represented at that time: death, anemia/blood, cut, head wound, sun, a body pierced by steel needles. These detached signifiers recall the superego demand of the voices of the archaic Other embodied in his grandmother, whose imperious demand for jouissance reveals, among other things, a morbid interest in his body as, precisely, a sick body. Thus, it is as much through his suffering and threatened body as through his submissive obedience that Mishima responded to what he heard as a demand. To respond to the Other's jouissance in the hope of being freed from it is a double-edged sword, since to yield to the Other's jouissance is also to loose the liberty of enjoying one's own life.

The Failure of Masculine Identification

Some elements begin to fall into place over the psychic structure that, in his early years, was constructed as the chessboard of Mishima's life. There were three events that formed the "preamble" to Mishima's life[10] as a subject abandoned to the Other's jouissance. As will be shown, they in fact provided the source for the production of a fantasy.

When Mishima was four, the sight of a young laborer, a ladler of excrement wearing a dirty roll of cloth around his head for a sweatband and close-fitting blue trousers called "thigh-pullers" haunted him "with a strangely vivid image" which gave him the presentiment "that there is in this world a kind of desire like stinging pain" and made him feel his "first summons by a certain strange and secret voice."

> I was choked by desire, thinking, . . . I want to *be* him [a night-soil man in close fitting thigh-pullers]. . . . toward him I felt something like the yearning for . . . a violent, body-wrenching sorrow. His occupation gave me the feeling of "tragedy," in the most sensuous meaning of the word . . . like a remarkable mixture of nothingness and vital power."[11]

At the same age, Mishima often sat, secretly contemplating a picture representing a magnificent knight on horseback brandishing a drawn sword in a terrifying manner to confront Death. Mishima imagined that the knight was going to be killed, and he cherished "sweet fantasies . . . concerning *his* death." A magnificent coat of arms emblazoned the knight's silver armor. When Mishima was told that the knight was in fact Saint Joan of Arc, a woman who went to war dressed as a man to save her country, he felt he had been "knocked flat." He *was* her. "If this beautiful knight was a woman and not a man," he asked, "what was there left?" Suddenly overtaken by a feeling of disgust, deceived by the world of perceptions to which he was confined, Mishima felt he was the victim of a cruel "revenge by reality."[12] Even so, the smell of soldiers soon "drove [him] onward," overpowered him, and violently aroused in him what he named a "violent, sensuous craving for the destiny of soldiers, the tragic nature of their calling . . . the ways they would die."[13]

What is to be noticed in these preambles? The bizarre images which suddenly appear before Mishima "in truly masterful completeness"[14] are all related to approaching death (from soldiers who die for their country, to the tragedy of those who sacrifice themselves for others or for a cause) and to masculine associations (strong smells, military uniforms, swords). For Mishima, *das Ding* comes back in the drive as a "violent desire," and he must find something on which he can anchor the drive that hits him with random brutality. At age four, the phallic stage for a boy, the father's intervention becomes especially important, because it must link, under the phallus, the excessive investment of the letter of the body by the drive to masculine identification. It is crucial to note, however, that the phallic signification that allows the boy to access castration cannot simply be established through identification with images or through wearing symbols of masculinity such as armor, a sword, a uniform—as Mishima realized in the painful intensity of his disappointment with Joan of Arc. The phallic signification must be established by the signifier of the father's desire, and this is precisely what was missing for Mishima in the household of his grandmother. He had no father in his life.

It is around the age of four that the boy must lose his penis to bear the phallus, the signifier of desire and of castration. This is how masculine identification takes place. The privilege of the phallus, says Lacan, is to give order to the real of the body and to its mental scheme, to integrate it, so that even if it remains parceled out, it functions as the elements of the body's crest, or coat of arms.[15] Through its relation to the Name-of-the-Father, the phallus tempers for the child the intense and disorganizing energy of the drives by unifying them under a narcissistic image, which supports the integration of the subject in social life and in his articulation to others.

The failure of Mishima's masculine identification was reflected, later in childhood, both in his taste for feminine disguises—as if he had been on the lookout for a sign that would have recognized him as a woman, since masculinity had been blocked for him—and later in life in a symptom, homosexuality, which, in Mishima's particular case, can be seen as a quest for identification, since he was attracted to men precisely insofar as they displayed virile traits and warrior qualities.

The Unveiling of the Original Fantasy

But Mishima had other resources, as his numerous literary works attest. Rather than dying physiologically of illness and rather than dying socially in madness, he found in writing a last resort to represent his subjectivity that had been totally neglected by the members of his family circle. At five he started writing poems. Thus, it can be seen that an object, the *pen*, took the place of the father's phallus. This forced passageway to the signifier through writing will register the maternal Other's jouissance in a metaphorical form. In Mishima's artistic attempt to name what he was living, he created a break in the Other's rock of jouissance, which in turn attenuated the violence of its mortifying impact on the letter of his body. The usual solution would have separated the subject from the jouissance of the Other by going through the register of *desire* with the help of the phallic signifier. However, even if the transposition of aggressive parcels of Mishima's imaginary into his writing is an efficient solution from the standpoint of psychic economy, he cannot, in the end, make words represent the reality of experience. As Mishima himself wryly remarked, "My composition teacher would often show his displeasure with my work, which was innocent of any words that might be taken as corresponding to reality."[16]

The material which, in the preambles of Mishima's childhood were yielding elements for the building of the fantasy that would determine his subjectivity, were fed further by tales and storybooks, his best playmates. Cruelly murdered princes stabbed and decapitated by long knives, poisoned by stings, voraciously devoured by dragons—such images captivated young Mishima's imagination and drained the energy of his death drive. His imagination lingered, too, over exhilarating scenes in which he himself was killed on the field of battle. As Mishima was nearing adolescence, what had been invading his body in a diffuse, disorganized, and aggressive manner began to concentrate in penile excitement. "The toy likewise raised its head toward the naked bodies of young men, death and pools of blood and muscular flesh . . . , gory dueling scenes . . . pictures of young samurai cutting open their bellies, soldiers struck by bullets, clenching their teeth and dripping blood . . . hard-muscled sumo wrestlers . . . a tight-rope-walker who had fallen and split his skull open." Supported by such images which stage the tragedy of those who give their life for a cause, Mishima says that he "began to seek physical pleasure consciously."[17]

At age twelve, in one of his father's art books, Mishima saw a picture that had been "lying in wait" for him. It showed a remarkably handsome youth with muscular arms accustomed to wielding a sword, bound naked to the trunk of a tree. His crossed hands were raised high, and the thongs binding his wrists were tied to the tree. He had arrows with their shafts deeply thrust into his left armpit and his right side. "I guessed," wrote Mishima,

> it must be a depiction of a Christian martyrdom. . . . It is not pain that hovers about his straining chest, his tense abdomen, his slightly contorted hips, but some flicker of melancholy pleasure. . . . That day, the instant I looked upon the picture, my entire body trembled with some pagan joy. My blood soared up; my loins swelled as though in wrath. . . . Suddenly it burst forth, bringing with it a blinding intoxication.[18]

Mishima experienced his first ejaculation after "unconsciously" masturbating to the sight of Guido Reni's image of the martyrdom of Saint Sebastian, whose ultimate sacrifice for the Christian cause seemed to bring an ecstatic jouissance to the martyr, while the arrows piercing Saint Sebastian's body suggest metonymically the needles associated with Mishima's childhood illnesses.

This scene with Guido's Sebastian clearly reveals what had been building up for Mishima, piece by piece, since childhood and was to be the source of that brutal and violent experience: an originary fantasy about sacrificing his life for the Other's jouissance and Cause. His erection and ejaculation provided a means of expression through the sexual drive to the originary fantasy which, as the rest of his life attests, structured his imaginary: to bring jouissance to the Other by becoming the object that completes the Other and works for the Cause of the Other, the object ready to die for the Other. Elements of his fantasies that have been judged perverse by many critics prove to be, upon analysis, a representation of the various expressions of the fantasy of the original scene, which one also finds expressed elsewhere in works of art, for example, the paintings of Hieronymus Bosch. Struggling with the real of the Other which demands jouissance, struggling with *das Ding*, the subject experiences emotions which are translated, in the imagination, into scenes of devourment, of bruised bodies, of bodies riddled with bullets or pierced with knives, of bodies bloodied or decapitated or subjected to

cruelty; of encounters with terrifying wild beasts, of obscenities haphaz-
ardly built with the signifiers that the subject has grasped in the first periods of life. The fantasy in which the subject is brutally captured by the
Other's jouissance and abandoned to this jouissance is the fantasy that
lies at the heart of the psychotic structure.

From the Pen to the Sword: The Quest for the Phallus and for a Meaning to His Death

Thus, Mishima was far from the denial of the phallus that grounds
the perverse structure. Indeed, Mishima would sacrifice his adult life to
the restoration of the Father and the reign of the Emperor. All his life, he
was very concerned with the conventions of the masculine code of ethics
and was serious about respectability. Moreover, despite his psychotic
structure,[19] his was not the life of a madman. He applied great psychic
ability and intelligence to confront the death drive that was tormenting
him and he turned it into something that others would recognize.

But Mishima's pen was not enough to fill the void left by the foreclosure of the Father and to give meaning to his life. So he began to body
build, as he wrote in *Sun and Steel*, to reverse the corrosive effect of words
on his flesh "until the whole physical being became a suit of armor forged
from the metal of that concept, to intellectualize the flesh in order to
achieve through it a closer intimacy with ideas than with the spirit itself."[20] He sought to neutralize the devastating effect of words on his
being by creating a new language without failure, the language of muscles
submitted to the sun and constrained by the steel, and he came to believe
that the body could have "its own logic, . . . its own thought, . . . its own
loquacity."[21]

Where Mishima had failed to achieve masculine identification under
the symbolic phallus, the violent reformation of his body in bodybuild-
ing, where muscles are torn and rebuilt in repeated painful efforts, became his mode of masculine identification, and forged for him the
missing link between the letters of his body and the signifiers that
marked his history. Thus was Mishima able to compensate for the foreclosure of the Father's phallus which had abandoned him to a meaningless imaginary. Through body building, Mishima reconstituted what
language had cruelly fragmented and provided the death drive a channel
to regroup. In the third period of his life, the phallic symbol of the samurai's *sword* replaced the *pen* to give a public form to the original fantasy
that organized his life.

At the end of his life, after Mishima had formed his private army, the
Shield Society, and had publicly engaged himself to defend the Emperor,

he also rehearsed through artistic representation, films and photographs, his future heroic death. By cutting open the belly with his own sword to commit *seppuku,* the most painful suicidal act, the Japanese samurai makes his sincerity visible, an important point, as Mishima said in a press conference, adding, "I cannot believe in Western sincerity since it is invisible."[22] Mishima figured as a tragic hero dedicated to a cause for which he would die in blood and pain, and in the first instance through the violence of his fantasy. But the same elements reappear in the clever and subtle transposition of his fantasy on the social stage: his seppuku, which according to Japanese tradition is the perfect ethical act of a warrior, returned to Mishima his masculinity, while at the same time placing him in a lineage—that of his aristocratic grandmother's samurai family, of course, but also that of the Sun, which according to myth, guarantees the succession of Japan's gods, from whom all Japanese are descended. Mishima also credits the sun with his discovery of the importance of body building.[23] Moreover, through his seppuku, an act he committed in uniform and whose theatrical character was exaggerated by intensive physical training, Mishima reunited his head and his belly, the signifiers and the flesh, the pen and the sword, in two successive dramatic moments: once the samurai has pushed his sword into his own belly with all his strength, his head is lopped off by his best comrade-in-arms.

In a letter written and sent to a collaborator just before his death, Mishima declared, "Dress my body in the uniform of the Shield Society, don me my white gloves, and put the saber in my hand. . . . I want it testified that I died not as a man of letters, but as a man of arms."[24] Through this death, Mishima accomplished his mission: to unite, in the violence of muscles, words and flesh in a new language supported by masculine ethics—and in so doing, to give meaning to his death. He also unveiled, in the most dramatic way possible, the obscene and aggressive work of the death drive in his own flesh.

The life of Mishima had been a constant struggle against the excess of the death drive that had ravaged his body like sharp daggers since his early childhood, and that would have carried him away, had it not been channeled into his writing, then projected onto the social scene on the path of the samurai warrior. The world might otherwise have missed its encounter with a body of work marked by an uncommon intensity and a true, vital urgency.

Notes

1. Henry Scott Stokes, *The Life and Death of Yukio Mishima* (New York: Noonday Press, 1995), 6.

2. Yukio Mishima, *Sun and Steel* (New York: Kodansha International, 1980), 8–9.

3. Jacques Lacan, *The Seminar of Jacques Lacan, Book VII: The Ethics of Psychoanalysis, 1959–1960*, ed. Jacques-Alain Miller, trans. Dennis Porter (New York: W. W. Norton and Co., 1992), 93, translation modified by author. Original edition (Paris: Éditions du Seuil, 1986), 112.

4. Lacan, *The Seminar of Jacques Lacan, Book VII*, 118.

5. Willy Apollon, "L'événement ou l'avènement de l'Autre," *L'universel, perspectives, psychanalytiques* (Québec: Collection le savoir analytique, Gifric, 1997): 51–91.

6. Lacan, *The Seminar of Jacques Lacan, Book VII*, 52.

7. John Nathan, *La vie de Mishima* (Paris: Gallimard, 1980), 20.

8. Yukio Mishima, *Confessions of a Mask* (New York: New Directions, 1958), 6–7.

9. ———, *Confessions of a Mask*, 10.

10. ———, *Confessions of a Mask*, 20.

11. ———, *Confessions of a Mask*, 8–10, translation modified.

12. ———, *Confessions of a Mask*, 12.

13. ———, *Confessions of a Mask*, 14, translation modified.

14. ———, *Confessions of a Mask*, 14.

15. Lacan, *Écrits: A Selection*, 302.

16. Yukio Mishima, *Sun and Steel* (New York: Kodansha International, 1980), 9.

17. ———, *Confessions of a Mask*, 35, translation modified.

18. ———, *Confessions of a Mask*, 38–40.

19. The question of Mishima's psychic structure is further developed in another text forthcoming in *(a): the journal of culture and the unconscious*, II (Spring 2001).

20. Mishima, *Sun and Steel*, 16, translation modified.

21. ———, *Sun and Steel*, 18.

22. Stokes, *The Life and Death of Yukio Mishima*, 6.

23. Mishima, *Sun and Steel*, 23, and 25.

24. Nathan, *La vie de Mishima*, 304–305.

Contributors

Authors

Willy Apollon has his doctorate in philosophy from the Sorbonne in Paris and is a practicing psychoanalyst. He is a founding member of Gifric (Groupe interdisciplinaire freudien de recherches et d'interventions cliniques) and has been President of Gifric for ten years. He is the consulting psychoanalyst and director of training of the staff at Center for Psychoanalytic Treatment of Young Psychotic Adults and is the director of the clinic for the psychoanalytic treatment of families. He is also director of the Center for research and training of Gifric. He is on the editorial board of the journal, *Savoir*. Since the early 1970s, Dr. Apollon has worked to introduce Lacanian theory in Québec. He is the author of numerous works and articles in a wide variety of journals speaking to issues fundamental to the practice and theory of psychoanalysis, from questions of psychoanalytic training, the ethics of analytic action, and the logic of psychoanalytic treatment, to the psychoanalytic treatment of families and psychoses. He is also responsible for a number of notable texts on the stakes of psychoanalytic knowledge in relation to broader cultural problems and social practices.

Danielle Bergeron, M.D. is a Training Analyst, Psychiatrist, and Associate Professor of Psychiatry at the University of Laval in Québec City. Since its inception twenty years ago, Dr. Bergeron has been the Director of the Center for the Psychoanalytic Treatment for Young Psychotic Adults. She has several publications on the psychoanalytic treatment of psychosis including *The Treatment of Psychosis* with W. Apollon and L. Cantin. She is Director of Training of Psychoanalysis at Gifric's Center for Research and Development and is on the editorial board of the journal, *Savoir: A Journal of Psychoanalysis and Cultural Analysis*. She is also the author of a number of publications on femininity, art and aesthetics, the analytic treatment of neurosis, and the formation of the analyst.

Lucie Cantin, is a psychoanalyst and psychologist. Since its creation in 1982, she has been Assistant Director of the Center for Psychoanalytic Treatment for Young Psychotics Adults. She is co-director of training for psychoanalysts at Gifric. She is a professor of clinical psychology at University of Laval. She is Vice-President of Gifric and in charge of publications and teachings of the Center for research and training of Gifric. She is the editor of the international journal, *Savoir: A Journal of Psychoanalysis and Cultural Analysis.* Her other publications include a book on the treatment of psychosis and she is author of numerous articles on femininity, masculinity, perversion, the logic of psychoanalytic treatment, the nature of psychoanalytic knowledge, as well as the training of analysts.

Editors

Robert Hughes, is an Assistant Professor of English at Augusta State University, where he teaches courses in literature and literary theory. He is also a Ph.D. candidate in Comparative Literature at Emory University, where he is writing a dissertation, entitled *Writing Out of Death: Literature, Ethics, and the Beyond of Language,* on nineteenth-century American literature and twentieth-century continental thought.

Kareen Ror Malone, Ph.D. is Professor of Psychology at the State University of West Georgia and on the Women's Studies faculty. She is coeditor, with Stephen Friedlander, of *The Subject of Lacan: A Lacanian Reader for Psychologists* (Albany: State University of New York Press, 2000).

Index

195